LEARN, TEACH...

SUCCEED...

With **REA's TExES™ English as a Second Language Supplemental (154)** test prep, you'll be in a class all your own.

WE'D LIKE TO HEAR FROM YOU!
Visit **www.rea.com** to send us your comments

TExES™ ESL SUPPLEMENTAL (154)

TEXAS EXAMINATIONS OF EDUCATOR STANDARDS™

Jacalyn Mahler, M.A.

Beatrice Mendez Newman, Ph.D.

Sharon Alverson, B.A.

Loree DeLys Evans, M.A.

 Research & Education Association

Research & Education Association
61 Ethel Road West
Piscataway, New Jersey 08854
E-mail: info@rea.com

TExES™ English as a Second Language Supplemental (154) with Online Practice Tests

Published 2015

Printed in the United States of America

Library of Congress Control Number 2013916779

ISBN-13: 978-0-7386-1147-1
ISBN-10: 0-7386-1147-6

Cover image: © iStockphoto.com/CEFutcher

Developed and produced by Focus Strategic Communications, Inc.

Contents

About the Authors

Jacalyn Mahler

Jacalyn Mahler is a language teacher, author, and educational resource developer. She holds a master's degree in Translation and Interpretation from the Monterey Institute of International Studies and a B.A. in Spanish from Tufts University.

Mahler was instrumental in developing two research-based programs adopted by the Texas State Board of Education for English-language learners: *High Point* (Hampton-Brown, 2001) and *Avenues* (Hampton-Brown, 2003). She was also a co-author of the *Teaching Reading Sourcebook* (Arena Press, 1999), a core text for preservice teachers endorsed by the National Council on Teacher Quality.

Mahler has received awards for K–1 Spanish picture books, multimedia intervention for adolescent readers, and National Geographic's classroom magazines. She is a member of Innovation Through Inclusion, the Association of Educational Publishers' diversity recruitment initiative.

Beatrice Mendez Newman

Dr. Beatrice Mendez Newman is a professor in the English Department at The University of Texas-Pan American where she regularly teaches first-year writing courses and writing methods classes. Her Ph.D. is from Texas A&M University where she specialized in rhetoric and composition and linguistics. She has a lifetime Texas teaching certificate in secondary English and Journalism, including ESL certification, and works extensively with local teachers in creating student-centered, engaging writing units.

Mendez Newman's book, *English Teacher Certification Exams in Texas,* published by Allyn and Bacon in 2005, is a study guide for the TExES ELAR exams. Mendez Newman's research has been published in collections on teaching writing at Hispanic serving institutions and writing center pedagogy; her recent articles have appeared in *Voices from the Middle*, *HETS Online Journal,* and the *English Journal*.

Mendez Newman is very active in the National Council of Teachers of English (NCTE), serving as a National Council for Accreditation of Teacher Education (NCATE) reviewer, as a reader for NCTE journal manuscripts, and as a national judge for the NCTE Achievement Awards in Writing.

Sharon Alverson

Sharon Alverson has been a certified elementary teacher in Texas for over 20 years and has held her ESL and Early Childhood certifications for 14 years. Alverson was an ESL District Coordinator in a North Central Texas district for three years, and as the district grew, she became an elementary ESL campus coordinator.

As the Language Proficiency Assessment Committee (LPAC) chairperson, she trained all members, ordered and administered current tests to students, and conducted meetings. As TELPAS coordinator for the school district, she trained teachers to be raters and administered the RPTE—both paper and online versions. She has administered many versions of the state-mandated tests.

Alverson has mentored other campus ESL coordinators and teachers of Pre–K through high school who received their ESL certification. She has also coordinated family involvement events and programs. She has a B.A. in Elementary Education from Olivet Nazarene University.

Loree DeLys Evans

Loree DeLys Evans has been a teacher of English, English as a Second Language, Special Education, and reading intervention in the Dallas, Texas, area for the past eight years.

Evans holds a master's degree of Education in Curriculum and Instruction, Triple Literacy Studies from the University of Texas at Arlington, and a B.S. in Marketing Management from Western Governors University. She is certified in the state of Texas as a Master Reading Teacher and as a Reading Specialist in the state of Texas, as well as nationally.

In addition, Evans holds certifications in English, Language Arts and Reading (8–12), English as a Second Language Supplemental, Business Education (6–12), Special Education, and Generalist (4–8).

About Research & Education Association

Founded in 1959, Research & Education Association (REA) is dedicated to publishing the finest and most effective educational materials—including study guides and test preps—for students in middle school, high school, college, graduate school, and beyond.

Today, REA's wide-ranging catalog is a leading resource for teachers, students, and professionals. Visit *www.rea.com* to see a complete listing of all our titles.

REA Acknowledgments

We would like to thank the people at Focus Strategic Communications, Inc., for their work on this study guide. We extend special gratitude to Focus's principals, Adrianna Edwards and Ron Edwards, for developing and producing the entire manual as well as putting together, overseeing, and supervising the writing, editorial, and production teams. We thank First Image for meticulously and patiently laying out and formatting the pages.

We would also like to thank Pam Weston, Publisher, for setting the quality standards for production integrity and managing the publication to completion; John Paul Cording, Vice President, Technology, for coordinating the design and development of the REA Study Center; Larry B. Kling, Vice President, Editorial, for his overall direction; Michael Reynolds, Managing Editor, for coordinating development of this edition; and Christine Saul, Senior Graphic Designer, for designing our cover.

INTRODUCTION

Passing the TExES English as a Second Language Supplemental (154) Test

Passing the TExES English as a Second Language Supplemental (154) Test

Congratulations! By taking the TExES English as a Second Language (ESL) Supplemental (154) test, you're on your way to a rewarding career working with exceptional students. Our book and the online tools that come with it give you everything you need to succeed on this important exam, bringing you one step closer to being certified to teach ESL in Texas.

Our *TExES English as a Second Language (ESL) Supplemental (154)* Book + Online test prep package provides these key features:

- Complete overview of the TExES English as a Second Language (ESL) Supplemental (154) test

- Comprehensive review of all 3 domains and 10 competencies

- Two full-length practice tests, both in the book and online, with powerful diagnostic tools to help you personalize your prep

- Detailed answer explanations that not only identify correct answers but also explain why the other answer choices are incorrect

There are many different ways to prepare for the TExES English as a Second Language (ESL) Supplemental (154) exam. What's best for you depends on how much time you have to study and how comfortable you are with the subject matter. Our Book + Online Prep has a plan that you can customize to fit both your lifestyle and study style.

How to Use This Book + Online Prep

About the Review

The review chapters in this book are designed to help you sharpen your command of pedagogical skills so you can pass the TExES English as a Second Language (ESL) Supplemental (154) test. Each of the skills required for all 10 competencies is discussed at length to optimize your understanding. Keep in mind that the education courses you have taken thus far have taught you what you need to know to answer the questions on the test. You already possess the know-how to understand and make important decisions about professional situations involving ESL students.

Our review is designed to help you relate the information you have acquired to Texas's specific competencies. Like the test itself, our review evenly covers the competencies within each domain. However, studying your class notes and textbooks together with our review will give you an excellent foundation for passing the exam.

This book is organized into three parts that correspond with the three domains on the test. The chapters in each part match up with the competencies within each domain.

About the REA Study Center

We know your time is valuable and you want an efficient study experience. At the online REA Study Center, you'll get feedback right from the start on what you know and what you don't know to help make the most of your study time.

Here's what you'll find at the REA Study Center:

■ **Two Full-Length Practice Tests**—These full-length tests cover everything you need to know for the TExES English as a Second Language (ESL) Supplemental (154) test and are a great way to evaluate what you've learned.

Each practice test comes with:

■ **Automatic Scoring**—Find out you how you did on your test, instantly.

■ **Diagnostic Score Reports**—Get a specific score on each of the 10 competencies, so you can focus on the areas that challenge you the most.

■ **Detailed Answer Explanations**—See why the correct answer is right, and why the other answer choices are incorrect.

■ **Timed Testing**—Learn to manage your time as you practice, so you'll feel confident on test day.

All TExES tests, with the exception of Braille (183), are given only as **computer-administered tests,** or **CATs**, so we recommend you take the online versions of our practice tests to simulate test-day conditions.

An Overview of the Test

The TExES English as a Second Language (ESL) Supplemental (154) test ensures that you have the essential knowledge and skills to teach the state-required curriculum, which is known as Texas Essential Knowledge and Skills, or TEKS.

Whether you are a student, a graduate from a Texas state-approved teacher preparation program, or an educator who has received certification in another state, you should carefully read the requirements for working with ESL students provided at the Texas Examinations of Educator Standards website *cms.texes-ets.org*.

What Is Tested on the TExES English as a Second Language (ESL) Supplemental (154) Test?

Ten competencies are covered on the TExES English as a Second Language (ESL) Supplemental (154) exam. These competencies represent the knowledge that teams of teachers, administrators, subject-area specialists, and others have determined to be important for beginning teachers who work with ESL students in the state's public schools.

Here is the approximate percentage of the total exam devoted to each domain.

Domains: Approximate Percentage of Exam		
Domain I	Language Concepts and Language Acquisition	25%
Domain II	Instruction and Assessment	45%
Domain III	Foundations of ESL Education, Cultural Awareness, and Family and Community Involvement	30%

What Is the Format of the TExES English as a Second Language (ESL) Supplemental (154) Test?

The 70 multiple-choice questions on the TExES English as a Second Language (ESL) Supplemental (154) exam are designed to assess your knowledge of the competencies and the related skills required to become an ESL teacher in Texas.

In general, the multiple-choice questions require critical thinking—mirroring the classroom imperative to promote exactly this among your future students. You are frequently expected to demonstrate more than an ability to recall factual information; you may be asked to evaluate the information, comparing it with knowledge you have, or are making a judgment about.

The multiple-choice questions are set up straightforwardly. Each question has four choices labeled A, B, C, and D. The test is scored based on the number of questions you answer correctly, and no points are deducted for wrong answers. Therefore, do not leave any item unanswered, since you will not be penalized for guessing.

You are given five hours to complete the test—which may seem like a lot—but be aware of the amount of time you are spending on each question so you allow yourself time to complete the whole test.

Keep a steady pace when answering questions. Taking our online practice tests with timed testing conditions will help you use your time efficiently. However, if you choose to take the printed versions of the tests in the book, be sure to time yourself.

When Should the TExES Test Be Taken?

Traditionally, teacher preparation programs determine when their candidates take the required tests for teacher certification. These programs will also clear you to take the examinations and make final recommendations for certification to the State Board for Educator Certification (SBEC). For those seeking certification right out of college, the TExES English as a Second Language (ESL) Supplemental (154) exam is generally taken just before graduation.

The TExES Registration Bulletin offers more information about test dates and locations, as well as information on registration and testing accommodations—for those with special needs. The registration bulletin is available at *cms.texes-ets.org/ registrationbulletin/*.

Registration bulletins are also available at the education departments of Texas colleges and universities. To address issues that cannot be solved at the teacher preparation program level, you can contact the offices of SBEC at (888) 863-5880 or (512) 469-8400. You can also find information about the test and registration on the SBEC website at *cms.texes-ets.org/*.

How Do I Register for the Test, and Is There a Registration Fee?

The TExES exams are administered by Educational Testing Service (ETS), which has very specific rules for registering for the test. It is important that you read the registration information on ETS's website (*cms.texes-ets.org/texes*) and follow the instructions given there.

To register for an exam, you must create an account in the ETS online registration system. Registration will then be available to you online, 24/7, during the regular, late, and emergency registration periods. You must pay a registration fee to take the TExES, and you will also incur additional late fees if registering after the scheduled date.

When Will I Receive My Score Report?

On the score report release date, you will receive an email notifying you that your score report is available in your online account. Test scores are released on Tuesdays after 10 p.m. Eastern time within six weeks of the test date.

Can I Retake the Test?

If you don't do well on the TExES English as a Second Language (ESL) Supplemental (154) test, don't panic! You can take the exam again, and in fact, many candidates do. However, you must wait 60 days to retake it.

Studying for the Test

When Should I Start Studying?

It is never too early to start studying for the TExES English as a Second Language (ESL) Supplemental (154) exam. The earlier you begin, the more time you will have to sharpen your skills and focus your efforts. Do not procrastinate. Cramming is not an effective way to study, since it does not allow you enough time to learn the test material. Work out a study routine and stick to it. Reviewing your class notes and textbooks along with our book will provide you with an even better foundation for passing this exam.

Study Schedule

Although our study plan is designed to be used in the six weeks before your exam, it can be condensed to three weeks by combining each two-week period into one. Be sure to set aside enough time—at least two hours each day—to study. The more time you spend studying, the more prepared and relaxed you will feel on the day of the exam.

When you take the practice tests at the online REA Study Center, simulate the conditions of the test as closely as possible. Turn your television and radio off, and sit down at a quiet table free from distraction.

As you complete each test, review your score reports, study the diagnostic feedback, and review the explanations to the questions you answered incorrectly. However, do not review too much at any one time. Concentrate on one problem area at a time by reading the question and explanation, and by studying our review until you are confident that you have mastered the material. Give extra attention to the review chapters that cover your areas of difficulty, as this will build your skills in those areas.

Week	Activity
1	Take Practice Test 1 at the online REA Study Center. Your score report will identify topics where you need the most review.
2-4	Study the review, focusing on the topics you missed (or were unsure of) on Practice Test 1.
5	Take Practice Test 2 at the online REA Study Center. Review your score report and re-study any topics you missed.
6	Review your score reports from both practice tests, read the detailed answer explanations for the questions you got wrong and study those competencies. If you have extra time, take Practice Test 1 again and see how much your score has improved.

Note: If you are studying and don't have Internet access, you can take the printed versions of the tests in the book. These are the same practice tests offered online, but without the added benefits of timed testing conditions, automatic scoring, and diagnostic score reports.

Test-Taking Tips

Taking an important standardized test like the TExES English as a Second Language (ESL) Supplemental (154) test might make you nervous. Here are tried-and-true tips to help alleviate your test-taking anxieties.

Tip 1: Become comfortable with the format of the test. When you are practicing, stay calm and pace yourself. After simulating the test only once, you will boost your chances of doing well, and you will be able to sit down for the actual TExES English as a Second Language (ESL) Supplemental (154) exam with much more confidence.

Tip 2: Familiarize yourself with the directions on the test. This will not only save time, but it will also help you avoid anxiety (and the mistakes anxiety causes).

Tip 3: Read all of the possible answers. Just because you think you have found the correct response, do not automatically assume that it is the best answer. Read through each choice to be sure that you are not making a mistake by jumping to conclusions.

Tip 4: Use the process of elimination. Go through each answer choice and eliminate as many as possible. If you can eliminate two answer choices, you will give yourself a better chance of getting the item correct since there will only be two choices left from which to make your guess. Do not leave an answer blank; it is better to guess than to not answer a question on the TExES English as a Second Language (ESL) Supplemental (154) exam as there is no penalty for wrong answers.

Tip 5: Work at a steady pace and avoid focusing on any one question too long. Taking the timed tests at the online REA Study Center will help you learn to budget your time. Remember to time yourself when taking the practice tests in this printed book.

Tip 6: When taking computer-based tests like the TExES battery, be sure your answer registers before you go to the next item. Look at the screen to see that your mouse click causes the pointer to darken the proper oval. If your answer doesn't register, you won't get credit for that question.

Test Day

As test day draws near, here are a few things to keep in mind so that you'll be prepared for the TExES English as a Second Language (ESL) Supplemental (154) test.

Before the Test

Check your registration information to find out what time to arrive at the testing center. Make sure you arrive early. This will allow you to collect your thoughts and relax before the test, and will also spare you the anguish that comes with being late. (If you arrive late, you might not be admitted to the test center.) Check your admission ticket 24 hours before the test in case there is a change. If there is a change, you will have to print out a new ticket.

Before you leave for the test center, make sure you have your admission ticket and two forms of identification, one of which must contain a recent and recognizable photograph, your name, and signature (e.g., a driver's license). All documents must be originals (no copies). You will not be admitted to the test center and you will forfeit your test fees if you do not have proper identification. (More information about proper forms of ID is listed on the official TEA website: *cms.texes-ets.org*.)

Dress comfortably, so you are not distracted by being too hot or too cold while taking the test. You may wear a watch to the test center. However, you may not wear one that makes noise, because it may disturb the other test-takers. Do not bring cell phones, smartphones, or other electronic, listening, recording, or photographic devices into the test center. Food and drink, dictionaries, textbooks, notebooks, calculators, briefcases, or packages are also not permitted. If you bring these devices into the test center, you will be dismissed from the test, your fee will be forfeited, and your test scores will be canceled.

During the Test

Procedures will be followed to maintain test security. Once you enter the test center, follow all of the rules and instructions given by the test supervisor. If you do not, you risk being dismissed from the test and having your scores canceled. The test administrator will provide pencils and scratch paper. You may not take your own scratch paper into the test center.

After the Test

When you finish your test, hand in your materials and you will be dismissed. Then, go home and relax—you deserve it!

Good luck on the TExES ESL Supplemental test!

TExES
ENGLISH AS A
SECOND LANGUAGE (154)

Domain Reviews

PART I: DOMAIN I

Language Concepts and Language Acquisition

Language Concepts and Language Acquisition

Domain I addresses Competencies 001 and 002.

Competency 001: The ESL teacher understands fundamental language concepts and knows the structure and conventions of the English language.

The beginning ESL teacher:

A. Understands the nature of language and basic concepts of language systems (e.g., phonology, morphology, syntax, lexicon, semantics, discourse, pragmatics) and uses this understanding to facilitate student learning in the ESL classroom.

B. Knows the functions and registers of language (e.g., social versus academic language) in English and uses this knowledge to develop and modify instructional materials, deliver instruction and promote ESL students' English-language proficiency.

C. Understands the interrelatedness of listening, speaking, reading and writing and uses this understanding to develop ESL students' English-language proficiency.

D. Knows the structure of the English language (e.g., word formation, grammar, vocabulary and syntax) and the patterns and conventions of written and spoken English and uses this knowledge to model and provide instruction to develop the foundations of English mechanics necessary to understand content-based instruction and accelerated learning of English in accordance with the English Language Proficiency Standards (ELPS).

Competency 002: The ESL teacher understands the processes of first-language (L1) and second-language (L2) acquisition and the interrelatedness of L1 and L2 development.

The beginning teacher:

A. Knows theories, concepts and research related to L1 and L2 acquisition.

B. Uses knowledge of theories, concepts and research related to L1 and L2 acquisition to select effective, appropriate methods and strategies for promoting students' English-language development at various stages.

C. Knows cognitive processes (e.g., memorization, categorization, generalization, metacognition) involved in synthesizing and internalizing language rules for second-language acquisition.

D. Analyzes the interrelatedness of first- and second-language acquisition and ways in which L1 may affect development of L2.

E. Knows common difficulties (e.g., idiomatic expressions; L1 interference in syntax, phonology and morphology) experienced by ESL students in learning English and effective strategies for helping students overcome those difficulties.

Competency 001

Competency 001

The ESL teacher understands fundamental language concepts and knows the structure and conventions of the English language.

Chapter 1 will focus on Competency 001—the fundamental language concepts, structure, and conventions of the English language.

The English language is enormously rich and complex. Its multilayered structure is the by-product of invasion, conquest, and scientific advancement. English has been shaped over thousands of years by many different groups—Anglo-Saxon tribes, Viking invaders, Norman conquerors, Renaissance scholars, New World explorers, Native Americans, slaves from West Africa, Mexican ranch hands, and generations of immigrants. In terms of vocabulary, it is the richest language in the world. There are more than 500,000 words listed in unabridged dictionaries, and it is estimated that there are another half million technical and scientific terms (McCrum, 1986).

The Structure of English

Mastering the vocabulary, pronunciation, sentence structure, and working grammar of English is very challenging. Yet, beneath its confusing and often frustrating surface is an underlying structure that students can learn and educators must be prepared to explain. Research has shown that in addition to providing many opportunities to use English in meaningful and motivating situations, effective second-language instruction explicitly teaches the features of the second language—syntax, grammar, vocabulary, pronunciation, and conventions of social use (Lyster, 2007; Genesee, 2006; Norris and Ortega, 2006).

Phonology

At its most basic level, English is comprised of individual sounds, or phonemes. A *phoneme* is the smallest unit of spoken language that makes a difference in a word's meaning. The first phoneme in *cap* is /k/. Changing the phoneme /k/ to the phoneme /m/ creates a word with a different meaning: *map*.

Linguists do not agree on the precise number of phonemes in English. General estimates are between 42 and 44, depending on variables such as dialect and changes in stress (Honig et al., 2008). There are about 25 consonant phonemes in English. Eighteen are represented by a single letter such as /n/ spelled *n*. Seven consonant phonemes are represented by two letters such as /sh/ spelled *sh*.

Consonant phonemes can be classified according to how they are produced:

- **Place of Articulation**—where the sound is produced in the mouth, position of the tongue, open or closed lips, open or closed throat

- **Manner of Articulation**—how air flows through the mouth or nasal cavity

- **Voiced or Unvoiced**—whether or not the vocal chords vibrate

Standard American English has 15 vowel phonemes represented by the letters *a, e, i, o, u* singly and in combination. The pronunciation of a vowel may differ between U.S. regions and dialects. Often, vowel combinations with the phoneme /r/ are considered vowel sounds. The three most common *r*-controlled vowels are /ûr/ as in *her*, /är/ as in *far*, and /ôr/ as in *for* (Moats, 2000).

Vowel phonemes can be classified according to the place of articulation:

- **Tongue Position**—front to back, high to low

- **Lip Position**—wide and smiling, rounded and wide open, rounded and partially open

Phonological awareness is the ability to detect, identify, and manipulate the various parts of spoken language: words, syllables, onsets and rimes, and phonemes. A *syllable* is a word or part of a word that is pronounced as a unit. Each syllable contains one vowel sound. A syllable has two parts: the *onset* and *rime*. The onset is the part of the syllable that comes before the vowel. The rime is the vowel and everything that comes after it. *Phonogram* is a nonlinguistic term that means the same thing as *rime*. The most common syllable division patterns in English are VC/CV (*rab•bit*), V/CV (*ti•ger*), VC/V (*clos•et*), VC/CCV (*hun•dred*), VCC/CV (*ath•lete*), and consonant-*le*, which forms a separate syllable.

Phonological awareness skills follow a developmental sequence from awareness of the larger units of spoken language to the smallest unit—the phoneme. Within each unit of focus, tasks vary in terms of difficulty. Blending spoken parts is easier than segmenting or counting them, which is easier than manipulating the parts by deleting, adding, or substituting them.

Phonemic awareness is the most sophisticated and most critical level of phonological awareness. Being able to blend individual sounds into words and segment words into individual sounds is both a predictor of and contributor to later reading achievement (National Reading Panel, 2000). As teachers plan activities, they need to be aware of these points:

- Blending words with two phonemes (*so*) is easier than blending words with three phonemes (*soap*).

- Blending words with continuous sounds such as /s/, /m/, /f/, and /l/ is easier than blending words with stop sounds such as /d/, /p/, and /k/.

- For segmenting tasks, it is easier to isolate an initial phoneme in a word (/z/ in *zoo*) than a phoneme in the final = (/z/ in *nose*) or medial position (/z/ in *easy*).

Phonological Awareness: Blending and Segmenting Examples Across Levels

Word ⟶		Syllable	Onset-Rime	Phoneme
Blending	Students listen to two small words (*good, bye*) and orally blend them to make a new compound word: *goodbye*	Students listen to a word broken into syllables (bas • ket) and orally blend the parts to say the whole word: *basket*	Students listen to a word broken into its onset and rime (/s/, /ing/) and orally blend the sounds to say the whole word: *sing*	Students listen to a word broken into phonemes (/s/ /o with macron symbol/ /p/) and orally blend the sounds to say the whole word: *soap*
Segmenting	Students listen to a sentence and tap one time for every word in the sentence.	Students listen to a word (*basket*) and clap out the number of syllables (two)	Students listen to a word (*pots*) and orally break the word into its onset and rime: (/p/, /ots/)	Students listen to a word (*soap*), count the individual phonemes, and say the sounds aloud: (three sounds, /s/ /o with macron symbol/ /p/)

Phonological Awareness Instruction for English-Language Learners

The National Literacy Panel (August and Shanahan, 2000) found that just like their English-speaking peers, English-language learners benefit from structured, direct instruction in the essential components of literacy: phonemic awareness, phonics, fluency, vocabulary, text comprehension, and writing. To align instruction with best practice, teachers should do the following:

- Plan activities that build phonological awareness and develop students' appreciation for the rhythm and sounds of English. Keep the activities lively and fun. Focus on no more than one or two skills per lesson.

- Progress from easier to more difficult tasks, helping students reach the point where they can blend and segment sounds in words.

- Have students point to or place chips, buttons, and blocks as they count and manipulate sounds. The use of manipulatives has been shown to make sounds less abstract and more concrete.

- Build on what students know. Skills, concepts, and knowledge transfer across languages. For example, if students already know that words are made up of sounds, they will transfer that understanding to English words and sounds.

- Directly teach the sounds that make up English words. Know which sounds do not exist in students' home languages and are therefore "new." Teach students how to produce the sounds, and give ample opportunities for students to hear and say words that contain those sounds.

- Capitalize on the many sounds that Spanish and English share. For example, when working with the sound /ch/, teachers should point out that it's the same sound students hear and say in the Spanish words *ocho* and *chaqueta*.

- Consider if students are making errors because they are correctly applying the "rules" of their home languages. For example, consonant clusters with *s* never appear at the beginning of Spanish words, so Spanish-speaking students may add the long vowel sound ā to the beginning of words like *stop* and *scrape*. It is important to work with students to identify these differences and build on their dual language skills.

Morphology

Morphemes are the meaningful parts of words. A morpheme may be an entire word like *play* or part of a word like *–ful*. Morphemes are the building blocks of English words. Most came from one of three ancient languages: Anglo-Saxon, Greek, and Latin. These different origins have had an influence on letter-sound correspondences, syllable patterns, and morpheme patterns. Teaching students to recognize these patterns improves their decoding, spelling, reading fluency, and comprehension (Henry, 2003).

There are two basic types of morphemes: free and bound. Free morphemes can stand alone as words. Bound morphemes must be attached to other morphemes to make words. Anglo-Saxon root words, or base words, are free morphemes. They are the short, common words used in everyday speech: *help, night, dog, work, house, love, spell*. They can stand alone, be combined into compound words (*doghouse*), or have prefixes and suffixes added to them (*misspell, spelling*).

Two types of suffixes are added to Anglo-Saxon root words. Derivational suffixes often change the root word's part of speech (*playful, lovely*). They may also alter the base word's meaning (*loveless*), pronunciation, or spelling. Inflectional suffixes usually don't change a word's part of speech. They show possession or plurality (*boxes*), verb tense (*helped*), and comparison (*louder*).

Latin roots cannot stand on their own or be compounded. They must have a prefix and/or suffix added to them. For example, the Latin root *struct* is part of the affixed English word *construction.* The prefix *con-* and the suffix *-ion* were added to the root to make a complete word. Words with Latin roots abound in technical texts, English literature, and textbooks in general.

Greek roots are also bound morphemes. They are usually combined, not affixed. For example, *microscope* is made up of the two Greek combining forms *micro* and *scope.* Words with Greek roots primarily appear in scientific texts, though some like *photograph* and *symphony* are part of everyday speech.

■ Morphemic Analysis for English-Language Learners

Examining how words are put together helps students recognize recurring patterns and provides strategies for decoding, understanding, and spelling multisyllabic words (Moats, 2005). Rather than teaching English-language learners a set of rules and generalizations, teachers should develop students' morphemic awareness through hands-on, interactive, and cooperative activities. The goal is for students to become "word detectives" who enjoy analyzing words and playing with language. To align instruction with best practice, teachers should do the following:

- Focus on English morphemes that are useful to know because they occur most frequently. Limit the number of morphemes introduced at one time, and initially teach prefixes and suffixes in separate lessons.

- Teach derivational suffixes when introducing parts of speech. For example, students can learn to recognize that the suffixes *-y, -al,* and *-er* are endings for adjectives, or words that describe.

- Build on what students know. Many different languages have borrowed English scientific and technology terms. When Spanish-speaking students are shown how to look for cognates, they tap into an extraordinary storehouse of knowledge because Spanish is based on multisyllabic words with Latin roots. In fact, a two-syllable Anglo-Saxon compound like *bathtub* is far more daunting for Spanish speakers than a five-syllable word like *educational.*

- Help students discover and remember patterns through multisensory, multimodal experiences. Ask students to write words on index cards, sort them, color-code the shared root words or affixes, and then read the words in each group aloud. Use graphic tools like semantic maps and word sums to show relationships between words' structures, spellings, and meanings.

- Guide students in using morpheme patterns to examine related words, pointing out how adding prefixes and suffixes can change the pronunciation and stressed syllable of the shared root (*nation, national, nationally, international*).

Syntax

Syntax refers to the rules of grammar that govern how sentences are formed, such as never splitting an infinitive or ending a sentence with a preposition. The term also refers to word-order patterns. Understanding how words, phrases, and clauses are combined into a meaningful sentence requires a great deal of knowledge—from sentence types and sentence structures to parts of speech function and the mechanics of written language.

A *sentence* is a group of words that express a complete thought. Every sentence has a *subject* (whom or what the sentence is about) and a *predicate* (what the subject is, has, or does). As English-language learners use their speaking skills in meaningful interactions, they construct four different sentence types:

- A *declarative sentence* tells something. Students use declarative sentences when they identify objects, share prior knowledge, make comparisons, or describe people and places.

- An *interrogative sentence* asks a question. Students use interrogative sentences when they ask for information, exchange greetings, make requests, or ask for clarification.

- An *exclamatory sentence* shows surprise or strong emotion. Students use exclamatory sentences when they express gratitude, express likes and dislikes, or give opinions.

- An *imperative sentence* gives a command. Students use imperative sentences when they give directions, conduct a transaction, or make a request.

Unlike spoken language, academic texts contain sophisticated sentence structures:

- A *compound sentence* has two independent clauses that are joined with a conjunction such as *or, and,* or *but.* Example: *The femur is the largest bone in the body, and the ossicle bones located in the middle ear are the smallest.*

- A *complex sentence* has one independent clause and one or more dependent clauses. Example with two dependent clauses: *Nerve messages are sent <u>from receptor cells to the brain</u>, <u>which interprets the messages as sounds</u>.*

Syntax Transfer Issues

Students' home language experiences may affect how quickly and consistently they use correct English word order and sentence structures. Teachers can accelerate learning when they build on the ways that students' home languages parallel English. At the same time, it is important to know sentence and word-order patterns that may transfer negatively to students' learning of English so that teachers can provide focused support in those skill areas.

Syntax in Academic Texts

In order to read and respond to content area texts, English-language learners need strategies for unpacking the meaning of long sentences with multiple ideas. To develop their content knowledge, they can't merely read for the gist of the text or look for discrete pieces of information. They have to learn how to dig into long sentences to analyze the hierarchical relationships between clauses and figure out the main idea of the sentence (Scarcella, 2002; Snow et al., 1998). Best practice suggests that teachers do the following:

- Discuss English syntax in the context of real reading and writing. Model how to break long sentences into chunks, interpret the chunks, and then sum up the main idea. Teach students how to look for and use words that introduce a dependent clause and signal certain relationships. For example:

  Cause: *because, since, due to, as a result, therefore*

  Time: *when, before, after, as, until, during, throughout*

  Location: *above, below, across, under, between, within*

  Condition: *if, unless, although*

  Relative Pronouns: *that, which, who, whom, whose*

- Teach students how to identify long strings of words that make up noun groups and analyze what they mean. Example: _This intricate branched network of increasingly smaller tubes_ ends in clusters of tiny airbags called alveoli.

- Teach students how to identify the passive voice and restate the idea in active voice or paraphrase it in their own words. Example: _Smooth muscle is located in the walls of some internal organs_ vs. _There is smooth muscle in the walls of some internal organs_.

- Encourage students to incorporate complex sentence structures into their own writing by providing sentence frames or graphic organizers that guide them in building basic sentences and then extending the sentences with dependent clauses.

Semantics and Pragmatics

Semantics is the study of the meaning of language—the meaning of words, phrases, sentences, passages, and entire texts. It includes the study of word origins, words with multiple meanings, how word meanings change over time, and shades of meaning differences among words (_cool, cold, freezing_). _Pragmatics_ is a branch of semantics. It focuses on the language choices people make in social contexts and the effects those choices have on other people.

English-language learners are engaging with semantics and pragmatics every day. They are not only learning the meanings of new English words, they are also learning how and when to use those words appropriately in their own speaking and writing. The same word or sentence may convey a different message depending on the situation and the speaker and listener. English-language learners may be so focused on the literal meaning that they don't understand how a speaker's tone of voice and emphasis can change a message such as _That guy's a real genius!_ from heartfelt praise to criticism.

Word Choice and Norms of Social Usage

Finding "just the right word" for the right social context is a complex task. It involves knowing the difference between a word's dictionary definition (denotation) and the feelings it evokes in other people (connotation). On the surface, the phrases _an inexpensive dress_ and _a cheap dress_ both mean the same thing (the dress does not cost much money). However, for fluent English speakers, the word _cheap_ has a negative connotation that suggests poor quality. Selecting appropriate language also requires understanding how people will interpret and react to word choice and levels of formality based on their relationship with the speaker/writer and the situation.

Phrasal Verbs

For English-language learners, phrasal verbs are one of the most confounding features of the English language. A phrasal verb is the combination of a verb and a preposition or adverb such *go out, go over, go about, go on*. Phrasal verbs are abundant in spoken language and informal writing. They're problematic for English-language learners for several reasons:

- The meanings of many phrasal verbs can't be inferred from their individual elements. Examples: *come off, make up*.

- They often have more than one meaning. Example: *go on* can mean "continue to do," "happen," "speak at length," "participate in," or "begin to operate."

- When students use them in a sentence with an object, they aren't sure where to position the adverb or preposition.

Other Figurative Language

Phrasal verbs are one example of figurative language, which is words and phrases that have meanings beyond their literal definitions. Figurative language makes oral and written language rich and interesting. English-language learners grapple with several types of figurative language, including the following:

- **Idiom**—a set phrase that expresses an idea in a colorful way (for example, *hit the books, a piece of cake, rain cats and dogs*)

- **Simile**—the comparison of two things using the word *like* or *as* (for example, *Your hands are like ice. The lake is as still as a statue.*)

- **Metaphor**—a comparison of two things without the words *like* or *as* (for example, *The sun shone fire red. That football player is an absolute machine!*)

Accelerating Students' Semantic Knowledge

For most English as a Second Language learners, it takes years of experience to fully understand and use all the nuanced features of the second language. There are, however, proven ways to accelerate students' learning and help them incorporate what they learn in their own speaking and writing. To align instruction with best practice, teachers should do the following:

- Plan clear content and language outcomes for each lesson, which is the essence of effective content-based learning. Structure lessons around content-based tasks and interactions that require students to negotiate meaning through the four modalities: speaking, listening, reading, and writing. This develops their ability to understand and produce discourse styles specific to particular content areas (Robinson & Ellis, 2008).

- To ensure that students at all language proficiency levels are engaged and challenged, modify learning outcomes, tasks, and grouping configurations accordingly.

- Provide robust vocabulary instruction that goes beyond a student-friendly explanation of a word or its dictionary definition. Create opportunities for students to explore the word in multiple contexts so that they truly learn it: when to use it and with whom, its level of formality, how its meaning changes in different contexts or subject areas, its connotations, and how it differs from words with similar meanings.

- Use graphic aids to deepen and consolidate what students are learning. These include the following:

  - photographs, videos, picture dictionaries, props and other visual representations

  - semantic webs, word maps, synonym scales

Academic English

Academic English is the language of school and the pathway to educational and occupational opportunity. It refers to the abstract, challenging language that enables students to fully participate in the classroom experience. It involves understanding and actively using the content vocabulary, complex sentence structures, and discourse styles specific to mathematics, science, literature, and social studies. It also involves understanding and carrying out complex directions such as comparing and contrasting events, explaining causal relationships, inferring motivation, developing a persuasive argument, and writing a procedural text.

Although young English-language learners can reach fairly high levels of conversational English in just two to three years, research has shown that proficiency in academic English may require six, seven, or more years (Genesee et al., 2006). This underscores the importance of *content-based learning*, which accelerates students' content-area knowledge while supporting their English-language development. For detailed information about aligning subject-area instruction and assessment to English Language Proficiency Standards (ELPS), see *Educator Guide to TELPAS: Grades K-12* at *www.tea.state.tx.us*. Search under Student Assessment Division.

Language Functions

According to Halliday's Systemic Functional Linguistics (SFL) approach (Halliday, 1994), language is both content and a resource that allows students to participate in new academic contexts and build discipline-specific knowledge. In an academic setting, students use oral and written language for a number of purposes. As teachers plan opportunities for students to practice these language functions in authentic contexts, they should identify the specific vocabulary and grammatical structures that students will need to learn. For example, in order to make comparisons, they will need to know words such as *both, also, similar, different,* and *unlike.* They will also need to know how to form comparative (*smaller, more colorful*) and superlative adjectives (*smallest, most colorful*).

Examples of Academic Language Functions

- Repeat spoken language
- Express greetings and social courtesies
- Ask and answer questions
- Express likes and dislikes
- Express feelings, needs, and opinions
- Give commands
- Describe people, places, objects, and events
- Recite
- Give directions
- Dramatize or role-play
- Ask for information

- Make comparisons
- Engage in discussion
- Retell a story or events in sequence
- Define and explain
- Summarize
- Persuade and justify with evidence
- Verify or confirm information
- Support ideas with evidence
- Clarify ideas with elaboration
- Negotiate

Language Register and Levels of Formality

Register refers to the variety of language appropriate in a given situation. Most fluent speakers are able to communicate in a variety of registers: *formal* with strangers, *informal* with friends, *technical* in the workplace, and *slang* on the basketball court. Most English-language learners understand the concept of adapting language as a sign of respect for older family members and adults. In Spanish, there are different words for *you* as a form of address—*tú* is used only to address children and close friends and family. *Usted* is used when addressing everyone else. In Japanese, levels of formality are shown through the choice of verbs, which have "honorific" and "humble" forms.

Although English-language learners may understand the concept, they do not have the same intuitive sense as native speakers about the appropriateness of specific English words and grammatical structures in a given situation with certain people. That is why it is important to teach students explicitly when and with whom to use the vocabulary and sentence patterns they are learning.

Integrating Listening, Speaking, Reading, and Writing

Initially, English-language learners' listening and speaking vocabularies are much larger than their print vocabularies. They understand more words when they hear the words spoken or read aloud than they can understand when reading on their own. They also initially use more words when they speak than they use in their writing. As students' reading and writing skills develop, their print vocabularies begin to play a more important role. At this point, they know the meanings of many words in print that are not part of their oral vocabularies.

Effective instruction gives English-language learners ongoing, targeted practice listening, speaking, reading, and writing as they learn new subject matter. To prepare students for academic success, teachers need to plan content-based instruction carefully so that it will support the development of two sets of discourse skills: content-specific and general.

Mathematics: Language Development in All Domains

	Listening and Speaking	Reading	Writing
Content-Specific Discourse	Measure and confirm dimensions with partners Restate a problem Discuss operations Explain a solution	Word problems Equations Proofs Data sets Graphs Surveys	Solutions Proofs Data sets Graphs Surveys
General Discourse	Engage in a discussion Listen actively Ask for information Ask for clarification Conduct an interview	Highlight key words Identify main ideas and details Identify relationships (cause-effect, time sequence) Use knowledge of word parts to infer meaning (prefixes, inflectional endings, Greek roots,)	Summaries Comparisons Notes Lists Charts Self-assessments

Based on Sherris, 2008

■ Review Questions

Use the information below to answer questions 1 and 2.

Jose is a middle school student whose family recently emigrated from Argentina. He has limited English-language skills and has difficulty explaining to his teacher why he did not complete his homework. He has the following conversation with his teacher regarding a missed homework assignment.

Jose: Is because I lose . . . uhmmmm . . . my notebook. Is no finish. Uhmm-mmm . . . the homework.

Teacher: You were unable to complete your assignment, Jose? [speaking slowly and clearly enunciating]

Jose: Yes. No do it.

Teacher: Do you think you could complete your homework during your study period? [speaking slowly and clearly enunciating]

Jose: Uhmmmmm . . . Estudy time. Yes. Finish.

Teacher: That's great, Jose. I hope to get your completed assignment later today.

Jose: Is good.

1. Which of the following statements best explains Jose's teacher's responses during the conversation about homework?

    (A) The teacher seems to be encouraging Jose's oral-language competence by responding to him in complete sentences that reflect Jose's communicative intentions

    (B) The teacher wants Jose to understand the connection between homework and academic success

    (C) Because of Jose's limited English proficiency, the teacher probably does not understand what Jose is saying

    (D) The teacher thinks Jose does not understand what she's saying to him, so she repeats her responses to Jose to create meaningful redundancy

    The correct response is (**A**). The teacher respects Jose's efforts to communicate by focusing on content rather than incorrect forms. By responding in complete sentences that reflect Jose's message, the teacher is promoting Jose's oral-language development through modeling and reinforcement. (B) is incorrect because the teacher seems to be using discussion of the assignment to provide scaffolding for the student's L2 development rather than to pressure Jose into completing the homework assignment. (C) is incorrect because the teacher's responses indicate that she clearly understands Jose. (D) is incorrect because nothing in the dialogue indicates that Jose does not understand; the teacher is aware that Jose does understands.

2. This conversation between Jose and his teacher reflects which of the following types of second-language acquisition as described in Texas English Language Proficiency Standards documents?

    (A) Cognitive Academic Language Proficiency (CALP)

    (B) Comprehensible input

    (C) Basic Interpersonal Communicative Skills (BICS)

    (D) Higher order thinking skills

    The correct response is (**C**). TELPAS materials describe two types of second-language acquisition: (1) Cognitive Academic Language Proficiency (CALP), which refers to students' understanding of course content (i.e., math, science, social studies, English), and (2) Basic Interpersonal Communicative Skills (BICS), which enables students to communicate in routine interactions. The exchange in this scenario reflects BICS because student and teacher are clarifying a routine class expectation. (A) is incorrect because this is a conversation about homework completion, not about understanding class content. (B) is incorrect, although the teacher is clearly creating comprehensible input by making sure Jose understands. However, comprehensible input is not one of the two types of L2 acquisition presented in TELPAS documents. (D) is incorrect because it does not reflect the communicative intentions in the conversation between Jose and his teacher.

3. Cindy, a tenth-grade ELL student, is writing an essay about how her sister has inspired her to aim high. She includes the following sentence in her draft: "It does not matter if the person is well known or even if they are family; anyone can be an inspiration." This sentence contains a grammatical error in

   (A) indefinite pronoun use.

   (B) pronoun number.

   (C) pronoun case.

   (D) pronoun antecedent.

   The correct response is (**B**). The student writes "person" singular and then uses the plural pronoun "they" to refer to the singular antecedent. (A) is incorrect because the indefinite pronouns in the passage ("it" and "anyone") are used appropriately. (C) is incorrect because the nominative case "they" is correct in this sentence; the problem is plural vs. the needed singular. (D) is incorrect because the antecedent-pronoun connection is correct; the issue is the plural-singular mismatch.

4. Which of the following sentences demonstrates the use of a subordinating conjunction in a grammatically correct string?

   (A) Since I started attending school, I was an average student.

   (B) Since I had started school, I had to give up afternoon backyard dirt wars.

   (C) Since first grade, I have been an average student.

   (D) Since I started attending school because I reached my six years birthday and had to turn to books instead of play things.

   The correct response is (**B**). This complex sentence includes correct use of past perfect in both the dependent and independent clauses, making it clear that "since" means "from the time that…." (A) is incorrect because the verb forms—simple past tense in both the dependent and independent clauses—suggests that "since" means "because" in this sentence when the writer is looking back to a much earlier time and actually is trying to say "from the time I started school, I have been an average student." (C) is incorrect because "since" is a preposition not a subordinating conjunction in this sentence. (D) is incorrect because, while the two subordinate structures are superficially correctly written, the string is a fragment, not a grammatically correct structure.

5.   Which of the following sentences shows correct use of an introductory participle phrase?

   (A)   Looking around, the boys noticed an open window.

   (B)   Looking around, someone was probably following the boys.

   (C)   Looking around, the truck seemed too close to the building.

   (D)   Looking around, it was getting darker and darker.

The correct response is (**A**). Introductory participle phrases frequently result in a syntactic error, labeled a dangling modifier. (A) is the only sentence in this group in which the initial participle phrase correctly modifies the noun. (B), (C), and (D) are incorrect because the introductory participle phrase does not modify the noun that is in the subject position in any of these options.

Competency 002

Competency 002

The ESL teacher understands the processes of first-language (L1) and second-language (L2) acquisition and the interrelatedness of L1 and L2 development.

Chapter 2 will focus on Competency 002—the first-language and second-language acquisition and how their development is interrelated.

How Children Learn Language

Over the past 75 years, many theories have attempted to explain how a young child learns the family language. The behaviorist view was influenced by the work of Ivan Pavlov, John B. Watson, and B. F. Skinner. Its proponents suggested that language is learned through repeated environmental stimuli and the child's response to those stimuli. When the child communicates a need and a parent fills that need, the child's use of language receives positive reinforcement. That reinforcement prompts the child to use the language form again. There are aspects of behaviorism in some current language teaching methods, including repeated audio-lingual drills and the learning until mastery approach.

Most experts now agree that learning a home language is more complex than imitating and receiving feedback from family members. Language is closely linked to social and cognitive development. Most children learn their home language effortlessly and naturally because they are motivated to communicate with the people who care for them—the family members and caregivers who satisfy their physical and emotional needs. Denise McKeon sums it up in this way: "people learn language because they are in real situations communicating about important and interesting things" (McKeon, 1994).

Language acquisition research also shows that children actively construct principles about language based on patterns of speech and generalize those understandings (Chomsky, 1969). That is what occurs when children say *goed* for *went* and *foots* for *feet* before they hear models of the correct irregular forms or get corrective feedback from family members.

Variations in Language Use

Among the speakers of any given language, there are significant variations. Geographic location, socioeconomic status, and culture shape the particular variety of language children learn—names for objects (*soda* vs. *pop*), pronunciation (how the vowel sound in *talk* is said in Chicago vs. New York), syntax (*standing on line* vs. *standing in line*), and general communication patterns. It's important for educators to be aware of social perceptions associated with language patterns and dialects. They also need to be aware of their own attitudes about "correctness" so that they can avoid judging a child's intelligence, motivation, or politeness based on the particular language forms learned in a speech community.

Poverty and Language Development

Poverty has an enormous impact on children's early language experiences. By the time they enter preschool, there is already a significant gap in the speaking vocabularies of many three-year-olds. Children from advantaged homes have oral vocabularies that are as much as five times larger than children from disadvantaged homes (Hart and Risely, 1995). Children's socio-economic status is also related to the type of language they learn and use at home. Children from middle-class communities have more experience with the type of language needed for success in school: how to label objects, answer questions, create extended narratives, predict events, and build on background knowledge (Heath, 1983).

Piaget's Stages of Cognitive Development

Jean Piaget's groundbreaking work in developmental psychology (Piaget, 1936) was inspired by the idea that children think differently than adults. His theories were a departure from the Empiricist view that children learn through experience, or the Nativist view that children are born with innate knowledge that matures over time. Piaget maintained that from infancy to adolescence, every child goes through four universal stages of cognitive development. At each stage, the child develops a mental construct of the world around her. As children go through the four stages, cognition develops from concrete and egocentric thinking to abstract reasoning and hypotheses.

Stage 1: Sensorimotor Stage (ages 0–2)

Stage 2: Preoperational Stage (ages 2–7)

Stage 3: Concrete Operational Stage (ages 7–11)

Stage 4: Formal Operational Stages (age 11 to adulthood)

Piaget's theories have influenced educational practice in many significant ways. Subsequent research built on his work and led to these educational practices:

- instruction that is developmentally appropriate
- discovery learning that actively engages students
- partner and group activities that promote collaboration
- instruction that helps students retrieve existing schema and build new schema

Vygotsky's Social Development Theory

Lev Vygotsky was a contemporary of Piaget. However, unlike Piaget, his theories took into account the role of social interactions and family culture in shaping a child's cognitive development. In his view, cognitive development is a source and effect of the particular language a child learns. Community plays a central role in the process of "making meaning" (Vygotsky, 1978).

Vygotsky also introduced the concept of the Zone of Proximal Development (ZPD). It is the difference between what a child can accomplish independently and what the child can achieve with guidance from a skilled partner such as a teacher, parent, or peer. According to Vygotsky, the greatest learning occurs when instruction is focused within a child's ZPD.

Cognitive Processes in Second Language Acquisition

Proficiency in a second language requires mental representations of the ways the language works (*analysis*) and the skilled attention and inhibition (*control*) that enable someone to access and activate those mental representations (Bialystok, 2001). The level of cognitive demand depends on the complexity of the language task. For example, a conversation with friends about something as concrete as the lunch menu in the cafeteria has a lower cognitive demand than a class debate about the scientific reclassification of Pluto.

The National Literacy Panel found that cognitive abilities are among several factors related to English-language learners' proficiency in reading and writing. Other key factors are a child's general language proficiency, English oral proficiency, age, previous learning, and the similarities and differences between the child's home language and English (August and Shanahan, 2006).

For information about the transfer of knowledge and skills between L1 and L2, see pages 31–35.

Stephen Krashen's Theory of Second Language Acquisition

Since the 1980s, Stephen Krashen's work has influenced the direction of second-language research and practice. His Theory of Second Language Acquisition (Krashen, 1981) contains five hypotheses:

1. **The Acquisition-Learning Hypothesis:** There are two ways of gaining knowledge and developing skills. *Acquisition* is a subconscious process that takes place when doing meaningful, authentic tasks—in the same way a child learns a home language. *Learning* is the passive process in which a teacher imparts information through direct teaching and lecture. According to Krashen's hypothesis, acquisition is the better way to learn a second language. Until recently, researchers were divided on the question of whether or not students could learn English by being taught directly. Several studies now support the

view that effective second-language instruction combines explicit teaching of the features of the second language—syntax, grammar, vocabulary, pronunciation, and norms of social usage—with ample opportunities to use the new language in meaningful and motivating situations (Goldenberg, 2008).

2. **The Monitor Hypothesis:** This is the conscious effort to monitor one's language use by applying known rules. It is of limited value in speaking since it requires immediate access to, and application of, the rules. It can be useful in the context of writing when the instructional goal is editing for the correct use of grammar and conventions.

3. **The Natural Order Hypothesis:** All second-language learners, regardless of age or L1, acquire the grammatical structures of the language they are learning in a predictable order. If a student is not yet ready to acquire a language feature, direct teaching cannot influence the natural order of acquisition.

4. **The Input Hypothesis:** Students learn best when they receive *comprehensible input*—input that is not too easy and not too hard but slightly challenging. This is a cognitive perspective focused on what takes place in the mind of an individual learner. Krashen expresses the idea of one step beyond the learner's current stage of language competence as $i + 1$. (For more information about comprehensible input, see pages 70–71.)

5. **The Affective Filter:** Variables such as motivation, self-confidence, and anxiety level can form a type of filter, or mental block, that impedes language acquisition. To be effective, second-language instruction must lower the affective filter.

Stages of Second Language Acquisition

Krashen and his colleague Terrell identified five stages of second-language acquisition (Krashen and Terrell, 1983). Regardless of their age or home language, all second-language learners progress through these stages, and each stage has an approximate time frame. How quickly a student progresses through these stages varies depending on the student's prior educational background, sociocultural experiences, and initial knowledge of L2.

1. **The Preproduction Stage:** In the Preproduction Stage (0–6 months), the student has minimal comprehension and remains silent, internalizing the new language and making connections to L1. Responses are nonverbal, including nodding "yes" or indicating "no," as well as pointing, drawing, and using gestures.

2. **The Early Production Stage:** In the Early Production Stage (6 months–1 year), the student has limited comprehension and communicates with telegraphic speech (one key word) and formulaic speech (short familiar phrases). The student also begins to use present-tense verbs.

3. **The Speech Emergence Stage:** In the Speech Emergence Stage (1–3 years), the student has good comprehension and can produce simple sentences with grammar and pronunciation errors. The student frequently misunderstands idioms and other types of nonliteral language.

4. **The Intermediate Fluency Stage:** In the Intermediate Fluency Stage (3–5 years), the student has excellent comprehension and communicates using newly acquired vocabulary. The student participates in discussions of an academic nature and makes few grammatical errors. The student may continue to misunderstand idioms.

5. **The Advanced Fluency Stage:** In the Advanced Fluency Stage (5–7 years), the student has near-native fluency.

Jim Cummins' Proficiency Types: BICS and CALP

In the 1980s, Jim Cummins identified two essential types of language proficiency. The first is BICS, Basic Interpersonal Communication Skills. They are the skills that students use to communicate in everyday social situations and routine classroom interactions. Since students have access to visual cues and receive continuous feedback that conveys and builds meaning, BICS is considered *context embedded*. Most second language learners develop near-native BICS fluency within two years of living, where the target language is the dominant language.

The second type of proficiency Cummins identified is CALP, or Cognitive Academic Language Proficiency. It is the academic language of school that focuses on more abstract ideas in context-reduced situations such as listening to a lecture or reading a content-area textbook. Since CALP requires higher-order thinking skills, CALP takes students much longer to develop than BISC—approximately five to seven years (Cummins, 1981).

In Cummins's construct, BICS and CALP involve more than words. BICS includes social cues and nonverbal gestures such as waving to a friend or getting a "thumbs-up" from a teacher. CALP involves the complex thinking skills required to carry out instructional tasks such as categorizing, analyzing, and summarizing. For further information about BICS and CALP and the relationship between academic language proficiency and academic achievement, see *Educator Guide to TELPAS: Grades K-12* at *www.tea.state. tx.us*. Search under Student Assessment Division.

Metacognition and Language Learning

Metacognition is the awareness of one's mental processes. It enables a student to control his or her learning by defining his or her learning goals, monitoring his or her progress, and applying or adjusting strategies as needed (Bransford et al., 2000). The metacognitive skills in the Learning Strategies strand of Texas ELPS Student Expectations are designed to help students become active and strategic language learners.

A metacognitive approach to teaching grew out of cognitive theories about the way the brain retrieves and applies information. In the context of language instruction, teachers support learning when they do the following:

- explicitly present and review the content and language goals for each lesson (Sherris, 2008)

- assess and activate background knowledge

- use graphic organizers to explain the relationships between ideas (hierarchy), objects (category), and events (sequence)

- teach students strategies for learning language such as asking clarifying questions or practicing formal language with an adult

- use think-alouds that model how good readers use text and visual clues to infer a word's meaning

- teach students how to monitor their comprehension through predicting, visualizing, identifying main ideas, and asking questions (Chamot & O'Malley, 1994)

- incorporate student self- and peer assessments into the class routine

The Relationship of L1 and L2

In today's classrooms, there is tremendous linguistic diversity among young English-language learners. The vast majority speaks Spanish, but English-language learners also include students whose families speak Vietnamese, Hmong, Chinese, Korean, Khmer, Laotian, Hindi, Tagalog, Haitian Creole, and Russian. There may not be many similarities between some of these home languages and English, yet the experiences children have in their primary language have a direct effect on their acquisition of English. There is considerable evidence that knowledge and skills transfer across languages (August, 2005; Gillon, 2004; Jiménez, 1997; Durgunoglu et al., 1993; Cummins, 1981). Once a child learns the concepts of "water," "cloud," and "rain" in her/his primary language, she/he can draw upon that knowledge to learn about the water cycle in English. Cummins refers to this as *common underlying proficiency* (CUP). If a concept is already known, students can more easily learn the English label for that concept and understand how it fits into a broader context.

The Bridge Between L1 and English

A student's proficiency and literacy experiences in L1 provide a strong foundation for academic achievement in English. Research shows that English-language learners are able to transfer the following:

- background knowledge

- phonological awareness (for example, the understanding that individual sounds can be blended into meaningful units—words)

- reading comprehension skills (for example, summarizing and making predictions)

- decoding skills if L1 is an alphabetic language

- knowledge of specific letter-sound correspondences and spelling skills if L1 uses the Roman alphabet (for example, the letter *m* spells the sound /m/)

Students may not realize that what they know in their home language applies to English. Jiménez (1994) found that less successful bilingual readers saw their two languages as separate and unrelated. In fact, students viewed their L1 background as a disadvantage rather than a valuable repertoire of knowledge and skills. Educators cannot assume that the transfer from L1 will be automatic. When they know what L1 experiences students bring to the classroom and value these experiences, they can accelerate learning by explicitly pointing out what does and doesn't transfer between the two languages.

Capitalizing on Cognates

Cognates are words in two languages that share a similar spelling, pronunciation, and meaning. Due to their common Latin and Greek roots, English and Spanish share a large number of cognate pairs (*information/información, example/ejemplo, science/ciencia, music/música*). According to some estimates, as many as 30 to 40 percent of English words have a related Spanish word.

Building cognate awareness requires explicit instruction because English-language learners do not automatically recognize and make use of cognates. Identifying specific cognates pairs and teaching students to use their knowledge of Spanish supports English-language acquisition (August et al., 2005; Bravo, Hiebert, and Pearson, 2005). Instruction should focus on words that students are likely to know from their everyday use of Spanish—that is, words they frequently hear or read. Teachers should point out any differences in pronunciation or stressed syllable since these differences may prevent students from recognizing that the words are related.

When planning instruction, it's also important to confirm that the word pairs have the same meaning. *False cognates* are words in two languages that have similar spellings but different meanings. These "false friends" can lead to confusion and embarrassment. For example, in Spanish *pie* means "foot," *actual* means "current," and *éxito* means "success."

Possible L1 Interference With L2

The differences between a student's home language and English lead to *negative transfer*. That occurs when students apply a rule or pattern from their home languages and produce an inappropriate form in English. Ellis (1997) makes a distinction between *errors* and *mistakes*. *Errors* are caused by gaps in a student's knowledge and can be traced to the phonology, letter-sound correspondences, morphology, or syntax of L1. *Mistakes* are occasional lapses in performance. This distinction has important implications for the teaching and learning process. When teachers are aware of a student's L1 knowledge, they can predict the types of errors the student is likely to make in English and adapt instruction accordingly.

Negative Transfer: Spanish Phonic Elements

Able readers in Spanish have mastered a number of important literacy skills that are transferrable to reading in English. As teachers introduce English phonics, they can draw on a large number of phonic elements that the two languages share. However, certain features of the Spanish letter-sound system are likely to cause difficulties due to their negative transfer. These include the following:

- The five vowel sounds represented by *a, e, i, o, u* are relatively invariable.

- *g* before *e* or *i* has a guttural sound similar to English /h/.

- *h* is a silent letter.

- The consonant digraph *ll* is pronounced /y/.

- *qu* before *e* or *i* is pronounced /k/, never /kw/.

- *v* is pronounced /b/.

- *z* is pronounced /s/ in the Americas.

There are also sound-spelling and syllable patterns in English that have *zero transfer* from Spanish because they do not exist in Spanish. These include short vowels, long vowels with silent *e*, long vowel digraphs, *s*-blends at the beginning of a word, final consonant blends such as *nd*, and consonant digraphs *sh, th, wh*.

Negative Transfer of L1 Syntax

In English, word order conveys meaning. English tends to follow a subject-verb-object syntax, but many languages are more flexible or convey meaning through inflected word endings. English-language learners frequently have difficulty ordering words correctly, especially when they begin to read and write academic texts that contain complex sentences and multiple clauses. The following table identifies some common negative transfer issues based on features of L1 syntax.

English Syntax: Examples of L1 Interference

English Structure	Transfer Issue	Languages
Word Order	Verb can precede subject.	Spanish
	Verb occurs at the end of the sentence.	Korean, Japanese
	Subject pronoun can be omitted.	Chinese, Korean, Spanish
	Adverbs can precede verbs.	Chinese, Korean, Spanish, Haitian Creole

(continued)

(continued)

English Structure	Transfer Issue	Languages
Word Order (cont'd)	Adjectives follow the nouns they modify.	Hmong, Vietnamese, Spanish (the position of the adjective may convey different meanings or emphasis)
	Negative marker goes before the entire verb phrase.	Korean, Spanish
Questions	Can be formed by adding an element to the end of a declarative sentence.	Chinese, Hmong, Korean, Vietnamese, Spanish
	Can be formed by adding a verb and its negative form within a declarative sentence.	Chinese, Vietnamese
	Verbs are used to respond to "yes/no" questions.	Hmong
Commands	Can be formed by adding an adverb after the verb for emphasis.	Hmong, Vietnamese
	Can be formed by adding a time indicator.	Hmong
	Can be formed by adding the verb *go* at the end of the sentence.	Vietnamese

Based on "Language Structure Transfer Chart." In *Avenues,* Teacher's Edition. Carmel, CA: Hampton-Brown, 2003.

Effective Second-Language Instruction

Language acquisition is a dynamic, complex process. For young language-minority children, learning English has significant social, cultural, cognitive, and linguistic dimensions. To support their ongoing English language development, best practice suggests that educators do the following:

- Create a supportive, risk-free environment for experimenting with new English language skills. Value all students' input, keeping the focus on *communication* rather than correctness. The goal is to lower what Krashen describes as the *affective filter.*

- Build on what students know—their knowledge, skills, and experience. This includes the patterns and structures of their home languages that have positive transfer to English.

- Value students' families and communities as *funds of knowledge* (Moll et al., 1992). Engage them as active partners in a broad-based learning community.

- Contextualize learning and make it meaningful for students from different cultural backgrounds. Provide ample opportunities for students to listen, speak, read, and write on relevant topics for authentic purposes. Include *cooperative learning* activities in which students work with a partner or a small group.

- Combine interactive and direct teaching approaches. Challenge students to higher levels of thinking, speaking, and reading in structured discussions and brainstorming activities. In addition, provide direct teaching of specific skills and language structures.

- Use a multisensory approach to enhance memory and learning. Present information in multiple ways, providing students with visual, auditory, and kinesthetic experiences. Use the *Total Physical Response* (TPR) method (see pages 68–69) in which students listen to a series of commands and carry out consecutive actions.

- Scaffold instruction by providing support that is appropriate for students' individual language proficiency levels. Scaffolding may include speaking more slowly and restating, pantomime and gestures, pictures and real objects, demonstrations, picture dictionaries, L1 translations, and extra response time. For more information about aligning instruction with proficiency levels, see Chapter 3.

- Provide robust vocabulary instruction. Use multimedia resources to teach the meanings and the usage norms (formality, register, connotation) of new words and phrases. Present multiple exposures of the new vocabulary in different contexts.

- Teach students strategies for learning and remembering words.

- Modify expectations of student performance, providing multiple pathways for them to show what they've learned regardless of language limitations.

Review Questions

1. A fourth-grade ESL teacher is preparing her students for their state-mandated writing exam where they'll be required to write a short expository essay. She hands out a practice prompt and asks for student volunteers to form a "think-aloud" panel as they consider the prompt and possible response strategies. What ESL model does this instructional activity most closely fit?

(A) Total Physical Response

(B) Cognitive Academic Language Learning Approach (CALLA)

(C) Immersion

(D) Suggestopedia

The correct response is (**B**). In encouraging students to explain how they would approach the prompt, the teacher is promoting their metacognitive understanding of the writing process, a content-specific skill. The Cognitive Academic Language Learning Approach (CALLA) smoothly integrates content and academic language skills and encourages metacognition, all of which are demonstrated in this teaching activity. (A) is incorrect because, while participating in a panel and being in a "fishbowl-type" class situation, the students are not responding to instructions, as is typical in TPR settings. (C) is incorrect because the students are in an ESL classroom where the instructor is clearly providing instructional scaffolding for content-area mastery. (D) is incorrect because the classroom is not structured in the typical Suggestopedia format (where music, seat arrangement, and relaxing movements create a soothing environment).

Use the information below to answer questions 2, 3, and 4.

Mr. Christopher, a middle school social studies teacher, has a mainstream class that includes a large number of intermediate ESL students. His ESL students are having trouble understanding the basic information in each chapter. Ms. Caranza, a colleague who teaches ESL classes, suggests two things: (1) that he break up his lectures into mini-lessons; and (2) that he create groups that include two or more native speakers in each and allow students to network with each other after each mini-lesson.

2. The language-learning scaffold that Ms. Caranza's advice reflects is

(A) syllabus-based instruction.

(B) reliance on universal grammar.

(C) the zone of proximal development.

(D) holistic assessment.

The correct response is (**C**). Vygotsky's zone of proximal development (ZPD) theory suggests that learners can be guided toward higher levels of understanding and independent learning through scaffolding offered by teachers and knowledgeable peers. Grouping that ensures the ESL students can network with native speakers will help them negotiate the ZPD. (A) is incorrect because the issue of a syllabus is irrelevant in this scenario. Clearly, the instructor is interested in promoting student learning rather than staying on some sort of schedule. (B) is incorrect because the concept of universal grammar does not figure into this learning transaction. It is a content-based situation. (D) is incorrect because the core issue in this scenario is comprehension, not assessment.

3. Which of the following statements best explains the value of mini-lessons in helping ESL learners acquire content knowledge?

   (A) Mini-lessons are short in order to keep ESL students from getting bored when they don't understand

   (B) Mini-lessons enable the teacher to divide a lesson into manageable "chunks" of information to help students receive comprehensible input

   (C) In mini-lessons, difficult concepts are omitted, so even beginning ESL learners are able to understand

   (D) Mini-lessons are delivered very quickly so that the teacher is able to cover a lot more information in a class session

   The correct response is (**B**). Although the mini-lesson approach is not restricted to ESL teaching, it is particularly suited to language-learning environments because presenting content information in smaller segments (rather than in a single, long lecture or presentation) promotes students' understanding of complex information. Typically, mini-lessons focus on a discrete learning objective and are delivered in 5- to 20-minute segments, depending on how much discussion and application are necessary. (A) is incorrect, although it could be argued that when students don't understand, they do demonstrate signs of boredom. Averting boredom borne out of lack of understanding is likely a positive side effect of mini-lessons, but not the central rationale for using this approach. (C) is incorrect because the mini-lesson approach does not leave out complexity. Instead, it is designed to make complex concepts accessible. (D) is incorrect because mini-lessons are short but not quickly delivered.

4. Mr. Christopher plans to use Ms. Caranza's mini-lesson and networking suggestion to promote his ESL students' understanding of social studies content. Which of the following additional classroom activities would help him meet his goal?

(A) After each networking session, each group offers the following report to the whole class: "We think the most important information in this mini-lesson is _____, but we want more explanation of _____."

(B) Before each networking session, the teacher asks each student to write down one word he or she doesn't understand. He then creates a class list of vocabulary words.

(C) As part of each networking session, students silently reread the section of the chapter just covered in the mini-lesson.

(D) At the end of each networking session, each student writes a paragraph summarizing the information in the mini-lesson.

The correct response is (**A**). In ending each mini-lesson and networking session with a one-sentence report of each group's understanding, the teacher is promoting English-language proficiency and content knowledge by integrating listening, speaking, reading, and writing skills in a nonthreatening class activity. Furthermore, this feedback while class is still in session enables the teacher to reinforce learning and to clarify misunderstandings. (B) is incorrect because the teacher has identified comprehension as the issue with which he is concerned. A vocabulary exercise would have limited or no impact on the bigger problem. (C) is incorrect because having students independently read something that they already don't understand will not address the teacher's goal to boost comprehension. (D) is incorrect because writing an effective summary requires holistic understanding of the content. Rather than promoting comprehension, writing a summary of content that they don't understand is likely to frustrate the students.

5. A high school with a large population of ESL students whose L1 is Spanish starts out newcomers and intermediate learners in content classes taught in Spanish. As students gain L2 competence, they are moved to content classes made up only of ESL students. When the ESL students demonstrate increased language proficiency, they are mainstreamed into content classes. This approach to ESL instruction is known as

(A) acculturation.

(B) bilingual education.

(C) sheltered instruction.

(D) immersion.

The correct response is (**C**). The scenario describes the typical sheltered instruction approach, which gradually moves language learners to mainstream classes. (A) introduces an aspect of language acquisition not germane to this teaching scenario. (B) misinterprets the scenario: mainstreaming is not focused on bilingualism but instead on learning academic content. (D) is incorrect because the sheltered-instruction approach offers substantive linguistic and content scaffolding for learners. The immersion approach is sometimes pejoratively referred to as "sink or swim," suggesting that scaffolding in that approach is limited or nonexistent.

PART II: DOMAIN II

Instruction and Assessment

Instruction and Assessment

Domain II addresses Competencies 003, 004, 005, 006, and 007.

Competency 003: The ESL teacher understands ESL teaching methods and uses this knowledge to plan and implement effective, developmentally appropriate instruction.

The beginning ESL teacher:

A. Knows applicable Texas Essential Knowledge and Skills (TEKS) and the English Language Proficiency Standards (ELPS) and knows how to design and implement appropriate instruction to address the domains of listening, speaking, reading and writing.

B. Knows effective instructional methods and techniques for the ESL classroom, and selects and uses instructional methods, resources and materials appropriate for addressing specified instructional goals and promoting learning in students with diverse characteristics and needs.

C. Applies knowledge of effective practices, resources and materials for providing content-based ESL instruction, engaging students in critical thinking and fostering students' communicative competence.

D. Knows how to integrate technological tools and resources into the instructional process to facilitate and enhance student learning.

E. Applies effective classroom management and teaching strategies for a variety of ESL environments and situations.

Competency 004: The ESL teacher understands how to promote students' communicative language development in English.

The beginning ESL teacher:

A. Knows applicable Texas Essential Knowledge and Skills (TEKS) and the English Language Proficiency Standards (ELPS) and knows how to design and implement appropriate instruction to address the proficiency level descriptors for the beginning, intermediate, advanced and advanced-high levels in listening and speaking strands.

B. Understands the role of the linguistic environment and conversational support in second-language development, and uses this knowledge to provide a rich, comprehensible language environment with supported opportunities for communication in English.

C. Applies knowledge of practices, resources and materials that are effective in promoting students' communicative competence in English.

D. Understands the interrelatedness of listening, speaking, reading and writing and uses this knowledge to select and use effective strategies for developing students' oral-language proficiency in English.

E. Applies knowledge of effective strategies for helping ESL students transfer language skills from L1 to L2.

F. Applies knowledge of individual differences (e.g., developmental characteristics, cultural and language background, academic strengths, learning styles) to select focused, targeted and systematic second-language acquisition instruction to English-language learners in grade 3 or higher who are at the beginning or intermediate levels of English-language proficiency in listening and/or speaking in accordance with the ELPS.

G. Knows how to provide appropriate feedback in response to students' developing English-language skills.

Competency 005: The ESL teacher understands how to promote students' literacy development in English.

The beginning ESL teacher:

A. Knows applicable Texas Essential Knowledge and Skills (TEKS) and the English Language Proficiency Standards (ELPS) and knows how to design and implement appropriate instruction to address the proficiency level descriptors for the beginning, intermediate, advanced and advanced-high levels in listening and speaking strands.

B. Understands the interrelatedness of listening, speaking, reading and writing and uses this knowledge to select and use effective strategies for developing students' literacy in English.

C. Understands that English is an alphabetic language and applies effective strategies for developing ESL students' phonological knowledge and skills (e.g., phonemic awareness skills, knowledge of English letter-sound associations, knowledge of common English phonograms) and sight-word vocabularies (e.g., phonetically irregular words, high-frequency words).

D. Knows factors that affect ESL students' reading comprehension (e.g., vocabulary, text structures, cultural references) and applies effective strategies for facilitating ESL students' reading comprehension in English.

E. Applies knowledge of effective strategies for helping students transfer literacy knowledge and skills from L1 to L2.

F. Applies knowledge of individual differences (e.g., developmental characteristics, cultural and language background, academic strengths, learning styles) to select focused, targeted and systematic second-language acquisition instruction to English-language learners in grade 3 or higher who are at the beginning or intermediate level of English-language proficiency in reading and/or writing in accordance with the ELPS.

G. Knows personal factors that affect ESL students' English literacy development (e.g., interrupted schooling, literacy status in the primary language, prior literacy experiences) and applies effective strategies for addressing those factors.

Competency 006: The ESL teacher understands how to promote students' content-area learning, academic-language development and achievement across the curriculum.

The beginning ESL teacher:

A. Applies knowledge of effective practices, resources and materials for providing content-based ESL instruction that is linguistically accommodated (communicated, sequenced and scaffolded) to the students' levels of English-language proficiency; engaging students in critical thinking; and developing students' cognitive-academic language proficiency.

B. Knows instructional delivery practices that are effective in facilitating ESL students' application of various strategies (e.g., preteaching key vocabulary;

helping students apply familiar concepts from their cultural backgrounds and prior experiences to new learning; using metacognition; using hands-on and other experiential learning strategies; using realia, media, and other visual supports [graphic organizers] to introduce and/or reinforce concepts) across content areas.

C. Applies knowledge of individual differences (e.g., developmental characteristics, cultural and language background, academic strengths, learning styles) to select instructional strategies and resources that facilitate ESL students' cognitive-academic language development and content-area learning.

D. Knows personal factors that affect ESL students' content-area learning (e.g., prior learning experiences, familiarity with specialized language and vocabulary, familiarity with the structure and uses of textbooks and other print resources) and applies effective strategies for addressing those factors.

Competency 007: The ESL teacher understands formal and informal assessment procedures and instruments used in ESL programs and uses assessment results to plan and adapt instruction.

The beginning ESL teacher:

A. Knows basic concepts, issues and practices related to test design, development and interpretation and uses this knowledge to select, adapt and develop assessments for different purposes in the ESL program (e.g., diagnosis, program evaluation, proficiency).

B. Applies knowledge of formal and informal assessments used in the ESL classroom and knows their characteristics, uses and limitations.

C. Knows standardized tests commonly used in ESL programs in Texas and knows how to interpret their results.

D. Knows state-mandated Limited English Proficient (LEP) policies, including the role of the Language Proficiency Assessment Committee (LPAC), and procedures for implementing LPAC recommendations for LEP identification, placement and exit.

E. Understands relationships among state-mandated standards, instruction and assessment in the ESL classroom.

F. Knows how to use ongoing assessment to plan and adjust instruction that addresses individual student needs and enables ESL students to achieve learning goals.

Competency 003

The ESL teacher understands ESL teaching methods and uses this knowledge to plan and implement effective, developmentally appropriate instruction.

Chapter 3 will focus on Competency 003—ESL teaching methods used to plan and implement effective and appropriate instruction.

Standards-Based ESL Instruction

Communication skills in listening, speaking, reading, and writing are at the core of all academic learning. English Language Proficiency Standards (ELPS) are designed to give every English language learner full opportunity to learn English and succeed academically. Approved by the Texas State Board of Education in 2007–2008, the ELPS are published with the Texas Essential Knowledge and Skills (TEKS) for each subject in the state-required curriculum.

Teachers must provide instruction that meets both the TEKS grade-level content area standards as well as the ELPS. To do so, they need to understand fully and become conversant with all the standards. To review the ELPS online or to download a copy, go to: *ritter. tea.state.tx.us*. Search under English Language Proficiency Standards.

Three Components

The ELPS identify the communication skills that students need to learn in order to understand and use English for grade-level academic instruction. The standards do not vary by subject, and with few exceptions, they are identical across grades K–12. The ELPS have three components:

1. **Student Expectations (SEs):** The SEs of cross-curricular second-language acquisition are essential knowledge and skills. These are categorized by Listening, Speaking, Reading, Writing, and Learning Strategies.

2. **Proficiency Level Descriptors (PLDs):** PLDs define stages of language acquisition as English language proficiency levels. There are four levels: Beginning, Intermediate, Advanced, and Advanced High. The PLDs describe how well a student at a given proficiency level can understand and use English to participate in grade-level academic instruction. There are separate descriptors for Listening, Speaking, Reading, and Writing. In addition, Reading and Writing are divided into K–1, which addresses emergent literacy and 2–12.

3. **Linguistic Accommodations:** These are special supports and accommodations that make content area instruction accessible to ELLs. Teachers select and implement accommodations based on students' English language proficiency levels. As students progress from one proficiency level to the next, they generally need fewer and fewer accommodations.

Overview of Language Proficiency Levels

The Language Proficiency Levels identified in the ELPS are not tied to any particular grade because progressing from little or no English to full proficiency takes place over time, not within a given school year. In addition, students may have different levels of proficiency in the different language domains. How quickly a student learns English depends on many factors, including the student's age, whether or not he/she was born in the United States, whether he/she has had continuous or interrupted schooling, his or her sociocultural experiences, and how much English he/she knows when he/she enrolls.

Although the PLDs are specific to the four language domains, there are global definitions and key features that provide a useful foundation for understanding the characteristics of each proficiency level.

Language Proficiency Levels: Global Definitions

Level	Definition	Key Features
Beginning	Beginning students have little or no ability to understand and use English. They may know a little English but not enough to function meaningfully in social or academic settings.	Little or no English ability
Intermediate	Intermediate students do have some ability to understand and use English. They can function in social and academic settings as long as the tasks require them to understand and use simple language structures and high-frequency vocabulary in routine contexts.	Limited ability, simple language structures, high-frequency vocabulary, routine contexts
Advanced	Advanced students are able to engage in grade-appropriate academic instruction in English, although ongoing second-language acquisition support is needed to help them understand and use grade-appropriate language. These students function beyond the level of simple, routinely used English.	Ability to engage in grade-appropriate academic instruction with second-language acquisition support
Advanced High	Advanced high students have attained the command of English that enables them, with minimal second-language acquisition support, to engage in regular, all-English academic instruction at their grade level.	Ability to engage in grade-appropriate academic instruction with minimal second-language acquisition support

Teaching Language Through Content

Given that it takes as long as seven years for English-language learners to reach the same level of academic language proficiency as their native-English-speaking peers, it is essential that teachers develop ELL students' content knowledge from the time they start school. Content-based ESL instruction achieves this by teaching language through content—building students' subject-area knowledge and their academic English proficiency. Content-based ESL instruction is grounded in several principles:

- **Problem-Based Learning and Student Inquiry:** Instruction is student-centered with students actively involved in solving problems, exploring concepts, debating solutions, making hypotheses, gathering data, and pursuing answers to questions they generate. Instructional conversations with teachers and peers develop students' critical thinking and academic language.

- **Communicative Competence:** English is used as a medium for learning content (Hymes, 1971). Emphasis is on developing students' ability to engage in content-specific discourse through speaking and writing (Canale and Swain, 1980; Diaz-Rico and Weed, 2010). For more information about communicative competence, see Chapter 4.

- **Interaction:** Students continually negotiate meaning through oral and written interactions with their teachers and peers. Content-based tasks spark purposeful communication. In the process, students have to notice content-specific language patterns, retrieve language from memory, and generate language (Robinson and Ellis, 2008; Long, 2007).

- **Integration of Four Language Domains:** Students have opportunities to improve their listening, speaking, reading, and writing skills in order to develop content-specific and general academic discourse. Speaking and writing are of particular importance because ELLs more readily *internalize* new English vocabulary and syntax when they actively practice using the language in speaking and writing activities.

- **Sheltered Instruction:** Teaching methods and materials make content comprehensible for English as a Second Language learners (Echevarria et al., 2004).

- **Review, Consolidation, and Assessment:** Students are involved in setting learning goals and know the criteria the teacher will use to evaluate their performance. Teachers and students work together to monitor student progress and target content for review (Echevarria et al., 2004).

Fostering Students' Critical Thinking

As long ago as the mid-1950s, Benjamin Bloom recognized that educational objectives must include higher-order thinking skills that challenge students to apply knowledge in new ways, compare objects' features, and critically evaluate information. In a revised version of Bloom's Taxonomy, intellectual behaviors fit into six categories. These behaviors build on one another and become increasingly complex (Anderson and Krathwohl, 2001):

Bloom's Taxonomy

Remember → Understand → Apply → Analyze → Evaluate → Create

Even in mainstream classrooms, students spend much of their time performing at the two most basic levels—remembering and understanding. Teachers prompt these low-order thinking behaviors by asking closed-ended questions and assigning tasks that direct students to name, define, select, or describe.

Unfortunately, this lack of rigor in instruction has been especially true for English-language learners. Limited language proficiency should not be confused with limited intelligence or limited experiences and skills. Historically, many erroneous assumptions and detrimental decisions were made based on ELLs' productive language skills. Spanish-speaking children in U.S. schools have been over-designated for Special Education services. It is important to remember that in the early stages of second-language acquisition, productive language usually lags far behind a student's receptive knowledge. A student may understand the concept of evaporation but may not have the speaking or writing vocabulary in English to express that knowledge.

At each stage of language development, it is possible to challenge English-language learners to be reflective and to think critically. The starting point is a classroom environment where students are encouraged to question information, evaluate each other's ideas, and examine their own assumptions and beliefs. To develop higher-order thinking skills, teachers should do the following:

- Select topics for listening, speaking, reading, and writing activities that are personally relevant to students. Invite students to formulate the questions they want to answer.

- Explore differing points of view in class discussions. Explain that there is no one "correct" answer. Model polite ways to express disagreement.

- When possible, shift from literal questions (*What? Who? When? Where?*) to questions that prompt higher-order thinking such as *What does this remind you of? How does this make you feel?* and questions that begin *Why…? Do you agree…? Do you think…?*

- Help students become critical "consumers" of the information they see, hear, and read in print and online. Discuss writers' and speakers' purposes as well as possible bias. Ask what experiences or cultural values might contribute to individuals' points of view.

Critical Thinking Across Proficiency Levels

Language Proficiency Level	Higher Order Skill	Sample Activity
Beginning	Categorizing Sequencing Organizing information	Sort picture cards. Number pictures to show the sequence of story events or the steps in a process. Draw the missing picture on a graphic organizer.
Intermediate	Categorizing Sequencing Comparing and contrasting	Sort words and record the lists in a notebook. Make a timeline of story events and use it to retell the story. Discuss family traditions with a partner and create a Venn diagram.
Advanced–Advanced High	Categorizing Sequencing Comparing and contrasting	Interview classmates to fill in missing sections of a tree diagram. Write a procedural text Work with two partners to place words on a continuum of degree or negative/positive connotation.

Developmentally Appropriate Instruction

To support each student's progress, educators need to understand how to differentiate instruction based on the student's English-language proficiency level. All instruction delivered in English must be linguistically accommodated—communicated, sequenced, and scaffolded. This approach has grown out of the second-language learning theory and research discussed specifically in Chapter 2:

- Piaget's *Stages of Cognitive Development*

- Vygotsky's *Zone of Proximal Development* (ZPD) and the sociocultural dimensions of making meaning

- Krashen's *Natural Order Hypothesis, Input Hypothesis, Affective Filter,* and *Stages of Language Acquisition*

Scaffolding is another concept closely tied to developmentally appropriate instruction (Graves and Fitzgerald, 2003; Gibbons, 2002). It is based on Vygotsky's view that optimal learning takes place when teachers provide support within a learner's ZPD. The support can take many forms including modeling, prompts, direct explanation, and visual aids. Scaffolding involves the gradual removal of these supports as a student begins to demonstrate independently targeted behaviors and skills. This approach has been widely incorporated into educational practice since the 1990s.

In the context of ESL instruction, it is important not to overlook a critical aspect of scaffolding. In order for students to progress, teachers must make gradual and deliberate efforts to move students from their current level of English proficiency to higher levels. Communicating with ELLs *only* at their current level of understanding or continually providing simplified versions of academic content will not achieve this. The linguistic accommodations identified in the PLDs are teachers' road maps for effective scaffolding. They provide the pathway from meeting students where they are to helping them reach the next level.

Even students who are at fairly advanced levels may require scaffolding when they are learning about completely new topics, navigating texts with complex vocabulary and sophisticated syntax, or completing assignments that require communicating with adults such during interviews or public speaking. As teachers make instructional decisions, they must be aware of the demands of particular lesson, including the demands of the learning objectives, materials used, and the social context.

Implementing Linguistic Accommodations

There are many proven techniques for making academic content accessible to English-language learners. The best way to select linguistic accommodations aligned to specific strands and proficiency levels is to consult the ELPS.

Broadly speaking, adjustments are made in three areas: instructional delivery, student materials, and assessment. Following are examples of widely used linguistic accommodations for content-based ESL instruction.

Instructional Delivery

- Adjust your speech. Speak slowly and clearly. Use basic vocabulary and simple sentence structures. Repeat information as needed.

- Present content in multiple ways, engaging students in all modalities: visual, auditory, and kinesthetic. Have students practice and apply what they are learning in active, hands-on tasks.

- Make concepts and vocabulary concrete using demonstrations, real objects, props (realia), pictures, photographs, video, and audio.

- Use gestures, pantomime, role play, and nonverbal cues to reinforce meaning. Teach students the meanings of the gestures and cues as these are often cultural-specific.

- Clearly explain each learning task, both orally and in writing. Provide models and real examples of good work.

- Respond to student errors by focusing on their ideas and praising their efforts. In the course of conversation, model appropriate usage by restating their ideas correctly.

- Provide daily oral language activities. When pairing students with more proficient classmates, make sure that the interaction will be instructionally meaningful and will give each student an opportunity to participate fully.

- Use cooperative learning structures such as Think/Pair/Share, Three-Step Interview, Jigsaw, Fishbowl, and Four Corners.

- Provide robust vocabulary instruction. Display visual representations of new vocabulary (objects, photographs, videos). Use graphic organizers to show the relationship between new words and concepts and those that are known by students. Provide multiple opportunities for students to hear and use the words in speaking and writing activities.

- Teach students how to recognize and use English and L1 cognates.

- Use L1 strategically to clarify or explain. If a peer provides a translation, confirm that the information being shared is accurate.

- Lead students in a picture walk to preview reading materials. Prepare them to engage with new content by activating prior knowledge and building background for any cultural or linguistic content that may be unfamiliar. This may include preteaching basic vocabulary that native English-speaking students are likely to know such as prepositions or phrasal verbs. (See Chapter 5 for more about vocabulary in the context of reading instruction.)

- Explicitly teach strategies for learning language such as requesting assistance, asking for clarification, interrupting politely, and using circumlocution.

Student Materials

- Select from a variety of media to enhance multimodal learning.

- Use songs, poems, and chants to introduce new content vocabulary, develop listening skills, build oral fluency, and make language memorable.

- Make instruction relevant, focusing on familiar topics with content that mirrors students' own lives and cultural backgrounds.

- Use reading material that has built-in print or digital support such as low text density, purpose-setting questions, labeled photographs, diagrams, on-page glossaries, L1 translations, read-aloud functions, cumulative timelines, or summaries that recap important information. (See pages 56–62 for more information about using technology with English-language learners.)

- Provide students with picture dictionaries, labeled picture cards, bilingual dictionaries, and dictionaries designed specifically for second language learners.

Assessment

- Offer multiple pathways for students to demonstrate their understanding of content. Assess content knowledge separately from language proficiency.

- Focus on meaning and content rather than language conventions and correctness.

- For students at the beginning level, structure assessment so that students can provide nonverbal responses or one- or two-word utterances.

- Allow additional time for oral responses.

- Have students practice responses with a partner before sharing their ideas with the entire class.

- For more formal assessment, consider adapting written tests to students' proficiency level. This may include adjusting the item format, language level, text density, and level of teacher support during administration.

Using Technology to Enhance Learning

Technology has revolutionized communication. Today's students have access to a staggering amount of information and learning tools delivered across multiple platforms: handheld devices, smart phones, tablets, interactive whiteboards, desktop computers, audio CDs, video, and DVDs. Digital literacy is not only an essential life skill but a prerequisite for ELLs' future academic and professional success.

According to standards set forth in the ELPS, technology plays an integral role in developing English-language learners' listening and speaking skills. Students are expected to listen to and derive meaning from a variety of media to build and reinforce concepts and language. They are also expected to respond orally to information presented in print, electronic, audio, and visual media. As is true of any instructional resource, quality matters more than quantity. The best educational technology motivates students, is easy to use, and is highly interactive.

To obtain the best results, teachers must actively plan and organize media for prior to use and monitor students' learning and engagement. The first step is to become familiar with the resources that are available from school and local libraries and educational service centers. All selected media must be prescreened by the teacher and meet district acceptable use policy. Teachers should apply strict criteria when evaluating audiovisual, multimedia, computer, and human resources for classroom instruction. First and foremost, each resource must have a clear curricular objective.

Technology can be used in many different ways to plan, organize, deliver, and evaluate ESL instruction. Some examples are shown on the next two pages.

Technology Applications in the ESL Classroom

Objective	Resources
For Professional Development	TEA website *http://www.tea.state.tx.us*
	District and school websites
	Online staff development
	Websites of professional organizations, research institutions, and clearinghouses (See the References section on page 245 for recommended Web resources.)
	Online college courses
	Internet browsers (e.g., Microsoft Explorer, Netscape)
	Search engines (e.g., Yahoo, Excite, Lycos, Google, Bing)
For Classroom Management	Cooperative group assignments
	Learning center design plans
	Electronic attendance charts
	Supply lists and order forms
	Electronic grade books
	School-based wikis
To Create Curriculum Maps	Electronic templates and archived files
	Email with colleagues
	School-based wikis
To Build Background and Present Language in Context	Video clips or video streaming from approved websites
	Videodiscs with images and sound
	PowerPoint presentation software
	Films, filmstrips, and audiotapes
	Websites with photos (per *fair use* guidelines)
To Demonstrate Procedures	Simulation software
	Interactive whiteboard lessons
	Video clips and video streaming from approved websites
	Videodiscs with images and sound
To Promote Multicultural Awareness	Live video conferences with other schools
	International forums and networks that connect schools
	Video clips and video streaming from approved websites Videodiscs with images and sound
	Films, filmstrips, and audiotapes
	Websites with photos (per *fair use* guidelines)

(continued)

(*continued*)

Objective	Resources
To Foster Critical Thinking	Live video conferences with other schools
	Electronic templates of graphic organizers
	Online articles and opinion pieces from news organizations
	Spreadsheet software
To Provide Targeted Language Practice	Computer-assisted instruction (tutorials and educational games)
	Recording equipment (practice and self-assessment)
To Develop Reading Comprehension	Audiotapes
	E-Books
	Computer-assisted instruction (tutorials and educational games)
	Interactive whiteboard lessons
To Build Reading Fluency	Computer-assisted instruction with voice-recognition recording equipment (practice and self-assessment)
To Develop Writing Skills	Word processing software with spell- and grammar-checkers
	Web-page design software
To Teach Research Skills	Internet browsers with safeguard filters
	Search engines with safeguard filters
	On-line databases
	Online glossaries and dictionaries
To Teach Presentation Skills	Presentation software (PowerPoint)
	Graphic software
	Student podcasts
To Communicate with Students	Networked devices that allow instant feedback to whole class or individual students
	E-mail
	School-based wikis
To Communicate with Families	E-mail
	Templates for newsletters
	Graphic software for flyers, awards, and notices
Assess Student Progress	Electronic assessment systems that generate reports and allow users to aggregate and disaggregate data
	Multimedia portfolios (videos, students' digital work)
	Computer-assisted instruction with "save" features

Language Learners and Computers

Computers can be fantastic learning tools when they are used appropriately for purposeful learning tasks. Simply placing a student at a computer does not guarantee positive learning outcomes. Computers are often used for drill, practice, and error correction. However many of these programs give students very little feedback, cannot recognize or reward responses that are acceptable language variations, and offer fixed course content in a lock-step sequence. Perhaps the greatest drawback to many computerized language courses is that they require students to spend hours on their own in front of the screen instead of developing their language skills for meaningful communication in the social context of a school community.

Though the research is fairly limited, findings have shown that computer-assisted language learning (CALL) can have positive results for second-language learners when the tasks are meaningful, interactional, and have a clear purpose. According to a summary of research published in the *CAL Digest* (LeLoup and Ponterio, 2003):

- Students tend to produce more language in chat rooms than in face-to-face discussions.

- Unlike regular classroom interactions, computer-mediated discussions aren't dominated by a small number of students. There is also a greater ratio of student talk to teacher talk.

- Being able to use email reduces students' anxiety and increases their motivation for social interaction.

- Learners express a preference for social interaction between and among native speakers and nonnative speakers.

- Writing-assistant software helps students become more aware of their errors. It also helps teachers identify students' interlanguage.

- There is some evidence that the language produced while engaged in CALL is more coherent, cohesive, and expressive than in face-to-face classroom communication.

- The multimedia nature of CALL enables learners to engage in complex listening activities, supported by visual cues.

Privacy and Safety

Educators must be concerned about what students see and share on the Internet. Even when school-approved filters are in place, students may be able to access information that is inappropriate or potentially harmful. In addition, websites and domain names change and may lead students to unsuitable content. Teachers must explicitly teach students how to use the Internet safely and closely monitor their use of this powerful resource.

According to the *Children's Internet Protection Act* (CIPA) and the *Neighborhood Children's Internet Protection Act* (N-CIPA), federal law requires that

1. the school or library use blocking or filtering technology on all computers with Internet access. The blocking or filtering must protect against access to certain visual depictions, including obscenity, child pornography, and materials harmful to minors. The law does not require the filtering of text.

2. The school or library must adopt and implement an Internet safety policy that addresses the key criteria, including

   a) access by minors to inappropriate matter on the Internet and the Web;

   b) the safety and security of minors when using electronic mail, chat rooms, and other forms of direct electronic communications;

   c) unauthorized access, including so-called "hacking," and other unlawful activities by minors online;

   d) unauthorized disclosure, use, and dissemination of personal identification information regarding minors; and

   e) measures designed to restrict minors' access to materials harmful to minors.

3. The school or library must hold a public meeting to discuss the Internet-safety policy; specifically, the law requires that the school or library "provide reasonable public notice and hold at least one public hearing or meeting to address the proposed Internet safety policy."

Accuracy, Credibility, and Bias

The Internet contains large amounts of inaccurate and false information. Teachers must help students become discerning consumers of information who are able to critically evaluate what they see, hear, and read. Students will benefit from direct instruction in distinguishing fact and opinion, evaluating writer's/speaker's credentials and purpose, and identifying supporting evidence for statements. Teachers should display a list of acceptable online websites and reference sources and explore the features that make these sources of dependable information.

Technology and Copyright Issues

Teachers must help students use technology resources ethically and legally by avoiding plagiarism and the improper use of work protected by copyright. Students and teachers must respect laws that protect people's intellectual property on the Internet and all print and digital media. It is illegal to violate the copyright that protects original works. This applies to music and images as well as text. The *fair use* doctrine allows the limited reproduction of works for research and educational purposes. To see suggested guidelines for applying fair use, go to: *www.utsystem.edu*. Search under Intellectual Property.

Effective Classroom Management

All classroom management strategies have the same goals: to keep students actively engaged, to motivate their participation, and to lower their anxiety. To create an organized and productive learning environment, teachers need to do the following:

- **Emphasize Collaborative Learning:** Organize instruction and the physical environment so that small groups of three to five students can work together on a task. In face-to-face interactions, they create a common product, complete a project, or achieve a new understanding. Students depend on each other, and each group member is responsible for the success of the entire group. Cooperative learning develops important social skills: active listening, listening without interruption, giving praise and encouragement, and making polite requests. It also develops students' critical thinking by requiring them to dialogue, negotiate meaning, and resolve differences with the common goal of understanding academic content.

- **Foster Mutual Respect and Value Diversity:** Teachers have to establish a positive atmosphere where students feel safe to be themselves and express their ideas (Krashen and Terrell, 1983). At the beginning of the school year, they should discuss the rules for engagement and clearly define parameters for acceptable behavior—how the teacher will treat students, how students will treat the teacher, and how the students will treat each other (Marzano and Marzano, 2003; Wolk, 2003). This includes zero tolerance for ridicule, sarcasm, or bullying. It also includes accepting and appreciating differences—diverse viewpoints, interests, cultural backgrounds, and home languages. Teachers set the right tone when they acknowledge students as individuals, each with interesting and important ideas to contribute to the learning community.

- **Establish Predictable, Consistent Routines:** Teachers need to explain classroom routines—everything that contributes to a smoothly functioning classroom from raising hands and sharpening pencils to taking attendance, moving into cooperative groups, and lining up for recess. Teachers also need to share their expectation that students will follow these routines automatically so that they can maximize learning time. To promote student ownership, teachers can ask for student input and allow them to determine some of the procedures. One form of effective scaffolding for ELLs is to display visual reminders of the routines and to regularly refer to them (Goldenberg, 2008). The reminders could be pictures, diagrams, lists, or easy-to-read schedules. Teachers can then connect physical gestures or other cues to specific routines and prompt students in a nonverbal way, as needed.

- **Praise and Correct Behaviors, Not Children:** Teachers must show the same respect for children that they expect children to show for others in the class. First and foremost, they need to convey high expectations for all students, assuring them that they are all capable of success. Singling out children for correction or public criticism undermines relationships and escalates disruptive behavior. Usually the best way to correct students is privately by moving close to the student and getting his or her attention. While maintaining eye contact, the teacher says what behavior needs to stop and what behavior needs to begin. The teacher then thanks the student and moves away.

English as a Second Language learners are dealing with many challenges inside and outside of school. Effective teachers realize that students may be under stress and experiencing a wide range of emotions that affect their classroom behavior and impede their learning. By modeling positive problem-solving skills and recognizing each student's potential, teachers keep students on track for a lifelong love of learning.

Review Questions

1. A middle school history teacher wants her class of intermediate ELL students to develop a stronger understanding of historical events. She creates email accounts with the names of the historical figures as the screen names. She gives students the following assignment:

    - With your group, writing in the character of the historical figure you choose, compose an email message and send it to an appropriate recipient from our list of historical figures.

- Your message must address an issue that would have mattered to your historical figure.

- Respond to each other's messages.

- Stay in the character of your historical figure.

This instructional strategy is best explained by which of the following rationales?

(A) Writing in the character of a specific historical figure will force students to re-read the chapter

(B) Integrating technology through this assignment will engage students in critical thinking and promote communicative competence

(C) By focusing on a single historical figure, the amount of information that students need to synthesize will be significantly reduced

(D) The email responses will provide an opportunity for the teacher to check the students' writing for accuracy in language use

The correct response is (**B**). The integration of technology encourages students to think about the content actively with greater engagement, promoting critical thinking. (A) is likely to occur as a result of this assignment but forced rereading is not the intent of the activity, so this is an incorrect response. (C) is incorrect because it overlooks the fact that the assignment calls for a broader rather than limited understanding of the historical events in order to perform the assignment satisfactorily. (D) is incorrect since it reduces this history content assignment to a grammar check, thereby misreading the intent of the assignment.

2. In an elementary class that includes beginning-level ESL students, which of the following strategies would best promote students' understanding of how the school day is segmented (for example, reading groups, recess, science time, lunch, and so on)?

(A) The teacher creates a large chart that displays the time each class activity starts and ends.

(B) The teacher creates a poster for each regular class-day segment with pictures that clearly illustrate the activity. Each poster is numbered to indicate the place of each activity in the class events sequence.

(C) When it's time for a new activity, the teacher sounds a chime and writes the name and time range of the new activity on the board (for example, 10:00–10:35: READING).

(D)   The teacher shows a video of students in reading circles, science centers, recess, art, and other school activities.

The correct response is (**B**). The fact that this is a *beginning*-level ESL *elementary* class points to the need to reinforce classroom management activities with illustrations and environmental print. The numbered illustrations will also give students greater understanding about the sequence of class-day events. (A) is incorrect because it overlooks the likelihood that beginning ESL students at the elementary level will not have sufficient L2 reading competence to understand a print chart. (C) is incorrect because it turns class-day activities into an arbitrary series of events abruptly announced by a chime, even though writing the time and event on the board would promote the young learners' graphophonemic awareness. (D) would be a good supplementary activity *after* students recognize that the school day is divided into predictable, stable segments. Therefore, (D) is an incorrect response.

Competency 004

Competency 004

The ESL teacher understands how to promote students' communicative language development in English

Chapter 4 will focus on Competency 004—promoting students' communicative language development in English.

Communicative Competence

Communicative competence is the ability to use language appropriately based on the demands of the social situation. Competent language users understand with whom they are speaking, the setting in which they are communicating, and the appropriate language for that setting. They have developed fluency in listening and speaking as well as extensive knowledge of word meanings, sentence structures, the participants' status, social and cultural norms, and even nonverbal cues such as gestures and changes in a speaker's voice (Canale, 1983).

This sociocultural view of language competence has influenced educational practice in the following important ways:

- The focus of Second Language Learning is authentic communication—language is used to communicate real ideas to real people.

- Students are taught how to use language for a variety of settings, purposes, participants, and texts.

- Learning is a cooperative activity in which students are encouraged to interact in the target language and experiment with different ways of speaking and writing.

- Instruction links listening, speaking, reading, and writing in real-world tasks.

- Teacher feedback focuses on the content of students' efforts (efficacy of communication and meaning) rather than "correctness" based on grammar rules and conventions.

State Standards for Listening and Speaking

The TEKS and ELPS state-mandated standards define communicative competence in the context of the ESL classroom. Teachers need to fully understand and become conversant with these standards so that they can integrate the ELPS expectations of students' communication skills into subject-area instruction. The K–12 TEKS for English Language Arts include Listening and Speaking standards. Beginning in kindergarten, students listen and respond to others' ideas and contribute their own ideas in conversations and in groups. All students are expected to do the following:

- listen attentively, ask questions to clarify information, and follow oral directions

- share information and ideas by speaking audibly and clearly using the conventions of language

- work productively in teams following accepted rules for discussion such as taking turns and speaking only one at a time

As students progress through the grades, the TEKS for English Language Arts identify more sophisticated listening and speaking skills such as restating and giving multistep oral directions, asking relevant questions, employing eye contact, adjusting speaking rate and volume, answering questions with appropriate detail, interpreting a speaker's message, clarifying a speaker's purpose, determining the main and supporting ideas in a speaker's message, giving oral presentations, and identifying points of agreement and disagreement in group discussions. At the same time students develop these increasingly sophisticated skills, the TEKS require that they demonstrate increasing control of English grammar and usage in their speaking and writing. (To review or download the TEKS for English Language Arts, visit *www.tea.state.tx.us*. Search under TEKS.)

ELPS and Oral Language Proficiency

For English-language learners to be considered proficient in the domain of listening, they must be able to understand spoken English well enough to participate in grade-level academic instruction with minimal scaffolding. That involves understanding what students hear—both social and academic discourse—and extracting information. Ultimately, students use this information to develop content knowledge, make decisions, solve problems, and synthesize and evaluate ideas. Student expectations for listening also include discerning elements of the English sound system (phonology), using the pitch of a speaker's voice (intonation) to infer meaning, and applying strategies to monitor and confirm their understanding of language.

In addition to identifying nine Student Expectations for Listening, the ELPS present K–12 Proficiency Level Descriptors for listening at four levels: Beginning, Intermediate, Advanced, and Advanced High. For students in grade 3 and higher who are at the beginning or intermediate level, districts must provide intensive and ongoing foundational second-language acquisition instruction. (To review the ELPS online or to download a copy, go to: *www.tea.state.tx.us*. Search under ELPS.*)*

Listening and speaking are inextricably linked in the classroom. Students are expected to listen and then orally respond to what they hear. While listening is a receptive aspect of communicative competence, speaking is productive. Students must be able to produce a wide range of language forms in different contexts. For English-language learners to be considered proficient in the domain of speaking, they must use spoken English appropriately and effectively in learning activities and social interactions. That involves sharing information, asking questions, expressing opinions, providing detailed explanations, responding to information presented in different media, and participating in extended discussions on a variety of academic topics. Proficient English speakers can pronounce English in a way that is understandable, continually internalize new vocabulary, speak with varied syntax and sentence length, use content-area terminology, and adapt their speech based on the required level of formality.

In addition to identifying 10 Student Expectations for Speaking, the ELPS present K–12 Proficiency Level Descriptors at four levels: Beginning, Intermediate, Advanced, and Advanced High. For students in grade 3 and higher who are at the beginning or intermediate level, districts must provide intensive and ongoing foundational second language acquisition instruction. (To review the ELPS online or to download a copy, go to: *www. tea.state.tx.us*. Search under ELPS.)

Total Physical Response

Total Physical Response (TPR) is an effective method for developing the listening proficiency of English-language learners who are at the beginning level. James Asher first introduced the technique, building on the cognitive research that showed how learning and memory are improved when new language is connected to physical movements (Asher, 1982). In TPR, the teacher says a series of sentences in the imperative form that serve as rapid-fire commands. Students demonstrate their listening comprehension by performing the requested actions and thus obeying the commands. As students understand more oral English, the teacher gives commands with more advanced vocabulary and may also introduce silly commands to add interest and fun. By virtue of its design, TPR does the following:

- motivates student participation because it is like a game

- is concrete and hands-on

- is consistent with research in recognizing that language learners initially understand more than language than they can produce

- can be incorporated into instruction for different subject areas

- lends itself to scaffolding, allowing the teacher to model the desired action and then removing that support so that students respond solely to the verbal commands

Assessing Oral Language Proficiency

Performance-based assessments are an effective way to monitor and support English-language learners' oral language proficiency. When students feel relaxed, language production is enhanced. Teachers should observe students listening, speaking, and responding to a partner or a group of peers while they complete a collaborative task. When assessing students' speaking proficiency, it is important for teachers to resist the urge to jump in when English-language learners do not respond immediately. This extra wait time can improve the quantity and quality of student language production. The following listening and speaking activities are some opportunities for assessment:

- following and giving oral directions
- matching sounds or generating rhymes
- responding to texts read aloud
- learning the melody and lyrics of a song
- interacting informally with peers
- reacting to or giving an oral presentation
- participating in a role-play or skit
- dictating and responding to language experience stories
- retelling events or describing objects presented in a video
- understanding and applying a partner's feedback
- interviewing a family member
- following prompts while viewing an electronic book
- reflecting on group work or discussing future learning goals

Oral Language and Literacy

The National Literacy Panel's review of research underscored the importance of oral proficiency for minority-language students (August and Shanahan, 2006). Although it is often overlooked in instruction, oral proficiency in English is closely associated with ELLs' reading comprehension and writing skills. Once English-language learners move beyond word-level decoding to reading and writing connected texts, students' listening comprehension, vocabulary knowledge, and oral syntactic skills are strong predictors of reading and writing achievement. For this reason, the panel urged educators to include extensive oral English development as an integral part of successful literacy instruction for English-language learners.

The panel also recommended teaching students how to tap into their oral proficiency in their home languages and apply their understandings when they speak English. This includes their ability to produce and distinguish transferrable speech sounds; orally segment words into syllables; and their higher order skills such as providing definitions, interpreting metaphors, and using cognate relationships.

Creating a Language-Rich Environment

Developing English-language learners' oral language proficiency requires effective instruction and careful planning. The key is to structure daily activities so that they require students to produce language and to expose students to rich content that is worth talking about. In this way, language becomes the medium for students to develop content knowledge and to successfully collaborate with their peers. Research has shown that basic principles of good curriculum and instruction hold true for English-language learners. They benefit from clear goals and learning objectives; active engagement; meaningful and challenging contexts; and opportunities to practice, apply, and transfer what they are learning (August and Shanahan, 2006; Genesee et al., 2006).

For each lesson, teachers need to identify clear content and language outcomes. They should draw on the TEKS to target grade-level concepts and skills in the content area. For language outcomes, they should refer to the ELPS proficiency standards in each language domain as well as the learning strategies. Guided by the standards and assessments of students' proficiency levels, teachers then do the following:

- design course content

- plan content-related listening, speaking, reading, and writing tasks

- define student groupings

- select materials

Ari Sherris recommends making a list of the descriptive verbs that appear in standards documents and course materials. Teachers can then sort the words into separate content and language outcomes (Sherris, 2008). For example, the verbs *measure, compute,* and *graph* describe possible mathematics outcomes. *Listen, explain,* and *summarize* describe possible language outcomes. This approach has benefits for both teachers and students. It helps teachers clarify the separate goals for each lesson and refine their instructional delivery. When teachers explain the learning goals and post them in the room for student reference, students become more involved in directing and monitoring their own learning.

Providing Comprehensible Input

Once language and content objectives are defined, teachers need to plan activities that are cognitively demanding but accessible to students at their current level(s) of English proficiency. Perhaps the most effective way to ensure that students have access to meaning and *comprehensible input* is to design instruction around experiential, hands-on activities that foster student-to-student communication (Met, 1994). Abstract vocabulary and concepts become concrete when learners have a chance to work together in heterogeneous groups manipulating and observing objects. These context-embedded tasks provide a variety of multisensory supports for meaning that make language and the tasks understandable. Consider, for example, the difference between teaching students the meaning of *scale* by showing them a photograph and having pairs of students use a scale to weigh different objects.

As discussed in Chapter 3, there are many proven techniques for making academic content accessible to English-language learners (see pages 52–62). To select linguistic accommodations aligned to specific strands and proficiency levels, teachers should consult the ELPS. Although it's generally true that students need fewer instructional modifications as their proficiency increases, even at intermediate and advanced levels, students will require support when they are working with new topics or particularly difficult material. To maximize student engagement, teachers should do the following:

- Preview all material to identify potential challenges for English-language learners including unfamiliar concepts, cultural references, new vocabulary, difficult or unusual syntax, and idioms.

- Help students set a purpose for listening and speaking. Focus on the big ideas and essential questions to explore.

- Repeat information and directions when needed.

- Help students make connections to known words and concepts using graphic organizers or linking new vocabulary with known synonyms and definitions that contain familiar examples.

- Capitalize on the knowledge and skills students have in L1.

In the early stages of language development, students can use the same techniques that teachers use to get meaning across. Students with limited oral proficiency can be shown how to use verbal and nonverbal means of communicating including pantomime, facial expressions, and gestures. In a content-rich environment, students use objects, props, visuals, and other resources to help them participate in discussions.

Providing Supported Opportunities for Communication

In addition to planning content and language outcomes carefully, teachers need to teach students how to collaborate by modeling basic social skills, practicing group routines, and instilling in students a sense of belonging to the learning community. It is important for students to forge emotional bonds so that they can learn with and from one another. The goal is for children to see themselves and their classmates as helpful, responsible resources.

A collaborative language-rich classroom is a noisy place. To maximize interaction, the physical environment needs to be flexible. Small groups may gather at tables or learning centers. After a time, they may need to transition to whole-class instruction or to working on a project with a partner or working independently during quiet reflection. This means that furniture and materials have to be arranged to ensure access to resources and supplies, ease of movement around the room, and a level of privacy for one-on-one conversations with the teacher.

Teachers should devote approximately 90 minutes per week to activities in which pairs of students at different ability levels or different English language proficiency levels work together to practice and extend what has been taught (Gersten et al., 2007). As is often the case in monolingual English classes, ESL students are often assigned to static, ability-based groups, which greatly limits their opportunities. English-language learners need to experience varied speakers in different participation structures, such as the following (Johnson, 1994):

- whole-class experiences led by the teacher, with questions that prompt pairs of students to spend a few minutes negotiating meaning

- individual work when students have time to draw on resources, quietly reflect, and prepare ideas for group discussions

- pair work when partners have to work together to complete *information-gap tasks* with each one contributing information to meet a shared goal

- teacher with a small group

- cooperative learning groups that are linguistically heterogeneous with three to five students working together on a meaningful task

When forming pairs or groups, it is important for teachers to monitor student inter-actions to make sure that the students grouped together are compatible. No one student should dominate the group or take on the role of a "correcting" peer. Teachers may want to alternate between setting up pairs and allowing students to choose a partner because building new friendships is an enormous motivator for language learning. Even students at low proficiency levels can benefit from structured interactions with monolingual, native English speakers as long as the English-language learner is engaged and using receptive and/or productive language to contribute to the task in some way. Another effective approach is to pair students who share L1 but are at different proficiency levels in English. They can benefit from discussing concepts in their first language and then, as a culmination of the activity, be asked to produce English orally or in writing.

Cultural Attitudes and Classroom Interaction

Language, culture, and the classroom experience are all closely connected. Children's cultural backgrounds affect how they interact with teachers and peers. For example, in many cultures, children are taught not to initiate social conversations with adults, par-ticularly authority figures like teachers. In other cultures, maintaining eye contact while speaking is considered impolite. It is important for teachers to respect students' family customs and cultural attitudes while helping them learn the rules for successful social engagement in school.

As part of their day-to-day experience, English-language learners have to navigate conflicting cultural expectations. Teachers can help them by learning about students' past experiences with school and speaking with their family members about the way they perceive the role of teacher and student. When teachers enlist the support of families, stu-dents are able to participate effectively without feeling as though they are abandoning the cultural norms they have been taught at home.

Cooperative Learning Structures

Educators have developed many cooperative learning structures that require language production and active collaboration. These structures can be used to involve students of varying language proficiencies in content-rich activities:

- **Think, Pair, Share:** Students think about a topic. Then they discuss it with a partner. Individually, students share information from their discussions with the entire class.

- **Jigsaw:** Students are assigned to small "expert" groups that study one topic in depth. Students are regrouped so that each new group has at least one member from each expert group. The experts report on their study.

- **Four Corners:** Areas of the room are designated for focused discussion of four aspects of a topic. Students independently think about the topic for a short time. Then they select a corner based on their interest and participate in a discussion. Individually, students share information from their discussions with the entire class.

- **Fishbowl:** Half of the class sits in a circle facing inward. The other half sits in a large circle around them. Students in the inner circle discuss a topic. Those outside are given a purpose for listening such as identifying new information or evaluating the inner circle's discussion. Students in the outside circle report. Then groups switch roles.

- **Inside-Outside Circle:** Half the class stands in a circle facing outward. The other half stands in a circle facing them. Students on the outside ask a question and those inside answer. On signals, students rotate to work with different partners or trade roles.

Giving Effective Feedback

Errors are a natural and necessary part of learning a language. Everything a child says or writes should be valued as a sincere attempt at communication. Teachers must show that the child's message is important by praising all efforts and focusing on the child's ideas rather than the errors.

Here are some guiding principles for giving effective feedback:

- Provide ongoing, positive reinforcement when students participate. Acknowledge when they apply important language skills such as using new vocabulary, selecting more precise or more vivid terms, and experimenting with more complex sentence structures.

- Do not discourage the free flow of communication by overcorrecting students or focusing on errors of grammar and usage.

- Relate all feedback to the lesson's big ideas and key content-related vocabulary. As you acknowledge students' ideas and input, restate what they said using correct English. If a student's ideas are unclear, paraphrase what the student said or confirm the intended meaning in another way.

- When you respond, use vocabulary and sentence structures that are at or just above the student's proficiency level. Confirm that the student understands your verbal feedback.

- When students use *simplification* answering a question with a single word or phrase, restate what they said and model expanding the phrase or moving clauses around. You can also keep the conversation going by inviting classmates to expand on what the students said.

- Remember that the errors students make are windows into their thinking about the patterns and rules of English. They may be *overgeneralizing* English rules they have learned (*maked*, *foots*) or may be using *interlanguage* and therefore "correctly" applying structures and patterns from L1. To make instructional decisions based on observed errors, teachers need to understand the L1 skills, cultural background, and content knowledge that students bring to second-language learning.

- Give corrective feedback in one-on-one meetings, working with the student to set attainable language objectives. You can then group students together for brief, targeted practice based on shared language needs. Asking group members to rephrase or sum up what they learned can help reveal any misunderstandings.

- Teacher-student journals are another risk-free way for students to ask for clarification and for teachers to give corrective feedback.

The Intermediate-Level Plateau

In the early phases of second-language acquisition, English-language learners move from the beginning to intermediate level in three phases: the silent period, or *preproduction*; *early production* when they can say one to two words; and *speech emergence* when they can say longer phrases and sentences. In general, ELLs seem to progress through these early phases fairly rapidly—in two to three years. However, once they achieve intermediate proficiency, many students reach a plateau and do not begin to show higher levels for at least four years (Goldenberg, 2008). This may be explained by the fact that intermediate speakers need to master simpler vocabulary and sentence patterns than advanced speakers.

Another factor for plateauing may be that intermediate proficiency is sufficient for daily activities and normal conversations with friends. In these familiar and contextualized situations, ELLs have access to many supports including gestures, intonation, and environmental print. Advanced proficiency requires speakers and listeners to understand vocabulary and sentence structures used in the academic setting. It also involves abstract concepts and references to things that are not in students' immediate environment. Students with limited oral language proficiency in grades 3 and higher need the language to talk about and understand these abstract concepts precisely when grade-level material tends to become more complex. To accelerate their oral language proficiency, these students require focused, targeted, and systematic instruction in these key areas:

- English vocabulary

- English grammar

- English syntax and rhetorical structures

- English mechanics

Review Questions

Use the information below to answer questions 1 and 2.

All the students at an elementary school are going on a field trip to the zoo. The ELL teachers plan to integrate language-proficiency activities into this science-enrichment opportunity.

1. The third-grade teacher posts pictures of the zoo animals around the classroom. She has her class of beginning ELL students pick their three favorite animals and explains this assignment:

   - Look carefully at the three animals you picked. Pay close attention to what makes each of your three animals special. For example, if you picked a giraffe, you know that its long neck and big spots make it special.

   - Imagine a new animal made up of the qualities that make your three animals special. Draw a picture of this made-up animal.

   - When we all finish our drawings, we are going to show our pictures to the whole class and explain how we invented this new animal.

This instructional activity will promote the student's oral-language proficiency because

(A) it promotes students' content-area vocabulary in science.

(B) it gives students an opportunity to describe and explain in an informal class presentation.

(C) students will have an opportunity to apply nonacademic skills to a content-area lesson.

(D) Students will learn how to do an important class presentation.

The correct response is (**B**). This activity is tailored for young ELL students. It merges science content and oral-language proficiency in an activity that takes individual differences and distinct abilities into account. (A) is incorrect because, while some science vocabulary may be involved in identifying the features of the animals, this activity is far more targeted at developing oral language. (C) is incorrect because integrating art, a "nonacademic" area, is a side effect but not the focus of this science activity. (D) is incorrect because creating the picture of the invented animal showcases students' individual abilities through an oral-language activity. It is not intended to teach formal presentation skills.

2. The fourth-grade teacher, who teaches intermediate and advanced ELL students, is also creating a field-trip-based activity. Which of the following activities would best target development of her students' communicative competence?

(A) Students create a story with their favorite zoo animal as a main character. On the day before the zoo trip, the students take turns reading their stories to the whole class.

(B) The teacher assigns each student an animal as the subject of a research paper due before the zoo trip.

(C) The teacher shows a video of famous zoos in the United States and has students create a semantic map of concepts related to zoos.

(D) The teacher does book talks on several of Rudyard Kipling's *Just So Stories*. Students vote on the one they want to hear. On the day before the zoo trip, the teacher reads the winning story aloud to the class.

The correct response is (**A**). Sharing an original story will activate prior knowledge while also developing students' listening and speaking proficiencies. This activity shows the interrelatedness of the four language domains in promoting oral-language proficiency. (B) is incorrect since this option does not include a communicative language-development component. The research paper isolates each student in an independent task. (C) is incorrect because creating a semantic map is a prereading activity, not an oral-language proficiency activity. (D) is incorrect because reading the story aloud to students showcases the *teacher's* skills and limits the students' active listening and speaking opportunities.

CHAPTER 5

Competency 005

Competency 005

The ESL teacher understands how to promote students' literacy development in English

Chapter 5 will focus on Competency 005—promoting students' literacy development in English.

Becoming a Reader

Skilled reading is a complex process. At its most basic level, reading English involves looking at a word, connecting its written form (*graphemes*) to its sounds (*phonemes*), and using those sounds to identify the word's meaning. Converting a printed word to its spoken form is known as *decoding*. Many of the most common words in English, however, cannot be read simply by sounding out the letters. Some examples are *said, of, would, what,* and *some*. Irregular high-frequency words have to be learned as whole units by sight. To do so, the words need to be explicitly taught, practiced, and reviewed because readers need multiple exposures to an irregular word before they are able to recognize it automatically (Carnine et al, 2006).

What Good Readers Know and Do

Being able to sound out regular words and recognize sight words are merely starting points for reading English. Able readers develop a truly impressive repertoire of skills. They do the following:

- They understand the directionality and conventions of print (in books or on computer screens).

- They know the uppercase and lowercase letters of the alphabet.

- They can detect, identify, and manipulate the parts of spoken language—syllables, onsets and rimes, and phonemes.

- They use context and other clues to select the correct meaning of multiple-meaning words.

- They recognize letter patterns and use meaningful word parts (*morphemes*) to read and understand multisyllabic words.

- They read words accurately and at an appropriate rate.

- They read expressively and chunk words together in natural phrases.

- They know the text structures and features of different genres and media.

- They add thousands of words to their reading vocabulary per year through independent reading and class instruction.

- Most importantly, they extract meaning from texts by tapping into background knowledge, by relating new information to what they know, by synthesizing and summarizing information, by making inferences about the writer's intentions, by evaluating the writer's evidence and arguments, and by actively monitoring their comprehension as they read.

State Standards for Reading

The TEKS and ELPS state-mandated standards define reading skills and strategies in the context of the ESL classroom. Teachers need to understand fully and become conversant with these standards so that they can incorporate the ELPS expectations and content area TEKS in daily instruction. The K–12 TEKS for English Language Arts include a Reading strand that reflects the major topic areas of the National Reading Panel Report (NICHD, 2000). Beginning in kindergarten, students participate in activities that build on their natural curiosity and prior knowledge to develop their reading, writing, and oral language skills. Every day, students have opportunities to write and to read or listen to different texts. All students in kindergarten and grade 1—including English-language learners—receive comprehensive instruction in phonemic awareness, phonics, decoding, and word attack skills.

Given that English-language learners are being taught to read in a second language, the TEKS underscore the importance of providing additional scaffolds and comprehensible input. To support ELLs' emerging literacy skills, teachers need to accelerate their vocabulary development and teach them comprehension strategies and grammatical conventions that expedite their ability to make sense of what they read.

The TEKS recognize that students' home language provides a foundation for learning in English, including the transfer of literacy skills and the use of cognates (see Chapter 2, pages 28–31 and 35–36). Students with no previous schooling or interrupted schooling will likely have fewer transferrable skills and need explicit and strategic support. With these special scaffolds in mind, beginning in kindergarten, all students are expected to do the following:

- understand how English is written and printed

- display phonological awareness

- use common letter-sound relationships to decode regular words and automatically identify a body of irregular high-frequency words

- use strategies such as making predictions and drawing conclusions to understand a variety of texts (narrative, procedural, and informational)

- use new vocabulary

- recognize and discuss theme and genre

- understand and respond to poetry

- understand fiction and point to evidence of their understanding in the text

- analyze the author's purpose in informational text and point to evidence of the purpose in the text

- understand expository informational text and point to evidence of their understanding in the text

- retell and summarize text

- glean and use information from procedural texts and documents

- analyze forms of media and the techniques used

- carry out research by identifying sources and gathering evidence from text

The TEKS for English Language Arts recognize that although young English-language learners are able to analyze, synthesize, and evaluate what they read and hear, they may not have sufficient speaking or writing proficiency to demonstrate their knowledge. Teachers need to consider the possible limitations of students' language production and offer alternative pathways for students to show what they learn. (To review or download the TEKS for English Language Arts, visit *www.tea.state.tx.us*. Search under TEKS.)

ELPS and Reading Proficiency

For English-language learners to be considered proficient in the domain of reading, they must be able to read, comprehend, and interpret grade-level texts. As their level of reading proficiency increases, students move from understanding texts read aloud to understanding environmental print and sight vocabulary to decoding and understanding grade-appropriate text with minimal support. In addition to identifying 11 K–12 Student Expectations for Reading, the ELPS present separate K–1 and 2–12 Proficiency Level Descriptors at four levels: Beginning, Intermediate, Advanced, and Advanced High. The descriptors for K–1 differ from those for 2–12 because they take into account the fact that students in K–1 develop decoding skills at different rates regardless of their stage of second-language acquisition. For students in K–1 who have not reached the emergent literacy stage of decoding written text, the descriptors related to understanding written texts are not used.

Throughout K–12, teachers should refer to the Proficiency Level Descriptors to select the linguistic accommodations that enable students at varying proficiency levels to engage with grade-level content area texts. For students in grade 3 and higher who are at the beginning or intermediate level, districts must provide intensive and ongoing foundational second-language acquisition instruction. (To review the ELPS online or to download a copy, go to: *www.tea.state.tx.us*. Search under ELPS.)

Assessing Emergent Reading Proficiency

As is true of K–1 instruction in general, teachers build English-language learners' foundational literacy skills by having students listen to texts that are read aloud and by having students read. Throughout the year, teachers use daily literacy activities to monitor and develop students' reading proficiency. In the spring, teachers trained as raters complete the summative TELPAS assessment using the PLDs to determine each student's proficiency level in reading. Holistic ratings are based on observations of the student during performance-based reading activities. The following activities are possible opportunities for gathering assessment data:

- sing-alongs and read-alongs, including chants and poems
- shared reading with big books, charts, or overhead transparencies
- paired reading
- guided reading with leveled readers
- reading subject-area texts and other materials
- cooperative group work
- reading-response journals
- independent reading

Early Screening and Intervention

In their practice guide for the U.S. Department of Education, Russell Gersten and his colleagues recommend that school districts screen English-language learners for reading problems in mid- or late kindergarten (Gersten et al., 2007). For students who are found to be at risk, they recommend ongoing formative assessments at least three times a year. Valid screening instruments for K–1 include measures of phonological awareness, rapid letter naming, matching letters to sounds, and reading single words in lists. After the middle of grade 1, students should be assessed using fluency measures based on the oral reading of connected text.

Gersten and his colleagues stress the importance of high expectations for all students. They urge school districts to use the same performance standards for English-language learners as they have established for native English speakers. Schools should not consider below-grade-level performance in reading as "normal" or something that will be resolved at a later time when a student's oral language proficiency improves.

English-language learners who enter first grade with weak reading skills and older elementary students with reading problems need focused small-group interventions provided for at least 30 minutes each day. This intensive early reading instruction for ELLs does not mean that the students have a learning disability or that they cannot learn to read as well as their classmates. It means that they face a unique challenge—learning a new language at the same time they are learning to read the language. (For more information about reading interventions for struggling English-language learners, visit *www.what-works.ed.gov.)*

Key Components of Effective Reading Instruction

In its comprehensive review of reading research, the National Reading Panel (NICHD, 2000) identified five essential components of reading instruction: phonemic awareness, phonics, fluency, vocabulary, and comprehension. There is some evidence that direct instruction in the first four areas has a positive influence on second-language literacy development (August and Shanahan, 2006). However, it cannot be overstated that English-language learners differ from their native English-speaking peers in terms of their cultural-linguistic backgrounds, potential for cross-linguistic transfer, and instructional needs (Escamilla, 2009).

Even among ELLs there is enormous diversity—their place of birth, home language, level of proficiency in that language, family's socioeconomic status, prior schooling, previous literacy experiences, and past exposure to English and U.S. culture. Teachers need to be aware of every student's strengths and academic challenges so that they can modify and adapt literacy instruction to meet each student's individual needs.

Print Awareness and Letter Knowledge

Print awareness is a child's earliest introduction to literacy. Children with emerging print awareness know the conventions and characteristics of a written language. They understand that printed words correspond to speech, white spaces mark the boundaries between words, and English print is read from left to right and from the top of a page to the bottom. They also know how to handle a book and can point to where they need to begin reading on a page. As their print awareness develops, students learn to recognize and use print conventions such as capitalization, punctuation, and paragraph indents.

Children with emerging *letter knowledge* understand that written words are made up of letters. They grasp the *alphabetic principle* that letters in print represent the sounds of spoken words. As their letter knowledge develops, children recognize the shapes of the 26 uppercase and 26 lowercase English letters, they associate these shapes with the letters' names, and they begin to use letters in their own writing to spell the salient sounds of words.

Implications for English-Language Learners

Many languages are *alphabetic*—the written form is comprised of a fixed set of letters that represent one or more sounds. English-language learners whose home language is alphabetic are likely to have some degree of print awareness and letter knowledge that they can transfer to English or can easily learn because the concepts are not new. For example, students who speak or read a language written with the Roman alphabet such as Spanish, Vietnamese *quoc ngu,* Haitian Creole, Portuguese, or Tagalog, will be familiar with letters in the English alphabet. These students will need to learn the English names for the letters and any differences in the sounds those letters represent. There are also alphabetic languages that use a different alphabet and in some cases right-left directionality and/or vertical rather than horizontal orientation. Some examples are Arabic, Korean, Urdu and Russian. Even so, English-language learners who have experiences with the written form of these languages already understand many essential concepts of print.

In contrast, English print conventions and letters of the alphabet may represent completely new concepts for students who have had interrupted schooling or no prior literacy experiences and for students whose home language is nonalphabetic such as Chinese, Japanese, and Amharic. In planning instruction for English-language learners, teachers need to consider these questions:

- What print experiences has the student had in L1?

- How is the L1 writing system similar to or different from English? Are there concepts and skills that I can help the student transfer to English?

- What prior experiences has the student had with English print?

To develop students' print awareness, teachers need to create a print-rich class environment, provide daily read-aloud experiences, and point out the conventions and features of print during shared reading activities. Print is everywhere—on street signs, labels, calendars, posters, bulletin boards, newspapers, magazines, cellphones, TV, and Web pages. Teachers can lead students on a school or class treasure hunt and invite them to bring samples of print from home. Another way to make print meaningful is to have students dictate stories that they then illustrate and share with their families.

Learning the letters of the alphabet involves becoming familiar with the shapes of uppercase and lowercase letters and learning their names. Since there is no relationship in English between the shape of the letters and their names, students have to memorize the links. It is helpful to plan instruction so that visually confusing letters are not introduced at the same time. The chance of confusion increases when look-alike pairs also have similar names. Some examples are *M* and *N, b* and *d*, and *e* and *a*. Alphabet books, alphabet blocks, letter cards, magnetic letters, and letter stamps are good resources for hands-on practice. Handwriting activities also have been shown to help the learning process.

When students begin to read, knowing the names of letters is enormously helpful. That is because most English letter names contain the letters' sounds (Trieman and Kessler, 2003). When students see the letter *f* and say its name, they hear the letter's most common sound in the name: /f/. Although the Spanish names for the letters of the alphabet are different from the English names, many contain the letter's *English* sound. When students have this powerful information, they can capitalize on their letter knowledge in Spanish.

Phonemic Awareness

Phonemic awareness is the ability to detect, identify, and manipulate the individual sounds, or phonemes, that make up spoken words. (For additional information, about phonemic awareness see Chapter 1.) Other phonological skills lay the foundation for phonemic awareness, helping students become familiar with the sounds of English. The three earlier developmental levels of phonological awareness focus on larger units of spoken language: word, syllable, and onset-rime. According to the National Reading Panel (NICHD, 2000), phonemic awareness is a prerequisite to students' reading and writing achievement. Blending phonemes and segmenting phonemes are the most critical skills for reading.

Phonemic awareness instruction should be provided in small groups for brief periods of 10–15 minutes. It should be fun and fast-paced, making use of games, rhythmical chants, puppets, and manipulatives that help students count and remember discrete sounds. Although incorporating letter-sound correspondences into phonemic awareness can be effective, it is better to wait until students have reached three milestones, as follows (Snow, et al., 1998):

1. They can orally blend and segment words with the consonant-vowel-consonant pattern (/m/ + /a/ + /n/ = *man*, *man* = /m/ /a/ /n/).

2. They know most of the letter names.

3. They know many of the sounds that go with the letters.

Implications for English-Language Learners

Research has shown that phonological skills and concepts transfer from one language to another. This transfer, however, does not occur automatically. Students need to be alerted to elements of their home language that apply to English and those that do not. Unfamiliar sound patterns can make phonemic tasks more complex for English-language learners. Although many phonemes are common to Spanish and English, students may be so attuned to the predictable patterns of spoken Spanish that they have difficulty discerning and reproducing known sounds in English words. For example, relatively few consonant sounds appear in the final position of Spanish words. As a result, Spanish-speaking students often have difficulty with final consonant blends such as *nk* and *st*. At the beginning of each activity, teachers need to explain sound pattern differences between English and students' L1 and give them a focused purpose for listening.

In addition to helping students transfer their phonemic awareness from L1, teachers need to teach explicitly the phonemes and phoneme combinations that do not exist in students' home languages. For example, the English phonemes /sh/, short /a/, and /z/ are sounds that do not exist in Spanish. English-language learners will need extra practice matching words with "new" sounds, identifying the position of those sounds in words, and producing the sounds as they orally blend and segment words.

Phonics

Phonics is a method of instruction that teaches students the relationship between letters or letter combinations and the sounds they represent. Knowing the letter-sound relationships of an alphabetic language helps beginning readers *decode* (read) and *encode* (spell) words that are phonetically regular. It is also useful for skilled readers when they come across an unfamiliar word.

Explicit phonics instruction teaches students how to look at the letters in a word, connect the letters to sounds, and orally blend the sounds in sequence to come up with a recognizable word or an approximate pronunciation. After successfully decoding a particular word multiple times, the reader stores all the relevant information about the word in a tightly bound neural model in the brain (Shaywitz et al., 2004). At that point, just seeing the word in print activates the neural model.

Accurate, automatic word recognition is the goal of phonics instruction because it allows the reader to develop reading fluency and focus more mental energy on constructing meaning from text. To help students develop automaticity, teachers need to provide repeated opportunities for students to practice reading words with target phonetic elements—in isolation and in decodable text, which contains a high percentage of words with known letter-sound correspondences. Students also benefit from hands-on activities in which they build, sort, and manipulate words with target elements.

According to the National Reading Panel (NICHD, 2000), the most effective phonics instruction is both systematic and explicit. Systematic instruction teaches a set of useful letter-sound correspondences in a carefully selected, logical sequence. Lessons are organized so that the alphabetic principle becomes evident, new skills builds on existing skills, and tasks progress from simple to more complex. Phonics instruction is explicit when the teacher clearly explains concepts and clearly models applying decoding skills. Studies have shown that systematic, explicit phonics instruction is more effective than approaches that rely on opportunistic teaching during storybook reading or approaches that require students to make inferences about phonics rules by "discovering" patterns.

Implications for English-Language Learners

The National Reading Panel emphasized that good phonics instruction is just one part of a comprehensive reading program. Reading instruction must focus on developing students' vocabulary and comprehension. This is even more relevant for students who are learning English. The goal of sounding out a word is to connect the printed word to its spoken form so that the reader can access the word's meaning from a store of oral vocabulary. Without the necessary background knowledge, English-language learners may become adept at sounding out isolated words and still have no idea what the words mean. Reading becomes more challenging when students are asked to read words in connected decodable text. To make sense of sentences, English-language learners have to know how to navigate syntax, grammar, and phonetically irregular high-frequency words, which are often abstract but essential for understanding.

In planning phonics instruction for English-language learners, teachers should consider the following guiding principles:

- Keep expectations high for all students. Support their ongoing efforts to develop reading skills in their home language. Engage family members in reading with students at home in L1 or in English.

- Read aloud to students every day from a variety of grade-appropriate fiction and informational texts.

- Integrate phonics instruction with oral language development, in-depth vocabulary instruction, and text comprehension strategies.

- Make reading experiences meaningful, contextualized, and fun. Before students are asked to read, introduce the words and phrases that may be unfamiliar. Use visuals, props, pantomime, graphic organizers, gestures, and technology resources to develop word meanings. Make learning experiential and hands-on. Have students hear and use target words and phrases in songs, chants, games, and role-plays.

- Help students transfer their L1 literacy skills to decoding and comprehending English text. This may include their understanding of the alphabetic principle, familiarity with letters of the alphabet, knowledge of letter-sound relationships, ability to recognize words that rhyme, ability to identify words that begin with the same sound, understanding that some sounds can be spelled in more than one way, awareness of word parts and syllables, awareness of word and sentence boundaries, use of cognates, and the ability to blend sounds to read words.

- If students read another language based on the Roman alphabet, determine which letter-sound correspondences in L1 have positive transfer to English, which have negative transfer because the correspondences are different, and which have zero transfer because they do not exist in L1.

- Acknowledge and praise students' efforts. Provide explicit instruction and extra support when teaching new concepts, new print conventions, or sounds that do not exist in students' home languages.

• Create opportunities for students to practice reading and writing English with different partners. When students speak the same home language, allow translation and conversation in that language as students work together on their English phonics skills.

Fluency

Fluent reading involves reading text accurately, at the appropriate rate, and with prosody (expression). These three aspects are interrelated. Improving one tends to improve the other. Fluent readers are able to read grade-level text smoothly and effortlessly. They recognize words automatically and group words together to form natural phrases. Fluent readers pause briefly between phrases and pause for longer intervals between sentences. They also use end punctuation and an understanding of the writer's tone to read with appropriate expression. Most importantly, fluent readers are good readers who understand what they read.

Accurate reading requires automatic word recognition, which is developed over time by successfully applying phonics knowledge to decode regular words. Instantaneous recognition also involves memorizing a large number of irregular high-frequency words. Reading with expression requires an understanding of English syntax and how groups of words work together in meaningful units.

Once students have mastered foundational decoding skills, there are a number of effective ways to develop their reading fluency, including the following:

• independent silent reading of texts at the appropriate reading level

• choral and echo reading of texts at the instructional reading level

• paired reading

• repeated oral readings

• readers theatre

• synchronized reading with a recording (computer, CD, or audiotape)

Implications for English-Language Learners

Even when reading silently, fluent readers "hear" the music of the language they are reading. Teachers must help English-language learners develop an ear and eye for the natural rhythms, pitch, and stress patterns of English. ELLs benefit from listening to models of fluent reading as they follow along in the text. These models may be teachers, peers, or virtual and digital audio resources.

Many variables impact how fluently a student reads a given text (Torgesen and Hudson, 2006). It is important for teachers to determine the underlying cause when students read a text haltingly word-by-word. Among the factors to consider are the following:

- mastery of foundation skills—letter knowledge, phonemic awareness, and letter-sound correspondences

- number of known sight words

- degree of self-monitoring and purpose for reading

- motivation for reading

- size and depth of the student's oral vocabulary

English-language learners are likely to benefit from fluency instruction that focuses on developing their oral and academic vocabulary and introducing them to a wide range of interesting sources of print (Francis et al., 2006).

Vocabulary, Comprehension, and English-Language Learners

Vocabulary is the knowledge of words and word meanings. It involves an understanding of how words are used in different social situations and across content areas. Vocabulary knowledge continues to grow over the course of a person's lifetime. In the context of reading instruction, it is impossible to separate vocabulary knowledge from comprehension. Readers cannot understand text without knowing what most of the words mean (NICHD, 2000). This, of course, has huge implications for students who are reading in English and learning the language at the same time.

In the early stages of literacy, many ELLs are able to keep pace with their English-speaking peers. That is because the instructional focus is on word-level decoding. When the focus turns to reading comprehension and writing, English-language learners lag behind (August and Shanahan, 2006). As students progress through the grades, their ability to read academic English becomes even more critical. In fact, native English-speaking students often experience a sudden drop-off in reading performance known as "the fourth-grade slump." This is due to a shift in focus to reading texts that contain words and concepts that are beyond students' oral vocabularies and knowledge base.

Given the close relationship between background knowledge, vocabulary, and comprehension, it makes sense that the most successful literacy programs for English-language learners are those that make oral language, vocabulary, and background building integral parts of reading instruction. Studies of vocabulary instruction show that English-language learners are more likely to learn words when the words are taught directly. ELLs also learn more words when the words are part of robust vocabulary instruction—embedded in multiple meaningful contexts in which students hear, say, discuss, pantomime, categorize, define, and write the words (Carlo et al., 2004). In this way, instruction goes beyond teaching words' meanings to teaching students how to use academic vocabulary and grammatical structures in authentic tasks. See Chapters 1 and 2 for more information about academic English and comprehensible input.

Enhancing Reading Comprehension

There are many ways to enhance English-language learners' reading comprehension. Best practice suggests that teachers do the following:

- Select text that is relevant and accessible. Incorporate reading material with themes and content that reflect students' own experiences and home cultures. For students at beginning proficiency levels in reading, consider using content-area texts that have built-in supports such as on-page glossaries, translations in L1, labeled visuals, and graphic summaries.

- Review reading selections and other content-area resources before introducing them to students. Identify potential obstacles to comprehension: difficult vocabulary, idioms, phrasal verbs, conditional verb tense, false cognates, cultural or historical references, and complex sentence structures. Areas of potential difficulty depend on individual students' level of proficiency, prior experiences and background, and L1 literacy.

- Build adequate background so that students are comfortable with the topic of the selection. One effective way to frontload their learning is to introduce new concepts through discussions and text in students' home language prior to reading and discussing the selection in English.

- Pre-teach key words and phrases that are essential to understanding the main ideas in the text. Also pre-teach basic vocabulary that may be unfamiliar or confusing to students.

- Lead students in previewing reading selections. Do a picture walk, paging through the selection. Teach students how to use the visuals and headings to predict what the selection is about and how it is organized.

- Work through difficult text passages with students, clarifying the meaning. Explain any cultural or historical references. Use think-alouds to model comprehension strategies such as using context clues and cognates to infer meaning, connecting new words and concepts to what students already know, and self-monitoring strategies.

- Prompt students to use higher-order thinking skills by evaluating the text, synthesizing information, and identifying the author's purpose. Encourage students to find evidence in the text to support their statements and opinions.

- Engage students in working together to make meaning. Provide opportunities for extended interactions with peers. Use instructional conversations to structure group discussion.

- Consolidate learning by guiding students in summarizing and paraphrasing key ideas. Use graphic organizers to record information and show the relationship between ideas.

- Allow students to respond first to texts by writing in L1 before they write a response in English.

Selecting Words to Teach

To help teachers determine if and how they should teach specific words, Isabel Beck and her colleagues developed a three-tier system for categorizing the words in student texts (Beck et al., 2002):

Tier One: Tier-One words consist of high-frequency words that are used in everyday speech such as *and, food, daddy,* and *the*.

Tier Two: Tier-Two words are words that occur frequently in academic texts, are central to comprehension, and cross content areas. Often, meaning changes across disciplines are subtle. Some examples are *product, concern, calculate,* and *conclusion*.

Tier Three: Tier-Three words are low-frequency specialized words that are used in specific content areas. Some examples are *photosynthesis, kayak, agriculture,* and *rectangle.*

Beck and her colleagues recommend that teachers select Tier-Two words for direct, explicit instruction prior to reading. That is because these words are used across academic disciplines and are critical for understanding and discussing academic content, including specialized Tier-Three words. Tier-Three words can be explained as they occur in context and as the need arises.

Margarita Calderón and her colleagues modified the tier system for English-language learners (Calderón et al, 2005). The framework views Tier-One from the perspective of ELLs' language proficiency and adds additional criteria for classifying and preteaching words. It recommends that teachers not assume that ELLs know the basic Tier-One words that native-English speaking students are assumed to know (for example, words that appear on published high-frequency word lists such as the Dolch List or Dale-Chall List). Teachers need to teach ELLs how to use Tier-One function words such as *on, more, next, because,* and *some* to understand the structure of a sentence. Tier-One content words carry information or meaning in text. In selecting instructional approaches for these words, the framework suggests that teachers consider how concrete or abstract the word is. If it is concrete, it may be sufficient to show students a picture prior to reading. If it is abstract, teachers can provide a brief explanation during reading, including an L1 translation.

Calderón and her colleagues also recognize the importance of drawing on what English-language learners know. When students have learned a concept or concrete term in their L1, providing the English "label" is often sufficient. Any time that text contains a cognate of a word in students' L1, teachers should point out the word and ask students to provide the L1 word they know. No additional discussion or explanation is needed, unless the word is a false cognate.

Teaching Grammatical Structures and Discourse Patterns

To develop students' academic English proficiency, instruction must go beyond teaching vocabulary. Students must be able to navigate and produce the complex grammatical structures that are part of content-area discourse. To do so, they need explicit instruction in the following:

- passive structures

- conditional clauses

- comparative constructions

- modals

- gerunds and infinitives

- noun and preposition combinations (*concern for, belief in, approval of*)

- adjective and preposition combinations (*interested in, opposite of, familiar with*)

Students also need to understand how texts in certain disciplines are typically organized. Robin Scarcella suggests teaching ELLs how to recognize phrases that signal discourse features (Scarcella, 2008). Examples of discourse features include the following:

- introductory statements (*This paper will examine…*)

- transitional sentences (*Before discussing X, it will be useful to define Y.*)

- ways to build on ideas (*This in turn leads to…*)

- concluding statements (*In conclusion,…*)

Becoming a Writer

Of the four language domains, writing proficiency is the last to develop. Skilled writers produce a variety of writing forms and tailor their writing for a specific purpose and audience. Their writing is clear and cohesive, with few spelling or grammar errors. Good writers carefully choose their words, create a rhythm with varied sentence structures, and include detailed descriptions. Ultimately, they develop their own unique voice and style. Skilled writers know how to conduct research and report information accurately with proper attribution. They also follow a process in which they draft, revise, edit, and proofread their writing to create a final, polished piece of writing.

State Standards for Writing

The TEKS and ELPS state-mandated standards define writing skills in the context of the ESL classroom. Teachers need to understand fully and become conversant with these standards so that they can incorporate the ELPS expectations and content area

TEKS in daily instruction. The K–12 TEKS for English Language Arts include a Writing strand. Once students in kindergarten and grade 1 have reached the stage of generating original text, they are expected to complete writing assignments in all content areas using newly acquired basic and content-based vocabulary. They are also expected to write with increasingly complex grammatical structures and increasing specificity and detail.

Given that English-language learners are being taught to write in a second language, the TEKS underscore the importance of providing additional scaffolds commensurate with each student's level of English language proficiency. Students' home language and L1 literacy provide a foundation for writing in English, including the possible transfer of conventions of print, letter-sound correspondences, and the use of cognates (See Chapter 2, pages 28–31 and 31–35). Students with no previous schooling or interrupted schooling will likely have fewer transferrable skills and need explicit and strategic support. With these special scaffolds in mind, once K–1 students begin to generate original text, they are expected to do the following:

- Use their knowledge of letter-sound correspondences to represent English sounds when writing.

- Use grade-level vocabulary when writing.

- Spell English words with increasing accuracy.

- Edit writing for standard grammar and usage based on grade-level expectations.

- Use grammatical structures based on grade-level expectations. This includes correct verbs, verb tenses, pronouns/antecedents, possessive case, negatives, and contractions.

- Vary sentence length and combine phrases, clauses, and sentences in increasingly accurate ways.

- Narrate, describe, and explain with increasing specificity.

ELPS and Writing Proficiency

For English-language learners to be considered proficient in the domain of writing, they must be able to produce written text with the appropriate content and format for grade-level writing assignments. As their level of writing proficiency increases, students move from emergent forms of writing to participating in shared writing activities to writing self-generated text that is free of errors. In addition to identifying seven K–12 Student

Expectations for Writing, the ELPS present separate K–1 and 2–12 Proficiency Level Descriptors at four levels: Beginning, Intermediate, Advanced, and Advanced High. The descriptors for K–1 differ from those for 2–12 because they take into account the fact that students in K–1 develop the ability to write original text at different rates regardless of their stage of second language acquisition.

Throughout K–12, teachers should refer to the Proficiency Level Descriptors to select the linguistic accommodations that enable students at varying proficiency levels to engage in content area writing activities. For students in grade 3 and higher who are at the beginning or intermediate level, districts must provide intensive and ongoing foundational second-language acquisition instruction. (To review the ELPS online or to download a copy, go to: *www.tea.state.tx.us*. Search under ELPS.)

Assessing Emergent Writing Proficiency

As is true of K–1 instruction in general, teachers build English-language learners' foundational writing skills through oral activities, emergent forms of writing, and activities that involve writing self-generated texts on familiar topics. Throughout the year, teachers use daily literacy activities to monitor and develop students' writing proficiency. In the spring, teachers trained as raters complete the summative TELPAS assessment using the PLDs to determine each student's proficiency level in writing. Holistic ratings are based on observations of the student during performance-based writing activities. The following activities are possible opportunities for gathering assessment data:

- journal writing for personal reflections
- language experience dictation
- shared writing for content development
- shared writing for literacy development
- prewriting activities to organize and sequence ideas
- making lists for specific purposes
- labeling pictures and objects
- first drafts

Writing Instruction for English-Language Learners

In planning writing instruction for English-language learners, teachers should consider the following guiding principles:

- Keep expectations high for all students. Support their ongoing efforts to develop writing skills in their home language. Engage family members in writing with students at home in L1 or in English.

- Read aloud to students every day from a variety of grade-appropriate fiction and informational texts.

- Integrate writing instruction into reading instruction.

- Provide models of student writing and discuss what makes them good examples. Encourage students to use these models as "anchors" for their own writing.

- Make writing experiences meaningful, contextualized, and fun. Use visuals, props, and technology resources to spark topics and ideas for students to write about. Display and teach interesting words and phrases that they can select for their writing.

- Collect examples of real-world print. Have students write their own signs, CD inserts, menus, news headlines, want ads, recipes, movie reviews, advice columns, comic strips, and advertisements.

- Help students transfer their L1 literacy skills to writing English text. This may include their understanding of the alphabetic principle, familiarity with letters of the alphabet, knowledge of letter-sound relationships, awareness of word parts and syllables, awareness of word and sentence boundaries, use of cognates, and the use of capitalization and punctuation.

- If students read another language based on the Roman alphabet, determine which letter-sound correspondences in L1 have positive transfer to spelling words in English, which have negative transfer because the correspondences are different, and which have zero transfer because they do not exist in L1.

- Acknowledge and praise students' efforts. Provide explicit instruction and extra support when teaching new concepts, new print conventions, or letter-sound correspondences that do not exist in students' home languages.

- Create opportunities for students to practice reading and writing English with different partners. When students speak the same home language, allow translation and conversation in that language as students work together on their English writing skills. To encourage collaboration, avoid making students responsible for correcting each other's written work.

- In the early proficiency stages, allow students to plan their ideas in L1. Provide bilingual dictionaries and access to translations from L1 via the Internet or hand-held devices. English-language learners also benefit from practice with filling in the blanks of a paragraph frame that makes the text's organization and thought transitions obvious.

- Once students are able to produce connected text, encourage the free flow of ideas during the draft stage. Have them focus on a limited number of new grammar or mechanics skills during the edit and proofread stages of the writing process. Encourage them to read aloud any piece of writing before they share it with classmates or the teacher.

Review Questions

1. An advanced ELL student in a high school class includes the following sentence in draft: "When the new teacher walks into the classroom, he supplants Mr. Keating's position." When the teacher praises the student for using "supplant," the student says, "I used 'substitute' first, but I wanted to use a better word, so I thought that in Spanish I would say '*suplantar*' because it means 'replace,' so I put it in English." The L1 to L2 transfer strategy that this student used is

   (A) approximation.

   (B) true cognate.

   (C) interference.

   (D) translation.

The correct response is (**B**). Cognates are words in different languages with the same etymological background and similar spelling in the two languages. (A) is incorrect because the student did not substitute a word similar in meaning or orthography. Approximation usually results in an L2 error. (C) is incorrect because the student has not used an L1 form to produce an L2 utterance. (D) is incorrect because the student has not translated an L1 form. The student started with an L2 string and replaced an L2 word using her knowledge of cognates.

2. ELL students in an elementary class tell their teacher that they don't know how to think of ideas for their writing prompts. The teacher knows that this signals a problem in which stage of the writing process?

(A) Drafting

(B) Audience awareness

(C) Discovery

(D) Publishing

The correct response is (**C**). The discovery stage of writing is the time when students generate potentialities and possibilities for responding to a writing task. Other terms for this stage of writing are "prewriting" and "invention." (A) is incorrect because drafting cannot occur until the student considers ideas that may apply to the writing task. (B) is incorrect because it is a consideration *after* the student generates possible ideas. (D) is the final stage of writing and so is an incorrect response.

Competency 006

6

The ESL teacher understands how to promote students' content-area learning, academic language development and achievement across the curriculum.

Chapter 6 will focus on Competency 006—promoting students' content-area learning, academic language development, and achievement across the curriculum.

Achievement Across the Curriculum

To reach their full academic potential, English-language learners must learn the knowledge and skills identified in the TEKS for each content area. In addition to English Language Arts and Reading, the foundation curriculum includes three critical content areas: Mathematics, Science, and Social Studies. For English-language learners, content-based instruction has three main goals:

1. to build deep subject-area knowledge
2. to develop academic language proficiency
3. to foster critical thinking

All English-language learners need to engage with rich, challenging grade-appropriate content. To do so, instruction must be *linguistically accommodated* to their level of proficiency in listening, speaking, reading, and writing. Content and learning objectives must be clearly *communicated* with comprehensible input. Subject-area knowledge and English language skills must be *sequenced* in a logical way so that successive lessons build on and reinforce previous learning. Instruction must also be *scaffolded*, with teachers or capable peers providing assistance to help students complete academic tasks. In scaffolded instruction, support is gradually removed as students begin to demonstrate the use of new language, concepts, and learning strategies on their own.

There are many ways to scaffold instruction for English-language learners. Some examples include the following:

- activating prior knowledge

- using home language to explain new words or concepts

- using graphic organizers to show relationships between concepts

- preteaching key vocabulary in multiple contexts

- using pictures, props, or realia to convey word meanings

- building word walls with key content vocabulary

- previewing a text's headings, visuals, and captions

- guiding students as a group through the steps of the writing process

The use of adapted texts that are simplified or abridged is another form of scaffolding that has been frequently used with students who have limited proficiency in English. However, this type of material should be viewed as a temporary scaffold because it limits the language, form, and content that students see. English-language learners need to learn how to navigate authentic content-area texts. In order to do so, they have to engage with rich grade-appropriate content and academic English that will stretch their reach to the next level of proficiency.

Aligning Instruction with Language Proficiency Levels

Given that students generally have different levels of English proficiency in the different language domains, school districts are required to assess separately proficiency in listening, speaking, reading, and writing. Based on the proficiency level descriptors in the

English Language Proficiency Standards (ELPS), a student's proficiency in each domain is identified as Beginning, Intermediate, Advanced, or Advanced High. This enables teachers to select the instructional methods and content-area materials that best meet each student's individual needs. It also helps teachers target specific English language objectives together with content objectives when planning lessons.

For students in Grade 3 and higher who are at the beginning or intermediate level, districts must provide intensive and ongoing foundational second-language acquisition instruction. To review the ELPS online or to download a copy, go to: *www.tea.state.tx.us*. Search under ELPS. For additional information about levels of language proficiency, see Chapter 2, page 30.

The Importance of Critical Thinking

Effective content-based instruction develops the communication skills and higher order thinking that prepare students for success as informed global citizens. As they learn the core ideas, concepts, and practices of each content area, they must also learn how to process information and connect it to the real world. Critical thinking involves abstract reasoning, recognizing cause-and-effect relationships, developing persuasive arguments, inferring motivation, making generalizations, forming hypotheses, and being a discerning consumer of information. To develop critical thinking, teachers must help students move beyond the facts on a printed page or the conditions of their immediate environment and provide ample opportunities for students to reason quantitatively and abstractly.

Examples of Students' Critical Thinking

Generate questions on their own.
Select learning tools and resources, including technology and digital media.
Gather information to answer their questions.
Evaluate the accuracy of information—separating fact from opinion and identifying fallacies in logic.
Evaluate the reliability of information—identifying assumptions and any bias that connected to culture, gender, or socioeconomic status.
Develop an argument based on evidence.
Identify alternative approaches to solving a problem or completing a task.
Relate instructional content to broader, real-world issues.

Experiential Learning and Group-Based Inquiry

Hands-on activities play an important role in content-based ESL instruction. They create excitement, promote engagement, and spark curiosity. For students with limited language proficiency, hands-on activities offer a concrete way to access and experience discipline-related content through multiple modalities: visual, auditory, and kinesthetic. Project-based learning also builds essential background knowledge and motivates students to apply what they are learning in each language area: listening, speaking, reading, and writing.

Research with English-language learners has shown that group projects such as science experiments serve as a basis for complex and abstract thinking (Lee and Avalos, 2002). Working in heterogeneous groups, students use their developing language skills to negotiate meaning and deepen their content knowledge, which includes an understanding of core ideas, concepts, and practices. In this way, students develop academic language in the context of authentic inquiry.

Agreeing to Disagree

For students to engage with peers around complex ideas, they need to feel that it is safe to do so. Teachers can set the right tone by explaining the ground rules for respectful argumentation. First, they should make it clear that every student has important ideas and is expected to contribute. Teachers can encourage participation by focusing on ideas, rewarding students' efforts to construct meaning, accepting flawed language, and helping students' get their message across by offering clarification, rephrasing students' utterances, and inviting classmates to expand on what they say (Quinn and Lee, 2012).

It is also important to support the practice of questioning peers. Requests for clarification and questions about supporting facts are important learning strategies that students need to develop. To keep conversations productive, it may be necessary for teachers to model how to focus comments on logic and factual evidence rather than judging the value of someone's ideas or the correctness of the language used (Anstrom et al., 2010).

Academic English in Content-Area Instruction

In its broadest sense, *academic English* is the language used to help students acquire and use knowledge. All students—including native English speakers—must learn how to communicate in the "language of school." Proficiency in academic English involves understanding and knowing how to use the *discourse* of each subject area—the written and oral communication patterns typical of a specific discipline. Among the different features of discourse are language functions, organizational patterns, grammatical structures, and vocabulary.

The language used in content-area learning is very different from the English children are exposed to in everyday conversation or in print and digital media. That makes sense when one considers the function, or purpose, of language in these different situations. In content-area learning, students are expected to use language to define a problem, analyze and interpret data, present and justify an argument, evaluate opinions, or describe a procedure.

Becoming proficient in academic English is a complex process for all students and presents special challenges for nonnative speakers. Unlike their native English-speaking peers, English-language learners don't have a built-in sensitivity to language *register* and the levels of formality that are appropriate in academic conversation. Depending on their level of proficiency in English, students may also lack the basic vocabulary that educators assume all children know. Limited levels of proficiency in their home language and interrupted schooling may also mean that students lack background knowledge about basic concepts, objects, people, and events.

To succeed in content-area classes, English-language learners need the basic language skills that are used outside and within school such as producing different sentence types and using appropriate verb tense. To participate in content-area learning fully, they also need extensive vocabulary knowledge, such as the following:

- A large body of commonly used words: the Tier-One content and function words that most native English-speaking children know.

- The language of classroom management, also known as School Navigational Language (Scarcella, 2008).

- The high-frequency essential academic language that is used across all content areas. This includes Tier-Two words *(represent, however, and illustrate)*, complex sentence structures, and features that signal how oral and written discourse is organized: transitions, introductions, and summations.

- Technical words that are specific to a given subject area: Tier-Three words.

(For more information about the tier classification system and how it informs instructional decisions, see Chapter 5.)

In 2003, Robin Scarcella has examined different areas of competency that K–12 students must develop in order to use English for academic tasks. Her framework identifies five linguistic components of academic English: phonological, lexical, grammatical, sociolinguistic, and discourse. Students need to learn the phonological features of English (sounds, stress, intonation) and letter-sound correspondences. They need to understand lexical components such as word meanings, word formation with affixes, and parts of speech. Students also need to learn how to make sense of grammatical components such as the following:

- morphology and syntax commonly used in argumentative compositions, procedural descriptions, and analysis

- rules that govern word order and the agreement of pronoun referents

- complex features of the verb system such as modal verbs

- complex rules of punctuation

The sociolinguistic components of academic English include understanding different language functions, navigating and creating different writing forms and genres, and knowing how to create cohesive communication with conjunctions, parallel structure, and sequencing of verb tenses. The discourse components include knowing transitions and other organizational signals that are typical of specific academic genres.

Sociocognitive Dimensions of Academic Language

Scarcella's research has also examined the special cognitive demands of content-based instruction as they relate to English-language learners. Teachers must be aware of students' backgrounds and the knowledge and experiences they bring to the classroom. English-language learners' prior knowledge about basic concepts, events, culture, and natural phenomenon may be insufficient to begin a course of study on a particular topic. In addition, proficiency in one subject area does not guarantee proficiency in another. That is because academic language varies greatly depending on the purpose and the context. For example, when students work on word problems in mathematics, they may not be able to apply what they have learned about particular words' meanings and language functions in their science or social studies lessons.

Given how much oral and written communication varies depending on the purpose and context, it is important for English-language learners to study academic vocabulary with grammar and discourse structures. Although extensive vocabulary development is essential for academic achievement, it is not sufficient for teachers to focus on building English-language learners' understanding of isolated academic terms (Anstrom et al., 2010). Students need to use and study the language of math during authentic tasks: gathering data, measuring objects, calculating estimations, discussing facts, forming hypotheses, and presenting arguments and claims. For example, a group activity that requires students to compare travel times provides a meaningful context for language instruction that examines comparative adjectives, *if/then* conditional constructions, the mathematical meanings of words such as *problem, rate, times,* and *product*, and the relationship between words, numerals, and symbols.

Metacognition and Learning Strategies

Metacognition is the awareness of one's thinking and the ability to monitor comprehension. Given the inherent challenges of learning content through a second language, English-language learners need to develop a level of awareness that helps them recognize when they do not understand something and a set of strategies for getting "unstuck." To align instruction with state-mandated standards, teachers should consult the cross-curricular Learning Strategies section of the English Language Proficiency Standards as well as the strategies that are identified within the TEKS for each subject area.

Initially, teachers will need to model learning strategies explicitly. After repeated guided practice, students will be able to internalize and apply the strategies on their own. Read-alouds and think-alouds are excellent ways to model metacognitive skills. As they verbalize their thoughts, teachers can show students how to link new information with prior knowledge, use text details to form mental images, and make predictions by combining what the writer or speaker says with what they know from their past experiences (Turkan et al., 2012).

To navigate complex content-area materials, students need to develop the habit of pausing from time to time to ask themselves: "Do I understand what I just read or heard? What is important for me to remember about this section?" If the answer to the first question is *yes*, students should identify the writer's or speaker's main idea and paraphrase it in their own words orally or in writing. If the answer is *no*, teachers should help students practice a number of fix-up strategies including rereading, reading more slowly, or continuing to read or listen for additional clarification. These metacognitive skills consolidate content knowledge and help create a lifelong love of learning.

Given the close relationship between vocabulary knowledge and comprehension, English-language learners also benefit from explicit instruction in strategies that help them figure out unfamiliar words and phrases they hear or read. In the context of oral communication, students may ask participants to repeat what they said, speak more slowly, rephrase, or clarify. Students may also respond by stating what it is they understand and requesting confirmation.

As has been previously discussed, prior to reading content-area materials, English-language learners need direct, robust instruction in key academic vocabulary. Given the enormous vocabulary growth required for academic success, English-language learners also need to become independent word learners. They have to develop strategies for figuring out the meanings of unfamiliar words that have not been explicitly introduced to them. Once learned, these word-learning strategies can be applied to other words and other texts. Teachers should provide explicit instruction in these effective word-learning strategies, such as the following:

- Think about other words you know that look like the unfamiliar word. The words may be part of a word family and have related meanings.

- Use what you know from your home language and identify cognates.

- Use surrounding context clues—words in the text as well as visuals.

- Think about the meaning of word parts—prefixes and base words. Use suffixes and inflectional ending as clues to part of speech or verb tense.

- Check the meaning of words in glossaries, bilingual dictionaries, or dictionaries designed for English-language learners. When more than one definition is listed, select the one that makes sense in the context.

Addressing Individual Differences

Each English-language learner is unique with a unique set of experiences, strengths, interests, and learning needs. Students learn at varying rates and differ in the ultimate levels of achievement they will reach. Successful teachers know how to motivate students and match instruction to each student's preferred learning style and abilities.

Students cannot be successful if they are not engaged. To motivate students, best practice suggests that teachers do the following:

- Teach content and language through hands-on, inquiry-based activities. Have high expectations and hold students' accountable for their learning. Teach at an appropriate pace—not too fast and not too slow.

- To reach all students, present material in multiple ways. Use visual, auditory, and kinesthetic approaches for instruction, guided practice, and assessment.

- Build on and value students' life experiences. Engage with members of their family and community as funds of knowledge. Use texts that reflect students' cultures and linguistic backgrounds. Incorporate cultural artifacts into hands-on activities. Provide opportunities for students to act as subject experts.

- Allow student inquiry to drive instruction. Invite students to select topics to explore, learning resources, and the type of work product that will show what they learned. Take advantage of teachable moments, allowing students to discuss what is personally relevant, surprising, or of special interest.

- Maintain the rigor of academic content, while providing linguistic scaffolding. Adjust the language load (length, complexity, and level of abstraction) based on students' levels of proficiency. Communicate at or slightly above students' level of communicative competence.

- Use home language support. Present key terms in multiple languages. Use cognates and allow code-switching between L1 and English. In group activities, allow students to read, discuss, and write about content in the home languages they share.

English-language learners' cultural backgrounds shape their attitudes and interactions. For many, content-area learning involves ways of thinking and communicating that conflict with the norms of their home cultures. For example, inquiry-driven science instruction promotes independent thinking, skepticism, questions about other people's assertions, and arguments that are based on evidence and logic. These habits of mind may seem new and even inappropriate to students whose family culture values cooperation, consensus, emotional support, and deference to the authority of teachers and elders (Lee and Avalos, 2002). To benefit from content-area instruction, these students have to learn an entirely new way of thinking, approaching problems, and communicating ideas.

Differences versus Disabilities

Teachers must keep in mind that many factors affect a student's performance and level of engagement. Speaking infrequently, refusing to answer questions, and poor comprehension are behaviors associated with the early stages of English-language proficiency. Yet these are the same measures by which thousands of English-language learners have been misidentified as having learning disabilities and referred to special education (Cloud, 2006). To assess English-language learners accurately and provide coherent educational programs, school districts need to do the following:

- Form collaborative teams made up of administrators, grade-level teachers, bilingual/second language teachers, and special educators. The core team members will need the support of special resources such as psychologists, speech therapists, and health providers.

- Conduct a comprehensive home language assessment that examines prior educational experiences and a student's present level of knowledge. Limited proficiency in a student's home language and limited background knowledge dramatically impede student achievement across the curriculum. In addition, prior instruction that was poor or inadequate may be why a student has not shown academic progress.

- Determine if there are external factors that may have caused a student's learning delays. These include disrupted schooling due to war, political unrest, refugee status, frequent moves within the United States, illness, or other instability at home.

- Build a trusting relationship with students and their families based on respect and confidentiality. Encourage them to share information about temporary situations that may be affecting a student's behavior and learning such as fatigue or the death of a relative.

- Use culturally and linguistically sensitive assessments to determine if the student has an intrinsic condition that limits the ability to learn and use language. Disabilities may be sensorial, neurological, psychological, cognitive, or linguistic in nature.

Once a student is diagnosed with a learning disability, the educational team will work together to develop an Individualized Educational Program (IEP), which includes the recommended instructional interventions and accommodations based on the nature of the disability. Examples of accommodations include learning-assisted devices and software, audio recordings of texts and lectures, adult classroom aides, additional time for completing assignments, and the use of dictionaries during tests. Teachers must comply with legally mandated procedures for developing and implementing a student's IEP.

Gifted Learners

Gifted learners thrive on choice and challenge. To keep them engaged, teachers should do the following:

- Collaborate with the a gifted education specialist.

- Actively involve students in planning their learning experiences by choosing topics, projects, materials, and partners.

- Pair them with classmates who can keep up with them. Do not expect gifted learners to assume the role of teaching less able students.

- Encourage them to think outside the box, suggesting alternative ways to solve a problem or complete a task. They may enjoy showing what they learn by inventing content-related board games, composing music, or creating multimedia presentations.

Equity of Access

To be successful, all students need to feel that they and their families are valued as important members of the school learning community. Yet students may be dealing with a lack of financial or emotional resources at home. Teachers need to be aware of students' home life so that they can sensitively address problems that are barriers to learning. Students who are anxious or lack self-esteem need opportunities to gain confidence through success. Teachers can select students to be a special helper for the day or an expert on a favorite topic. Students who have a chaotic home life benefit from extra structure in the classroom with predictable routines, schedules, and expectations.

If students do not have the financial means to purchase materials for a project, teachers have several options: supply the materials, have students select a different project, or have students work collaboratively on a group project. If students do not have computers or Internet access at home, teachers should come up with alternative plans that still allow students to develop critical technology skills. Some students might complete assignments while supervised by an adult at school or in a local library, or they might partner with a classmate and plan how to delegate tasks and responsibilities. Flexible, creative problem-solving ensures that all students have access to educational opportunities and achievement.

Review Questions

1. Ms. Oliver has an elementary class of beginning ESL students. During reading time, she integrates nonfiction picture books that focus on science, history, and social studies topics. She reads a book orally to her students and then rereads it several times. After several rereadings, she stops at key points in the book and asks students to fill in what comes next. Which of the following statements best explains how this teaching strategy reinforces students' content-area learning?

    (A) The repeated readings and student participation reinforces' students familiarity with discipline-specific terms and concepts

    (B) The oral reading reinforces students' phonological awareness

    (C) Reading picture books instead of actual textbooks simplifies the content-area material for learners who are not yet ready for challenging content

    (D) Working with picture books allows students to learn to spell high-frequency words in a meaningful communicative context

    The correct response is (**A**). The teacher is reinforcing content-area knowledge during oral-reading time. Rereading the books familiarizes the young learners with content-area concepts and vocabulary, but it also causes the listeners to "memorize" the text, which is a good language-learning strategy for beginning ESL students. Filling in words and sentences in a familiar text is also an effective language-learning strategy for this ESL level. (B) is incorrect because the teacher's goal is to reinforce content-area knowledge. (C) is incorrect because the teacher is not trying to simplify content, but to reinforce it. (D) is incorrect because the teacher's goal does not target high-frequency words.

2. A high school history teacher realizes that his ELL students are having significant difficulties in understanding the content of each new chapter of their history textbook. To introduce the next chapter, he creates an outline of the key points. Prior to starting the chapter, he projects the outline on the overhead and has students copy the outline. Which of the following adjustments should the teacher make to this activity to promote his students' understanding of history content more effectively?

(A) After they finish copying the outline, the teacher should have several students read the outline orally

(B) As a next step, the teacher should model how to create a graphic organizer to connect the key concepts in the outline

(C) After the students finish copying the outline, the teacher should check all the outlines to ensure the students copied everything correctly

(D) As a next step, the teacher should give students time to work in groups to discuss the outline and then administer a quiz to determine the students' understanding

The correct response is (**B**). The outline will prepare students for the new information they are about to get in the chapter. However, teaching them how to create a graphic organizer from the outline will foster learner independence. They will be able to transfer this knowledge to future new learning. (A) and (C) are incorrect responses because they do not directly support the teacher's objective. Reading the outline orally and checking for correct copying of the outline do not contribute to students' understanding of history content. (D) is incorrect because the outline is supposed to prepare students for new knowledge, so quizzing them on the preparation activity is illogical.

Competency 007

Competency 007

The ESL teacher understands formal and informal assessment procedures and instruments used in ESL programs and uses assessment results to plan and adapt instruction.

Chapter 7 will focus on Competency 007—assessment procedures, including formal and informal procedures, instruments used in ESL programs, and how assessment results are used for planning and adapting ESL instruction.

English-Language Learners and Assessment

Assessment is the process of discovering what students know, understand, and are able to do with that knowledge. Ideally, it measures students' mastery of certain learning objectives, identifies learning gaps, and plots student progress. For ELLs, it is essential to assess English language skills in order to assign students to the appropriate language program or course (in high school). Then, students are assessed throughout the program to determine their progress. In content-based ESL instruction, teachers need to assess students' language proficiency separately from their content knowledge, which is why Texas has two state assessment systems—STAAR and TELPAS. STAAR is the State of Texas Assessment of Academic Readiness test that is used annually to assess students' knowledge of grade level content areas—reading, writing, math, science, and social studies. TELPAS stands for Texas English Language Proficiency Assessment System, and it is designed to assess the progress students make in learning the English language.

There are two types of assessments—formal and informal. Formal, or summative, assessment consists of typical standardized tests (often written tests, quizzes, or essays) that measure a certain level of achievement or mastery of objectives. Traditionally, these types of tests were usually carried out at the end of a chapter, unit, course, or grade level, generally resulting in a numerical grade or test score. But times have changed, and today tests are given to assess mastery of objectives, not to assign a grade.

For beginning ESL teachers, it is important to know that summative assessment results show teachers what objectives (TEKS) students did not master, so they plan instruction accordingly. It evaluates student achievement by measuring certain objectives or expectations, which are reported to the student, parents, and others.

On the other hand, formative assessment is used throughout the school year to allow teachers to give students more frequent feedback on their progress. It is usually more casual, consisting of teacher observation or discussion or student self-evaluation; these are usually not part of the traditional numeric grade or mark. Teachers use a portfolio approach that combines observations, rubrics, student work samples, and the like with more formal measures. Formal formative assessments may be used to give grades for beginning or intermediate students whose reading and or writing is so limited that the results of a written test would not be valid. The teacher may use ELLs oral responses in grading.

ESL teachers must continually modify and accommodate instruction for individual students or groups. (See Chapters 5 and 6 for best practices to accomplish this.) This is mandated by state law as stated in the Commissioner's Rules (see below). Teachers use formative assessment to modify instruction based on the ELPS and TEKS to plan instruction based on test data for language proficiency levels or gaps in content knowledge. Details about how an ESL teacher may use formative assessment to adjust instruction will be given later in this chapter.

All laws for educating children in Texas are compiled in the Texas Education Code (TEC), which includes those that are mandated by the federal No Child Left Behind Act (NCLB). The Texas Education Agency (TEA) provides resources to school districts and oversees the implementation of the law. The Commissioner's Rules, Chapter 89, Subchapter BB (the most up-to-date version of the TEC) sets the policy for educating ELLs. It is the authority for all ESL/Bilingual Language Programs. The Rules state how the Language Proficiency Assessment Committee (LPAC) uses the Home Language Survey (HLS) to identify which students should be tested to determine if they are LEP.

The Rules also include polices for how ELLs are served, exited, and monitored; they state when assessments are given, how they are to be used, and the steps the Language Proficiency Assessment Committee (LPAC) uses to determine when the student is no longer considered LEP. It includes the rules for selecting a LPAC and the duties of the committee. This document may be revised and updated annually.

Initial Designation and Program Placement

A flowchart on the ELLTx website is helpful for LPAC members to follow the process for determining limited English proficiency—*www.elltx.org*, search under flowchart—beginning with the Home Language Survey, which is required by the No Child Left Behind Act (see Chapter 8).

Home Language Survey—Identification as LEP

When a student enrolls in a Texas public school for the first time, the parent must complete a Home Language Survey (HLS), which consists of two questions:

- What language is spoken in your home most of the time?

- What language does your child speak most of the time?

If the answer to either question is any language other than English, the student must be tested to determine if she or he is LEP (Limited English Proficiency). The LPAC must administer the OLPT (Oral Language Proficiency Test) and norm-referenced testing (also called standardized testing); they must meet to determine if the student is LEP or EP and place the student in an ESL or Bilingual Program within 20 school days of enrollment. LPACs must use the tests on the state-approved list. See pages 120–121, Oral Language Proficiency Tests (OLPTs), for details. If a school has just one possible LEP student, it must establish an LPAC and provide an ESL program to fulfill this requirement. However, if a district has 20 or more LEP students with the same language classification, it must offer a bilingual program.

Language Proficiency Assessment Committees (LPAC)

The Commissioner's Rules mentioned earlier in this chapter, are the authority for all ESL/Bilingual program policies. These include the following:

- when and how to establish an LPAC

    - membership

    - training

    - roles and responsibilities

- when a student should be tested, how, and why

- language program design and content

- training needed for teachers to implement and maintain appropriate instruction for the ESL or bilingual programs

- documentation required to be kept in the student's cumulative (permanent) folder; note that there is a separate folder referred to as the LPAC folder, which is kept with the "cum" folder and contains all of the LPAC documents for the individual student

- exiting students from the programs

- monitoring exited students for two years

- providing summer school for students entering kindergarten or first grade

The LPAC membership for an ESL program must include one or more professional personnel (this may be a school counselor, content subject teachers, ESL teachers, and Special Education teachers), an administrator, and a parent of an ELL participating in the program that is designated by the school district. The parent representative *may not* be employed by the district. All LPAC members must be trained in the roles and responsibilities of the LPAC and sign an oath of confidentiality to act for the school district.

The LPAC is established by the Texas Education Code to implement the Commissioner's Rules. The responsibilities are as follows:

- review all pertinent information on LEP students

- identify students as LEP (an ELL) or non-LEP

- designate language proficiency level of each student and initial placement of LEP students in a language program upon receiving parent/guardian permission

- facilitate ELL participation in other state/federally funded programs such as G/T (Gifted/Talented) or RTI (Response to Intervention), and so on

- document all meetings and decisions made with a minutes form and individual forms for the student's LPAC folder

- provide written notice to the parents/guardian of the student— including classification, approval for program placement, benefits on the program, and its role in the total school program in English and the parent's home language

- determine instructional interventions that are appropriate based on the students proficiency levels and prior schooling

- determine which state-mandated tests an ELL will take and accommodations for testing

- reclassify LEP students, including those with parent denials as EP when they meet exit criteria

- collaborate with the ARD, 504, and grade placement committees when the student is also served by these committees

- monitor the progress of students who exited the program within the past two years to determine if the students is academically successful based on grades, test scores, behavior, and subjective teacher data

To plan for individual needs, an ESL teacher must be keenly aware of the student's progress in each of the four domains—listening, speaking, reading, and writing—and how students are gaining content knowledge and skills. The teacher must try many interventions or diagnostic screenings to rule out physical or social problems that interfere with learning, such as earaches causing listening difficulty, dental issues or deformities causing speaking issues, bullying causing fear to speak in class, or lack of sleep causing inability to remember or focus on the lesson. Informal discussions with parents sometimes reveal if a student has these issues at home when using his primary language. The teacher should then make the necessary referral to the RTI (Response to Intervention) committee and increase linguistic accommodations for instruction. This committee helps the teacher with interventions and determines if the student qualifies for the next tier, which leads to testing for Special Education services (see Chapter 6).

The ELL student may need testing in his or her home language and English to determine if he or she qualifies for Special Education services. Parent permission is needed for this testing, and it is done by a certified test diagnostician—*not* the teacher. An ARD committee must meet within 30 days of the evaluations to determine if the student qualifies for Special Education services. These may include resource instruction (minutes in a small group to provide intensive targeted content instruction), speech, occupational therapy, physical therapy, sensory therapy, behavior therapy, and so on. If an ARD meeting is held for an ELL, the LPAC must be notified and represented at the meeting.

Annual LPAC meetings are held to determine ELL placement for the next school year. By examining each student's progress through test scores and other criteria, the LPAC determines if a student is still LEP. If so, the student will continue in the ESL program. If not, the committee must decide whether the student meets exit criteria.

Every year, reports are made to the school board about how many students advanced a level on TELPAS, how many exited ESL, how many are still on monitor, and how many passed each reading and math STAAR. This is all documented for the state AMAOs (see Chapter 8).

Oral Language Proficiency Tests (OLPTs)

Every summer, the TEA publishes the List of Approved Tests for Assessment of Limited English Proficient (LEP) Students on its website. This list outlines which tests may be used for identification of students as LEP, program placement, program exiting, student progress, and identification as gifted/talented (G/T). Each school district must determine which tests it will use from the list. Depending on the district, the Language Program Coordinator or the LPAC chairperson ensures that students are given the latest version of the tests and that updated norms are used for diagnosis. Teachers must attend training in test administration and interpretation by the test publisher and receive a certificate before giving any of the approved tests.

OLPTs are used to determine a student's oral English fluency. The list of approved tests for assessment of limited English proficient (LEP) students includes the scores indicating limited English proficiency in listening and speaking for each test. These tests are used by the LPAC to identify students in Pre-K–12 as LEP and for entry into an ESL/ Bilingual Program. They may be used to exit students in grades 1–12 from an ESL program. The OLPTs are as follows:

- Idea Proficiency Test (IPT), LAS Links

- Stanford English Language Proficiency Test (Stanford ELP)

- Woodcock-Muñoz Language Survey Revised with Normative Updates (WMLS-R NU)

- Comprehensive English Language Learning Assessment (CELLA)

- Texas English Language Proficiency Assessment System (TELPAS)

OLPTs in Spanish are used to identify students who qualify for Spanish bilingual programs. In addition, giving the test in Spanish to Spanish speakers in the ESL program provides a more complete evaluation of the student's language skills.

Norm-Referenced Standardized Achievement Tests

The reading and language portions of norm-referenced standardized achievement tests on the approved list are used by the LPAC in conjunction with the OPLT for identification as LEP and program placement of students in grades 1–12. Students in grades 1 and 2 only also take these assessments for exiting the ESL Program. STAAR scores are used for exiting students in grades 3–12. Scores below the fortieth percentile on both the reading and language portions indicate Limited English Proficiency. The tests currently on the approved list are as follows:

- Iowa Assessments—Survey Battery or Complete Battery, Stanford Achievement Test—Complete Battery, Abbreviated Battery

- Measures of Academic Progress for Primary Grades, Measures of Academic Progress, Texas

- STAR Reading Enterprise, Online—Reading ONLY

- Terra Nova CAT—Basic or Complete Battery

- Terra Nova CTBS—Basic or Complete Battery

- Terra Nova Survey

Testing for Gifted/Talented (G/T)

Ability Tests for identification of ELLs as Gifted/Talented (G/T) are included in the list of approved tests. They include the following:

- Cognitive Abilities Test (CogAT)—verbal, quantitative, nonverbal

- Cognitive Abilities Test (CogAT)—composite, verbal, quantitative, nonverbal

- Neglieri Nonverbal Ability Test— nonverbal, cognitive, higher order thinking

Assessing English Language Proficiency

The No Child Left Behind (NCLB) Act mandates that every state evaluate ELLs in grades K–12 annually for English language proficiency in listening, speaking, reading, and writing. The TELPAS (Texas English Language Proficiency Assessment System) fulfills this requirement.

TELPAS

Students who have a parent denial (parents have the right to deny their children entrance to an ESL program) must still take the TELPAS (Texas English Language Proficiency Assessment System) because they continue to be LEP until they attain English proficiency. The ratings count toward the Annual Measurable Achievement Objectives (AMAOs), which is discussed in Chapter 8, No Child Left Behind. The Reading Proficiency Tests in English (RPTE) is a computer-based reading test that is designed to rate students as beginning, intermediate, advanced, or advanced high levels. The beginning English proficiency level has the easiest questions, and the difficulty increases with each level—longer passages and more difficult questions. Beginning and intermediate students may not be able to answer all the questions.

The listening, speaking, and writing domains are holistically rated using formative assessment. Teachers must attend training to learn how to use the PLDs (proficiency level descriptors) to rate students, collect writing samples, and administer the RPTE when required to do so by the campus or district test coordinator. Those tests are usually administered annually. All rating is confidential.

Properly trained teachers know how to interpret scores and answer any questions parents may have. Each campus is sent individual score reports, cum folder stickers, and letters to parents in Spanish and English to explain what the score levels are and what the composite score is. The report also shows the composite and reading score from the previous year. The table below shows how each grade level is rated.

TELPAS Simplified

Grade Levels	Domains Assessed			
	Listening	Speaking	Reading	Writing
K–1	Use PLDs	Use PLDs	Use PLDs	Use PLDs, may collect samples
2–12	Use PLDs	Use PLDs	Online, RPTE	Rater collects writing samples for a specified time and rates them using PLDs

Formative Assessment Strategies

At the beginning of each school year, the ESL teacher is given a roster of all LEP students who attended a Texas public school the previous year. That document shows students' TELPAS levels for each domain. This information is used for test selection, adaptation, and to determine how to develop formative assessment used to modify instruction.

It is one thing to design an effective assessment and another to properly administer or execute it; and it is still another to gather the data and interpret the results. But perhaps the ultimate test of a well-crafted assessment is how that knowledge is used in the classroom. Teachers use formative assessment results to help them plan and adapt lessons to individual student needs.

Formative assessment may take the form of planned or unplanned observations of students during the lesson or at social activities such as recess and lunch. In the classroom, this type of assessment usually occurs when the student is working with the teacher in a small group or with a partner. The teacher may evaluate how often the student does a certain task such as "speaks in complete sentences" or the level at which the student participates, such as answering questions orally in sentences or just responding yes and no. Does the ELL use all English or a mixture of English and her or his home language?

Since ESL teachers must be prepared to rate students holistically in speaking, listening, and writing for the TELPAS, they will need documentation of observations. The teacher may make individual notes to record data later in the student's file, use a rubric to assess specific domains such as speaking and listening or content objectives, or prepare a check list of desired results. These take the form of the PLDs. For example:

The student is able to understand elaborated directions. Needs processing time
__always
__sometimes
__often
__never.

The ESL teacher must use the ELPS and TEKS to make sure the assessment is meaningful. Training is provided by the district or state centers to show how to correlate the ELPS and TEKS for each core subject. For example, a grade 5 language arts teacher should not give an ELL at beginning level a vocabulary test of 20 words or a test with open-ended questions that require writing in English. The test results would not be meaningful. The teacher should modify the test for the beginner ELL. For example, this modified test could include matching 10 vocabulary words to definitions by giving the student a word bank from which to select answers or pictures of vocabulary concepts used by the student to answer. For social studies or reading, an ELL could place pictures of events in the correct order to tell a story.

By using ongoing mini-assessments, the teacher will know if more accommodations are needed to remove language barriers. The teacher may need to simplify directions and questions, read test items aloud, allow "think time" for the ELL to mentally associate the lesson with prior knowledge in his or her home language, or use the computer to look up the concept in his or her home language.

Strategies include applying formative assessment to content area objectives—math, science, social studies, and reading vocabulary. Newcomer students or those who are still in "the silent period" may need a peer to translate. Other approaches include providing bilingual dictionaries, using books that have photographs of the content material, or having students work with partners so the ELLs feel more secure in participating in the activity.

It is possible to evaluate students in a number of ways. For example, students could solve math problems with manipulatives, do actual hands-on science experiments instead of just reading about them, and role-play for social studies in small groups. Each of these allows teachers to evaluate students who are not at the advanced level of reading or writing.

Assessing Content-Area Skills and Knowledge

Summative or formal assessment is used at a predetermined time, such as at the end of a unit, grade period, or annually. It is used to assess content knowledge and mastery of the TEKS.

STAAR

The State of Texas Assessments of Academic Readiness (STAAR) is a criterion-referenced test given to ALL students in grades 3 through high school in a variety of subject, depending on grade level. Students must get a certain number of questions correct to pass based on score scales determined by the state each spring. The table below helps explain who is eligible to take which assessment, with emphasis on STAAR L. This chart is based on the Linguistic Accommodation Form LPACs must use every winter to document test decisions made for every ELL. If the ELL is also served by Special Education or a 504 plan, test decisions are made jointly with the ARD and 504 committees. The ARD is the Admission, Review, Dismissal committee that makes decisions for students who are covered by the Individuals with Disabilities Education Act (IDEA) 2004. The programs are called Special Education (SpEd). Students who have other disabilities may be designated "504," based on Section 504 of the Rehabilitation Act of 1973.

The table on the next page does not include all available accommodations. However, a complete online manual explains each of the 20 accommodations listed on the tiered triangle. The accommodation manual—including the accommodation triangle—can be found at *www.tea.state.tx.us*. Search under Student Assessment Division.

It requires training to understand which students can use certain accommodations and how they can be used to be in compliance with test security.

STAAR—What, Who, How

Assessment	Eligibility/ Participation	Accommodations
STAAR	Assessment required for ELLs not eligible for another assessment	Limited, based on the accommodation triangle
STAAR Spanish	For ELLs in grades 3–5 for whom a Spanish version of STAAR most appropriately measures their academic progress; not permitted for an ELL whose parent or guardian has denied ESL/bilingual program services	Limited, based on the accommodation triangle
STAAR L	Linguistically accommodated STAAR mathematics, science, and social studies available for ELLs who: have been enrolled in U.S. schools for three school years or less starting with first grade (five school years or less if a qualifying unschooled refugee) are not most appropriately assessed with STAAR Spanish *and* have not yet attained a TELPAS advanced high reading rating in grade 2 or above Not permitted for an ELL whose parent or guardian has denied ESL/bilingual program services	Clarification of word meaning and oral reading of text is built into the online test May also receive extra time and use a bilingual dictionary
STAAR Modified	Available for students, including ELLs, receiving Special Education services who meet participation requirements for an alternate assessment based on modified achievement standards	The test is usually given orally; ELLs may also have clarification of word meanings in English
STAAR Alternate	Available for students receiving Special Education services (including a small number who are also ELLs) who meet requirements for an alternate assessment based on alternate achievement standards This can only be used when the student has a significant cognitive disability that severely limits reading and /or writing ability	The whole test is accommodated to set criteria based on the student's IEP

Formative Assessment Strategies for TEKS Subjects

The teacher can use the scores to address specific TEKS objectives that need to be retaught before the next round of testing. If the test is a unit test, students may go over the questions and answers in class and make sure they understand what they missed and why. If several ELLs missed the same question, the teacher may need to do mini-lessons in a small group using formative assessment to find out if the problem is due to a lack of content knowledge or limited English proficiency. Perhaps more instructional modifications are needed. Students may need practice in how to use a dictionary, which could help them on the STAAR and other tests. If the ELL misses an objective such as "reading a chart to interpret data," the teacher would need to reteach this using simple charts and work up to those used at the student's grade level. The teacher may use formative assessment to determine if lack of English vocabulary is the problem. For math, the teacher may ask students to "be the teacher" and explain to the group the steps to solve the problem.

Redesignation, Exit, Monitoring

Annual Language Proficiency Assessment Committee (LPAC) meetings are held to determine ELL placement for the next school year. The committee reviews each student's progress using test scores and other criteria to determine whether she or he is still LEP. If so, the student will continue in the ESL program.

If the student is not LEP, the committee reviews his or her test scores (OLPT, TEL-PAS, and STAAR reading and writing scores in addition to core subject grades) to decide whether the student meets exit criteria. The ESL teacher's role in these determinations is vital. All students who were M1 or M2 (monitor year 1, monitor year 2) are reviewed so status can be determined. Students may need to be reclassified as LEP and reenter an ESL program. A teacher's subjective evaluation is also considered. For example, the teacher may suggest alternative testing to determine if the student can exit if she or he gets high scores on class tests but gets test anxiety for the state tests and repeatedly does not pass them. The student may be tested individually or given other accommodations for the next round of STAAR in grades 5, 8, and high school.

All M1 or M2 (monitor year 1, monitor year 2) students are reviewed to determine their status. Students may need to be reclassified as LEP and reenter an ESL program if they are not successful in all-English instruction.

Review Questions

Use the information below to answer questions 1 and 2.

A fourth-grade teacher wants to assess her ELL students' reading proficiency. She designs several instructional assessment activities. The teacher asks students to select a book they have read more than one time during sustained silent reading. As the student reads, the teacher marks the following checklist.

> ☑ Reads with appropriate inflection.
> ☑ Voice modulation indicates the reader is engaged in the content.
> ☑ Notices miscues and self-corrects.
> ☑ Hesitations are infrequent.

1. This instructional activity will enable the teacher to assess her students' reading proficiency in

    (A) comprehension.

    (B) graphophonemic knowledge.

    (C) fluency.

    (D) pronunciation.

    The correct response is (**C**). The checklist targets features associated with fluency—reading smoothly at a developmentally appropriate rate without conscious decoding. (A) is incorrect because the teacher has selected a book that the students are highly familiar with, and a high level of comprehension would be expected. (B) and (D) are incorrect because they do not represent what the teacher is assessing through this oral reading activity. Because the students are already familiar with the book, they would have previously negotiated pronunciation and word-recognition problems.

2. As a follow-up classroom reading assessment, the teacher identifies a paragraph from the science chapter they will cover in two weeks. She gives these instructions to each student when they sit at the reading center in the classroom: "This paragraph is from a chapter we have not read in our science book. I want you to read it orally to me. When you get to a word or idea that is confusing or that you don't understand, I want you tell me what you're thinking. For example, you might tell me what you are doing to try to figure out the meaning. Okay…let's start." The area of reading that this instructional activity assesses is

    (A) content-area knowledge.

    (B) metacognition.

    (C) activation of prior knowledge.

    (D) decoding skills.

    The correct response is (**B**). The teacher's instructions indicate that she wants to see how students think about the problems they encounter when they read and how they work through them. Asking students to explain these strategies offers insight into the learners' metacognition. (A) is incorrect because the teacher's instructions clearly state that the learner's reading process, not retention, is the focus. (C) is incorrect because activating prior knowledge is considered a prereading strategy. However, in the process of describing their thinking about the paragraph, the students might mention prior knowledge. (D) is incorrect because the instructions do not specifically target decoding skills. However, in describing their thinking processes, students might explain how they work through new words.

PART III: DOMAIN III

Foundations of ESL Education, Cultural Awareness, and Family and Community Involvement

PART III: DOMAIN III

Domain III addresses Competencies 008, 009, and 010.

Competency 008: The ESL teacher understands the foundations of ESL education and types of ESL programs.

The beginning ESL teacher:

A. Knows the historical, theoretical and policy foundations of ESL education and uses this knowledge to plan, implement and advocate for effective ESL programs.

B. Knows types of ESL programs (e.g., self-contained, pull-out, newcomer centers, dual language, immersion), their characteristics, their goals and research findings on their effectiveness.

C. Applies knowledge of the various types of ESL programs to make appropriate instructional and management decisions.

D. Applies knowledge of research findings related to ESL education, including research on instructional and management practices in ESL programs, to assist in planning and implementing effective ESL programs.

Competency 009: The ESL teacher understands factors that affect ESL students' learning and implements strategies for creating an effective multicultural and multilingual learning environment.

The beginning ESL teacher:

A. Understands cultural and linguistic diversity in the ESL classroom and other factors that may affect students' learning of academic content, language and culture (e.g., age, developmental characteristics, academic strengths and needs, preferred learning styles, personality, sociocultural factors, home environment, attitude, exceptionalities).

B. Knows how to create an effective multicultural and multilingual learning environment that addresses the affective, linguistic and cognitive needs of ESL students and facilitates students' learning and language acquisition.

C. Knows factors that contribute to cultural bias (e.g., stereotyping, prejudice, ethnocentrism) and knows how to create a culturally responsive learning environment.

D. Demonstrates sensitivity to students' diverse cultural and socioeconomic backgrounds and shows respect for language differences.

E. Applies strategies for creating among students an awareness of and respect for linguistic and cultural diversity.

Competency 010: The ESL teacher knows how to serve as an advocate for ESL students and facilitate family and community involvement in their education.

The beginning ESL teacher:

A. Applies knowledge of effective strategies advocating educational and social equity for ESL students (e.g., participating in LPAC and Admission, Review and Dismissal (ARD) meetings, serving on Site-Based Decision Making (SBDM) committees, serving as a resource for teachers).

B. Understands the importance of family involvement in the education of ESL students and knows how to facilitate parent/guardian participation in their children's education and school activities.

C. Applies skills for communicating and collaborating effectively with the parents/guardians of ESL students in a variety of educational contexts.

D. Knows how community members and resources can positively affect student learning in the ESL program and is able to access community resources to enhance the education of ESL students.

Competency 008

Competency 008

The ESL teacher understands the foundations of ESL education and types of ESL programs.

Chapter 8 will focus on Competency 008—the foundation of ESL education and types of ESL programs.

History of ESL Education

For centuries, immigrants have come to North America seeking better lives and greater opportunities for their families. Their strength and resilience contributed to the early settlement and economic growth of the United States. Even before the first colonists arrived, this was a land of linguistic diversity. Native Americans spoke hundreds of different languages and dialects. To communicate with European traders, many became fluent in English, French, Dutch, or Spanish.

As long ago as the 1660s, newly arrived colonists received bilingual education in the first settlements in North America. During the 1700s, groups from different linguistic backgrounds continued to settle across the country. Starting in 1839, some states began to adopt bilingual education laws that authorized instruction in languages other than English.

Over time, immigration patterns have changed. So have people's attitudes toward diversity and the public policy that shapes English language instruction. In many ways, today's ESL classroom is an intersection of history, policy, and science.

Early Twentieth Century: Immigration and Assimilation

School's today are seeing the greatest influx of non-English-speaking students since the beginning of the twentieth century. Between 1899 and 1921, more than 14 million immigrants came to the United States (Jenks and Lauck, 1926). The vast majority came from Southern, Central, and Eastern Europe. Immigrants often received English instruction in classes organized by their own ethnic and religious communities. Some of these community-based centers provided instruction in students' home languages, but by 1900, support for bilingual education was rare (Young, 2008).

The prevailing attitude was that assimilation was the key to success. In 1906, the Bureau of Immigration and Naturalization added English language ability to the requirements for citizenship. Policymakers felt that cultural and linguistic diversity were obstacles to personal achievement and serious threats to national unity. Immigrants and their children had to be "Americanized" as quickly as possible. That meant that immigrants were expected to abandon their cultural traditions, including their home language. To support this effort, factories set up English-only classes in large cities across the country to teach immigrant workers about safety, health, and housekeeping.

Leading up to World War I, the United States enacted several laws that restricted immigration. During World War I, German-English bilingual schools were closed across the country. By the mid-1920s, most bilingual schools in the United States were dismantled (Young, 2008). English-only classrooms "submerged" students in English. They had to either sink or swim, without special instructional support and few remedial services. Many did not fare well. School dropout rates were extremely high, and many immigrants returned to their homeland (Mora, 2013a). Those who remained did not need high levels of education to fill millions of unskilled jobs in factories and farms.

Cold War Competition and Civil Rights

With the advent of the Cold War and a race into space with the Soviets, people began to reexamine the English-only approach to education. In the late 1950s, policymakers feared that the Soviets would outpace the United States. In 1958, new federal legislation was passed that provided funding for math, science, and foreign languages. In 1963, the first large-scale federally sanctioned bilingual program was established in Dade County Florida to meet the needs of children whose families had fled Cuba. Coral Way Elementary School's successful program became a model for bilingual instruction for ELL— English-language learners.

In its 1954 decision, *Brown v. Board of Education*, the Supreme Court established the principle of equal access to educational opportunity for all Americans. The Civil Rights Movement of the 1960s continued to focus the country's attention on equity and the need for greater social justice. It also helped shift attitudes toward a greater acceptance of diversity, including language diversity.

In 1964, Title VI of the Civil Rights Act prohibited discrimination in federally funded programs and established that every student has the right to meaningful and effective instruction. In 1966, in response to the increased demand for ESL methodologies and instructional materials, the professional organization TESOL (Teachers of English to Speakers of Other Languages) was founded.

Key Legislation and Court Rulings

Date	Legislation and Court Rulings
1968	**Title VII, Bilingual Education Act of the Elementary and Secondary Education Act (ESEA)** • Established federal policy for bilingual education. • Provided supplemental funding for innovative programs to meet the "special educational needs" of non-English-speaking children. • First national acknowledgment of the effects of poverty and educational disadvantages faced by cultural minorities.
1974	**Equal Educational Opportunity Act** Defined what constitutes denial of equal educational opportunity, including failure to take action to overcome language barriers that prevent equal participation in an instructional program.
1974	**Lau v. Nichols** In response to a suit filed on behalf of Chinese students against the San Francisco USD, the Supreme Court ruled that providing students who do not understand English the same facilities, teachers, textbooks, and curriculum does not constitute equality of treatment. "Basic English skills are at the very core of what public schools teach. Imposition of a requirement that, before a child can effectively participate in the educational program, he must already have acquired those basic skills is to make a mockery of public education."

(continued)

(continued)

Date	Legislation and Court Rulings
1981	**Castañeda v. Pickard** In response to a claim against the Raymondville, Texas ISD, the Fifth Circuit Court of Appeals established a set of standards for determining a district's compliance with the Equal Opportunity Act of 1974. The "Castañeda Test" includes three criteria: the instructional program must be based on sound educational theory, the program must be implemented with appropriate resources and personnel, and the program must produce positive results.
1981	**Plyler v. Doe** The Supreme Court struck down a Texas law as unconstitutional, thereby granting undocumented immigrant children the right to a free public education.
1988	**Amendments to Title VII** Expanded funding for "special alternative programs" where only English is used and established a three-year limit on participation in most Title VII.
1994	**Amendments to Title VII** New provisions reinforced professional development programs and increased attention to the maintenance of home languages.

Restrictions on Bilingual Education

Since the 1990s, there have been a number of state ballot initiatives designed to restrict bilingual education. As of today, 27 states have enacted laws that declare English as the state official language. These initiatives have been presented as ways to accelerate the assimilation of language minority families. Supporters of the initiatives have argued that bilingual services prevent immigrants and their children from learning English and thereby prevent them from accessing and participating in mainstream society and institutions (de Jong, 2011).

In 1998, California voters passed Proposition 227, which was authored by Ron Unz. It mandated that bilingual programs be replaced with a one-year structured English immersion program, followed by placement in mainstream classrooms. During the one-year immersion period, students are grouped by their language proficiency levels. They join fluent English-speaking peers when they acquire "a good working knowledge" of English. Similar "Unz Initiatives" have appeared on the ballot in other states. In 2000, Arizona voters passed Proposition 203, essentially ending bilingual education in Arizona. In 2003, Massachusetts followed suit. In 2003, Colorado voters rejected an English-only ballot measure, and in 2008, Oregon defeated a measure that would have abolished bilingual education in that state.

No Child Left Behind

In 2001, the No Child Left Behind Act (NCLB) reauthorized and restructured Title VII of the Elementary and Secondary Education Act (ESEA). NCLB affects nearly every school district and charter school in Texas. Its goal is to ensure that all children meet grade-level standards by 2014. By federal law, schools and districts are accountable for demonstrating that various subgroups of students—identified by race or ethnicity, special education status, and ELL status—make adequate yearly progress (AYP) toward the goal of 100 percent proficiency.

The Title III, Part A program aims to ensure that English language learner (ELL) and immigrant students attain English language proficiency and meet the same challenging State academic content and student academic achievement standards as all children are expected to meet.

States must follow strict compliance guidelines by administering a regime of standardized tests in reading, math, and science. Tests in reading and math must be given each year in grades 3–8 and once in high school. Science tests are administered in grades 5 and 8 and once in high school. To help districts prepare for statewide testing, significant funds have been provided for compensatory programs in reading and math.

English-language learners are exempt from taking the reading test for 1 year, and they do not have to take the math test their first year in U.S. schools. Under Texas law, recent immigrants may be eligible for a limited English proficient (LEP) exemption from testing for up to three years. In response to the federal mandate regarding reading, math, and science testing, the TEA administers TAKS with linguistic accommodations to recent immigrant ELLs who are exempt. For more information about ELL academic skills assessments and policies, see Chapter 7.

Under NCLB, each state is also required to develop English language proficiency standards and administer a test aligned to those standards. Regulations require states to set annual measurable achievement objectives (AMAOs)—targets for the percentage of students making progress on the test and the percentage of students classified as "proficient" according to test results. Following a student's reclassification, districts must monitor exited students for two years. For more information about NCLB, visit the TEA website at *www.tea.state.tx.us*. Search under NCLB.

ESL Educational Reform in Texas

Date	Reforms
1995	**Texas Education Code, Chapter B** **Texas Administrative Code, Chapter 89** Established bilingual education policy and laid out a comprehensive state plan for educating Limited English Proficient (LEP) students. School districts with 20 or more English-proficient students in the same grade level must offer a bilingual education program for ELLs in grades K–5. Grade 6 is included when it is part of the school site. Districts that don't meet the minimum of 20 students must provide an English as a Second Language (ESL) program to every LEP student, regardless of students' grade levels, home languages, or number of students.
1998	**English Language Standards, Texas Essential Knowledge and Skills (TEKS)** ELS standards for language arts and proficiency descriptors added to TEKS.
2006	**English Language Standards, Texas Essential Knowledge and Skills (TEKS)** ELS standards revised to reflect focus on language development in the content areas. Requirements included providing comprehensible content and developing students' academic language skills.
2007	**English Language Proficiency Standards (ELPS)** Cross-curricular ELPS standards in listening, speaking, reading, writing, added to TEKS as well as standards for Learning Strategies. Integrated language acquisition skills into every content area.

Program Models

Since 1995, Texas school districts have been required to provide a bilingual education program or an English as a Second Language program to every student with limited English proficiency. The program type depends on the number and language proficiency of students in each grade level. The state defines *Student of limited English proficiency* as "a student whose primary language is other than English and whose English language skills are such that the student has difficulty performing ordinary classwork in English." The term *LEP* is used interchangeably with *English language learner* (ELL).

Bilingual Education Programs

Across the country, bilingual education encompasses many different program types. Each reflects a philosophical orientation with a different pedagogical approach and educational goals. In general, programs can be defined as either subtractive or additive (May, 2008). *Subtractive* programs are like the "sink or swim" methods used through much of the early twentieth century. They promote monolingual learning in English and discourage the use of a student's home language. The ultimate goal is to for students to replace their L1 with English. Because they deemphasize the value and importance of a student's primary language, subtractive models have been discredited as pedagogically unsound, culturally biased, and in violation of the Equal Education Opportunity Act and the *Lau v. Nichols* Supreme Court decision.

Additive bilingual programs promote bilingualism and biliteracy by adding another language to the student's existing repertoire. Generally, these additive programs are provided for several years, recognizing the time required to develop full academic proficiency in both languages. *Language immersion* is a method of teaching in which the target language is used as both content and the language of instruction. *Two-way dual language immersion* programs integrate language minority students and fluent English speakers in the same classroom with the goal of academic excellence and bilingual proficiency for both student groups. Although they vary, dual language immersion programs generally share three characteristics: instruction is provided in two languages, one language is used at time, and learning is based on shared language experiences during peer interactions (Pacific Policy Research Center, 2010).

There are four models of bilingual education programs in Texas.

1. **Transitional Bilingual/Early Exit:** This is a bilingual program that serves students with limited English proficiency in both English and Spanish. It transfers students to English-only instruction not earlier than two or later than five years after the student enrolls in school.

2. **Transitional Bilingual/Late Exit:** This is a bilingual program that serves students with limited English proficiency in both English and Spanish. It transfers students to English-only instruction not earlier than six or later than seven years after the student enrolls in school.

3. **Dual Language Immersion/Two-Way:** This is a biliteracy program that integrates students proficient in English and students with limited English proficiency in both English and Spanish. It transfers students identified as having limited English proficiency to English-only instruction not earlier than six or later than seven years after the student enrolls in school.

4. **Dual Language Immersion/One-Way:** This is a biliteracy program that serves only students identified as students of limited English proficiency in both English and Spanish and transfers a student to English-only instruction not earlier than six or later than seven years after the student enrolls in school.

English as a Second Language Programs

Sheltered instruction is a hallmark of English as a Second Language (ESL) instruction. These techniques take into account a student's background knowledge and level of language proficiency to make English content comprehensible. There are two models of English as a Second Language (ESL) education programs in Texas.

1. **English as a Second Language/Content-Based:** This is an English program that serves students with limited English proficiency in English only by providing a full-time teacher certified under TEC §29.061(c) to provide supplementary instruction for all content-area instruction.

2. **English as a Second Language/Pull-Out:** This is an English program that serves students with limited English proficiency in English by providing only a part-time teacher certified under TEC §29.061(c) to provide English language arts instruction exclusively, while the student remains in a mainstream instructional arrangement in the remaining content areas.

For more information about these program models, visit TEA's ELL Web Portal *www.elltx.org/bilingual_esl_programs_english.html*.

Overview of Research Findings

It is important for every teacher to make instructional decisions that are informed by research. Understanding the evidence base allows teachers to provide sound instruction and advocate for their students' cognitive, linguistic, social, and emotional needs. Although there are still many open questions, important findings have emerged about educational models designed to serve English-language learners. Among these are the following two findings that have been corroborated by meta-analysis of data:

1. Instructional programs that extend and develop students' first language literacy promote higher levels of academic achievement in English. This is true at both the elementary and secondary levels (August and Shanahan, 2006; Genesee et al., 2006; Rolstad, et al., 2005; Slavin & Cheung, 2005; Greene, 1997).

2. Regardless of the type of educational model, certain instructional practices are associated with higher student outcomes (Levine, 1995; Marzano, 2003; Wenglinsky, 2000).

The Center for Applied Linguistics released a report that examined the teaching practices used in successful bilingual and immersion programs (Howard et al., 2007). The authors identified five common features, as follows:

1. **Equitable Interaction:** promoting positive interaction between the teacher and every learner

2. **Targeted and Varied Teaching Techniques:** adapting teaching to students' differing learning styles and language proficiency levels

3. **Student-Centered Teaching and Learning:** emphasizing active student participation and interactions in which they share their cultural and linguistic knowledge rather than teacher-centered transmission of knowledge

4. **Sharing Between Learners:** using cooperative learning strategies that require students to collaborate interdependently on common tasks and share work experiences with students from other ethnic and linguistic backgrounds

5. **Language through Common Task Orientation:** focusing cooperative activities around specific language tasks to ensure that students develop and share language knowledge

Review Questions

1. Which of the following descriptions defines two-way dual-language immersion education?

   (A) An educational approach that separates ELL students from native speakers in order to provide intensive, targeted instruction in English and L1

   (B) An educational approach that integrates native speakers and ELL students in a context that provides language- and content-area instruction in L1 and English

   (C) An educational approach that brings together ELL and native-language students in a supplementary class where all students learn both English and L1

   (D) An educational approach that integrates native English speakers and ELL students in a self-contained classroom, in which all instruction is in English, but students are strongly encouraged to cooperate in teaching each other English and L1

   The correct response is (**B**). The hallmark of two-way dual-immersion approaches is the integration of native speakers and nonnative speakers in all areas of instruction. Dual immersion is a bilingual-program approach that aims at biliteracy for both native speakers and nonnative speakers. (A) is incorrect because ESL programs strive to integrate learners rather than to segregate them. (C) is incorrect because dual-immersion programs are not supplementary. (D) is incorrect because it describes the traditional immersion approach that is sometimes referred to as the "sink-or-swim" approach.

2. Which of the following explains the English-to-L1 instruction ratio used in the majority of two-way dual-language-immersion programs?

    (A) There are two typical models: (1) 90/10 or 80/20 (English/L1) in early elementary grades moving gradually to 50/50 in about fourth grade; or (2) 50/50 starting with kindergarten

    (B) There are two primary models: (1) 90/10 or 80/20 (L1/English) in early elementary grades, moving gradually to 50/50 in about fourth grade; or (2) 50/50 starting with kindergarten

    (C) 50/50 from kindergarten through fourth grade when it becomes 90 percent English/10 percent L1

    (D) 100 percent English from kindergarten through second grade, when it becomes 90 percent English to 10 percent L1

    The correct response is (**B**). Two-way dual-immersion programs typically begin with a high L1 ratio, which gradually evens off to an ideal 50-50. (A), (C), and (D) incorrectly explain the typical approach to this type of ESL program.

3. Official regulations for the implementation of ESL programs in Texas are mandated by

    (A) the Texas Education Agency.

    (B) the U.S. Department of Education.

    (C) the Texas Education Code.

    (D) the No Child Left Behind Act.

    The correct response is (**C**). The Texas Education Code (TEC) officially documents all regulations impacting public education in Texas. Information from the TEC is integrated into the Texas Administrative Code (TAC), which is a compilation of all state agency rules in Texas. TEC regulations are integrated into Title 19 of the TAC. (A) is incorrect because TEA carries out the mandates of the TEC. (B) is incorrect because the Department of Education impacts education in all states, but specific aspects of Texas public education are managed through the state legislature and TEA. (D) is incorrect; NCLB is the federal impetus for bilingual and ESL programs in all states, but the specific Texas components are regulated by the TEC.

Competency 009

Competency 009

The ESL teacher understands factors that affect ESL students' learning and implements strategies for creating an effective multicultural and multilingual learning environment.

Chapter 9 will focus on Competency 009—factors that affect ESL students' learning and strategies for creating an effective multicultural and multilingual learning environment.

Student Diversity and Identity

According to the Texas Education Agency, English-language learners enrolled in special language programs reresent more than 120 different languages. Approximately 90 percent of these students are Spanish speaking. After Spanish, the languages with the largest number of speakers are Vietnamese, Arabic, Urdu, Korean, and Burmese (Texas English-Language Learners Portal).

Home language is just one aspect of the enormous diversity of students in today's classrooms. In addition to language, teachers must be aware of other factors that influence a student's identity, communication style, and classroom learning experiences. Among these factors are the student's ethnicity or race, culture, socioeconomic status, gender, temperament and personality, and home environment.

Respect for diversity involves understanding and valuing the whole child. It means being committed to developing every student's potential by teaching through and to individual differences. Students' cultural values and ways of thinking influence how they interact in the classroom—what they think, what they say, and how they behave. Their home language and communication style are intimately connected to their families, communities, and personal identity. When teachers convey the message that students' language skills are "deficient" or their communication style is "incorrect," they do irreparable harm to students' self-esteem and sabotage their academic achievement.

Understanding Communication Styles

To some extent, all children need to learn the basic rules and etiquette for communicating in the classroom. This process, however, is particularly challenging for many English-language learners. That is because the communication styles they use in their homes and communities are inconsistent with classroom practices. During whole-class discussions, teachers generally expect students to do the following:

- speak one at a time

- wait until they have permission to speak

- maintain eye contact with the speaker

- remain seated using little or no physical movement while listening and speaking

- provide answers that are brief, logical, and to the point

In contrast to this type of linear, directed conversation, ethnic groups including Latinos, African Americans, and Native Hawaiians use a conversation style that is much more active and participatory (Gay, 2010). During discussions, listeners engage with the speaker by vocalizing, responding, and moving *while the speaker is speaking*. In the context of a conventional classroom, this behavior might be misinterpreted as rude, disruptive, or speaking out of turn. Different cultures also have different ideas about the appropriateness of eye contact and the optimum physical distance between speakers. Children from some cultures, particularly girls, may feel it is disrespectful to address teachers or to question others' ideas critically.

Unlike the topic-centered discourse style of the classroom, many cultural groups use what is called *topic chaining*—speaking and writing about more than one topic at a time in a circular style with repetitions and flourishes. Teachers unfamiliar with this discourse style might dismiss students' responses as rambling, disjointed, and illogical (Gay, 2010). In addition to different speaker/listener relationships and discourse styles, some cultural groups emphasize the importance of establishing a personal connection before participants begin working together on a group task. Teachers who are unaware of this might think that students who socialize with peers in a cooperative learning group are wasting time off-task, ignoring instructions, or refusing to participate.

The bottom line is that teachers need to be aware of the ways that classroom practices contradict what students have learned in their linguistic communities. Too often, teachers jump to the conclusion that students are being uncooperative or just don't "get it." Learning about different communication patterns among students' ethnic groups has several positive effects. It helps the teacher to do the following:

- recognize when students are using discourse that is appropriate in other social contexts and languages

- develop students' awareness about different communication styles and the need to use different styles in different contexts, which is the essence of communicative competence

- examine classroom communication patterns to improve student comprehension and engagement

- avoid making erroneous judgments about students' attitudes, behaviors, and abilities

Creating a Culturally Responsive Learning Community

The first step in teaching respect for others is for teachers to examine their own attitudes about language minority students and the social status of immigrant families. It is unfortunate that many educators have failed to understand that students' backgrounds are rich foundations for learning. Often, teachers have adopted a deficit view—seeing diversity as something that needs to be overcome so that students can "catch up" to their English-speaking peers. By adopting this approach, teachers undermine the education of English-language learners.

Language bias is the belief that English is superior, more important, or more useful than students' home languages. Cultural bias is the belief that mainstream cultural practices are normal and more desirable than students' family customs. Cultural bias is reinforced when class activities and curricula focus only on the culture, contributions, and values of the dominant English-speaking culture. Bias negatively affects students' cognitive development and denies their access to equal educational opportunity.

To create an inclusive learning community, teachers need to teach explicitly students respect for others and develop their appreciation of linguistic, cultural, ethnic, and racial diversity by doing the following:

- cultivating a supportive climate where every student is praised and encouraged to participate

- working together with students to establish how they will treat their classmates, other peoples' possessions, and themselves

- establishing a zero tolerance policy for bullying and culturally insensitive remarks

- continuously helping students explore their cultural identities and encouraging them to take pride in sharing their knowledge and experiences

- developing students' awareness of different languages and cultures through multicultural content and media, classroom displays, guest speakers, demonstrations, field trips, and cooperative learning groups made up of students with varied skill levels and backgrounds

- ensuring that the images of people displayed in the classroom, hallways, and throughout the school equitably and positively represent students' cultural groups

- building students' appreciation of different languages and cultures—identifying similarities, and at the same time valuing differences

- arranging video conferences and joining networks that connect schools in different towns and countries

- vetting recordings, textbooks, and literature for culturally or racially offensive content

- helping students learn to recognize examples of bias in media such as prejudice, stereotyping, and ethnocentrism

- discussing historical events from the perspective of different ethnic, cultural, gender, or socioeconomic groups

Creating a Multilingual Learning Environment

English-language learners have tremendous potential for becoming successful global citizens of the future. They are already learning to communicate in English and have varying degrees of proficiency in their home language. They are also developing bicultural awareness and the social skills that enable them to act and speak with different people in different contexts. This repertoire of skills and knowledge is valuable in a multicultural society. It is also a necessity for competing in today's interdependent global economy.

Supporting the Continued Development of L1

In order for students to develop academically, cognitively, and socially, they need a strong sense of self that is rooted in their families and communities. Discouraging or attempting to eliminate the use of students' home language has negative impacts on English-language learners. Asking students with limited English proficiency to communicate only in English devalues their existing L1 language skills as well as the experiences, knowledge base, and cultural identities they have developed in that language. Students who stop speaking their home language lose important emotional bonds, cutting themselves off from family members and friends who do not speak English well.

Proficiency in the home language supports students' English language learning. Decades of research have shown that the more proficient a student is in his or her home language, the faster and better he or she learns English (Cummins, 1991; Tong, et al., 2008). This is likely due to the transfer of knowledge and skills to the context of learning English, as was discussed in Chapter 2. According to five meta-analyses of ELL research, learning to read in their home language promotes students' reading and mathematics achievement *in English* at both the elementary and secondary levels (August and Shanahan, 2006; Genesee et al., 2006).

Due to the many demonstrated benefits of bilingualism and biliteracy, teachers need to partner with families in order to provide opportunities for students to listen, speak, read, and write in their home language. Teachers may need to explain why it is beneficial to continue to develop students' home language and allay any unfounded concerns that doing so would confuse students or impede their mastery of English.

Promoting Authentic Communication

Language learning thrives when students use language in meaningful and purposeful ways—communicating about real ideas with real people. When planning lessons, teachers should incorporate authentic communication into activities throughout the day. As always, the starting point is defining high expectations for every student at every proficiency level. The goal is to design language-use tasks that challenge and stretch students' language development without frustrating them.

To promote authentic communication, students need to be motivated, engaged, and able to actively contribute to the learning process. Best practice suggests that teachers do the following:

- Learn about students and their communities. Focus on content that is relevant and meaningful to them based on their backgrounds and interests. For every lesson, plan language outcomes and content objectives.

- Give students opportunities to select topics they want to explore. Structure activities so that English-language learners can act as subject experts.

- Provide print, digital, and audio resources in students' home languages. Use these materials to frontload students' understanding of new concepts and vocabulary prior to providing lessons on the content in English.

- Use hands-on experiences such as projects, demonstrations, and experiments as springboards for speaking, reading, and writing activities. Include props, objects, and artifacts from students' cultures.

- Use cooperative learning activities, mixing students with different English proficiency levels and/or different home languages and backgrounds. Monitor the groups to make sure that every student is participating and that interactions are productive. At the beginning proficiency level, students may benefit from working with classmates in their shared home language. Such "risk-free" practice might include preparing answers to questions, explaining ideas, taking notes, and creating first drafts of written responses.

- Involve family members as important learning partners both at home and in school. Invite them to use their home language to communicate in a way that they are comfortable. For example, they might read a story or poem, teach students a new skill, share a personal experience with photographs, play music, demonstrate a dance, explain the importance of a holiday, or lead a hands-on demonstration. See Chapter 10 for more detailed information about how to engage families in the learning community.

Review Questions

Use the information below to answer questions 1–3.

An elementary school ESL teacher gives her students the following directions: "We are starting a unit on folk stories—stories that you learn from your parents and that are well known in your culture. A lot of times, stories like these are supposed to keep you from doing something dangerous. Or they might explain how or why something happens."

1. To explain what a folk story is, the teacher reads Tomie DePaola's *Legend of the Bluebonnet*, which offers a native American explanation for the apparent overnight appearance of bluebonnets in Texas in the spring. Which of the following statements best explains how this activity will help students' understand the assignment?

   (A) The teacher is creating a multicultural learning environment by showing students how folk stories reflect different cultures' beliefs

   (B) The teacher is illustrating that folk stories are most commonly associated with native American tribes

   (C) The teacher wants students to understand that folk stories usually involve mysticism or exaggeration

   (D) The teacher wants to promote students' active listening skills by illustrating that folk stories are passed down through oral storytelling.

The correct response is (**A**). These young learners are likely to be unfamiliar with the concept of folk stories. The teacher's activity provides a clear example of the concept that will allow learners to connect similar stories from their own culture. (B) is incorrect because it would not be likely following only one folk story. Furthermore, given the teacher's assignment, it is likely that she or he would follow up the reading with immediate class discussion of similar stories from the students' own backgrounds. (C) is incorrect because this is not supported by the activity. (D) is incorrect as it misrepresents the purpose of the teacher's oral reading.

2. When the students bring in their folk tales, the teacher hands out construction-paper booklets in which the students will write and illustrate the stories they brought. The teacher creates a folk story gallery where the students to post their booklets. When all the booklets are done, the students read each other's booklets and then have a class discussion about similarities and differences they found in their own stories and in their classmates' stories. As an ESL teaching strategy, this activity

(A) integrates several academic and nonacademic skills.

(B) allows the teacher to promote students' oral-language proficiency.

(C) creates a culturally responsive learning environment.

(D) promotes students' creativity by asking students to think like authors and to imagine how their story would be best presented through illustrations.

The correct response is (**C**). Even if all the students share the same L1, the folk-story assignment will generate significant variations in retelling stories specific to each child's family, thereby promoting a culturally responsive learning environment. (A), (B), and (D) are likely to be effects of this activity, but none of these responses targets the teacher's ESL instructional strategy and so are all incorrect.

3. The teacher wants to expand the folk-story unit in order to promote students' awareness of linguistic and cultural diversity. Which of the following activities would best meet this goal?

(A) The teacher collaborates with the school librarian to identify books that present children's versions of folk stories from around the world. She has each student pick a book from this collection to read and to present in reader's theater.

(B) The teacher assigns each student a specific country to research. The students create small posters presenting the following basic facts about the country: the language spoken, one story from that country, and a picture of a typical scene from daily life in that country.

(C) The teacher turns the folk-story unit into a geography lesson. She brings in pictures of scenes from countries throughout the world and tells students a few facts about each country as she shows the pictures.

(D) The teacher gives each group a picture of a scene from a foreign country. Each group has to write a folk story triggered by the scene.

The correct response is (**A**). By reading folk stories from different cultures and lands, the students' own folk-story experience will be reinforced as an aspect of their own cultural identity. Additionally, reading stories from other lands will create opportunities to introduce culture-specific concepts and words. (B) and (C) are incorrect because these activities deviate from the teacher's original goal to focus on culture via folk stories. (D) is incorrect because it misrepresents the foundation of folk stories, which the teacher established earlier in the unit.

Competency 010

Competency 010

The ESL teacher knows how to serve as an advocate for ESL students' learning and facilitate family and community involvement in their education.

Chapter 10 will focus on Competency 010—facilitating family and community involvement in students' education.

Partnering with Families

Families play a critical role in students' academic success. In addition to being student's "first" teachers, family members can provide important information about students' interests, learning styles, developmental milestones, and needs. At home, families can support specific learning goals that help students see the continuity between home life and school life. When families actively participate in activities at school, they foster students' self-esteem and help create a rich, multicultural learning community.

Although every family wants children to succeed in school, there are many factors that may prevent language minority parents from being actively involved. Multiple jobs or work shifts may leave little time for them to help with homework or may make it impossible for them to attend school events. They may lack transportation or have difficulty finding child care. Parents may feel they are unable to communicate, embarrassed by their limited English skills. They may feel uncomfortable speaking with teachers simply because they do not have much knowledge about the way schools operate in the United States. In fact, in many countries, parental involvement in school is neither expected nor encouraged.

Added to these challenges are differing expectations about classroom culture and the potential for miscommunication. Many immigrant parents are accustomed to schools where teachers do all the speaking while students sit quietly and listen. Therefore, parents are very surprised when they visit classrooms and see children moving around, working in cooperative groups, and questioning classmates and teachers. They may view this type of active, student-centered learning as undisciplined and even disrespectful.

Interactions with teachers may add to a family's discomfort and frustration.

As discussed in Chapter 9, different cultures have different communication styles and different ideas about eye contact, the appropriate distance between speakers, and even the volume and pitch of speakers' voices. The more teachers learn about different cultural expectations and communication styles, the more effectively they'll engage students and their families.

Making Families Feel Welcome

First impressions are very important. Families' experiences at a school site can cement productive relationships between home and school or make families feel overlooked or intimidated. There are many things teachers can do to make English-language learners' families feel like valued members of the school community (Coelho, 1994). The following are some examples:

- Create welcome signs in students' home languages, and display them prominently in the class and around the school site.

- Designate a welcome team, including someone who understands the school system and is fully bilingual in English and the family home language. This could be a teacher, school support staff, or professional interpreter. It is not appropriate to use another student as an interpreter, particularly when confidential or sensitive information is being shared.

- Allow plenty of time for first meetings with parents. Also, do not overwhelm them with too much information. Keep the focus on the overall structure of the school day and what the child needs to bring to school. Focus on giving the family time to ask questions and share information about the student.

- Ask if the family would like assistance obtaining school supplies, gym uniforms, clothing, or field trips. If so, provide information about school- and community-based funding and resources. Be sure to be sensitive to families' needs while respecting their privacy.

- Give parents a welcome booklet in their home language, including school staff contact information and what to do if the child is ill.

- Discuss the importance of helping students continue to develop their home language proficiency. Explain the many benefits, including the fact that it contributes to their English language development.

- Offer to give the family a brief walking tour of the school and a chance to participate in a hands-on activity.

- Share the expectation that parents and teachers will act as a team—communicating and working together throughout the school year. Ask about the best way and the best times to contact them for future follow-up.

Understanding Parental Rights

Teachers must make a concerted effort to connect with the family of every student and to communicate with the family regularly. Numerous federal and state laws require that they do so in the family's home language. Parents or legal guardians must be kept informed of students' academic progress and learning objectives as well as any behavior issues that arise. They must give their consent before the student receives a psychological examination or treatment, before a video or recording of the child is made, before the child participates in an educational field study, and before a child's photo or artwork is published. Teachers must not try to limit or prevent parents from exercising their rights.

Parents have the right to request information and to take action in their child's best interest. They have the right to the following:

- inspect all written records related to their child and respond to any statement

- obtain information about the academic requirements of the school program

- review all materials in the classroom

- have complete information about all school activities

- review tests after they have been administered

- make requests regarding changes in the assigned class or teacher, transfer to a higher grade level, and early graduation from high school if all course requirements are completed

- obtain easy-to-understand documentation regarding special education, including their child's ARD

- appeal the placement of their child in a special education class

- be informed of and appeal school policies

- be informed of and appeal administrative decisions

- have access to public meetings of the school board

Communicating with Families

To be effective advocates for their students, teachers need to establish a rapport with family members. Interactions with families must be positive, productive, and student-focused. Whether the interaction is an in-person meeting, phone call, email, or other parent communication, it is essential to keep the tone positive by focusing on student accomplishments and what is needed or expected. Regular communication about class topics, projects, homework, events, student performance, and learning goals promotes collaboration and builds mutual respect.

Respect and rapport are the foundation for successful parent conferences. Dina Castro and her colleagues, in their 2010 book, *The New Voices/Nuevas Voces: Guide to Cultural and Linguistic Diversity in Early Childhood,* offer guidelines for effective cross-cultural communication between teachers and English-language learners' families (Castro, et al., 2010). They recommend that educators do the following:

- Plan and prepare prior to the meeting. Consult colleagues to learn about the family's cultural and linguistic background. Ask about their preferred communication style and nonverbal cues. If an interpreter will be used, meet ahead of time to explain the purpose of the meeting, the expected role of the interpreter, and relevant terminology.

- Ensure that all materials are available in the family' home language. If materials need to be translated, beware of translation software! It is not an adequate substitute for a human translator and proofreader.

- Practice effective communication by role-playing with colleagues. Debrief about the overall interaction and any messages conveyed with facial expressions, posture, and tone of voice.

- When meeting with parents, begin by thanking them for supporting their child's education. Introduce everyone present, and discuss what each person hopes the outcome will be. Seats should be arranged in a triangle, with the teacher directly facing parents and the interpreter to the side. Explain that parents can stop the conversation at any time to ask the interpreter for clarification or repetition.

- Listen actively to what parents say, and respond in a nonjudgmental way. Show that you are listening by using empathetic facial expressions and verbal encouragers such as "Yes, go on" and "Mmm-hmm." Keep questions clear and simple. Look at parents while you speak, not the interpreter. Ask open-ended questions that begin with "How" or "What."

- Explain acronyms. Avoid professional jargon and colloquialisms.

- Ask permission to address sensitive topics. The goal is to be helpful without being intrusive. Emphasize that everything discussed will be kept confidential.

- Never argue with parents. Do not make assumptions about their behavior. Acknowledge their concerns and frustrations. Invite them to help you find solutions that meet the needs of their child.

- Help parents feel they have been understood by briefly paraphrasing what they share. Ask for clarification if needed.

- Summarize the conversation, and discuss next steps and follow-up plans. Assure parents that there will be a two-way flow of information and advice between parents and teachers.

Involving Families Outside School

When teachers build a positive relationship with parents, they can count on families to encourage students' educational efforts and share helpful insights about the student. There are many ways that extended families and friends can help support students outside of the classroom. They can provide opportunities for students to listen, speak, read, and write in their home language. They can teach students about the world and pass on valued cultural traditions. They can also check that homework assignments are completed, answer students' questions, help with home practice, read aloud with the child, take the child to the library and local museums, watch and discuss videos about a study topic, and provide rewards or consequences based on effort and performance. When teachers suggest specific home-based activities, they need to be sensitive to the family's circumstances including available time, space, resources, and supplies.

Involving Families at School

Partnering with families involves learning about the special talents, interests, and skills of each family member. In doing so, teachers develop a pool of experts that they can call on to enhance students' learning experiences. During initial meetings with parents, teachers should ask if they or other family members would like to help students during the school day.

To spark some ideas, teachers should give examples of meaningful ways parents can contribute in class even if they have limited English language skills. Some parents may feel it is not their role to teach at school, or that they do not have proper training to do so. The important message to convey is that teachers and students want their families to be part of the school community and share their skills and knowledge.

Facilitating Access to Community Resources

As teachers build trusting relationships with families, they may learn about difficulties students' families are facing. Teachers need to be both compassionate and professional. They must balance their concern for the family's well-being with respect for the family's privacy.

Being an effective advocate involves taking the family's lead. When asked for help or counsel, teachers must protect the dignity of the family and the student by offering assistance privately and respectfully. They should not *tell* families what they should do. Instead, they should provide information about possible solutions and allow families to select the solutions that are appropriate for them. For example, they can do the following:

- Provide a list of cultural networks and religious institutions that donate food, clothing, and holiday gifts to families in need.

- Provide a list of social service organizations and legal advocacy groups.

- Share information about English language programs and career counseling for adults.

- Share information about community programs for new immigrants and cultural centers where families can find support in their home language.

Review Questions

1. Parental involvement is linked to improved student achievement, student motivation, student attitudes toward language learning, and persistence in the ESL program. A fourth-grade teacher wants to increase parental involvement opportunities. As an initial attempt to involve parents in their children's school activities, the teacher should

    (A) invite ESL parents to join the school's parent-teacher organization (PTO) and encourage them to attend meetings.

    (B) send home a progress report every week and asks each parent to sign it.

    (C) work with students every two or three weeks to help them create a "Classroom Stories" booklet, which the students take home to show their parents.

    (D) set up a parent volunteer schedule to encourage parents to help out with class activities.

    The correct response is (**C**). Creating a booklet that showcases class experiences will give each student ownership of the class experience in a way not possible through teacher-generated progress reports. Additionally, because the students are creating the booklet, they will offer authentic experiences that will communicate to parents student attitudes about meaningful educational activities. (A) is incorrect because it does not specifically target ESL parents' potential involvement in their children's school activities. All parents are eligible for membership in PTO. (B) is incorrect because signing a progress report does not actively involve parents in school activities. (D) is incorrect because this would not be the best initial means to reach out to parents. A volunteer or parent guest schedule would be a good follow-up once parents know what their children are doing in the class via the booklet.

2. An upper elementary ESL teacher decorates the classroom with motivational reading posters, borrows grade-appropriate fiction and nonfiction books from the library, and

invites parents to a read-aloud demo in class. The teacher gives the parents a reading log (which the children have decorated with stickers and their own illustrations) on which parents and children are supposed to record at-home oral reading time. The teacher suggests several at-home reading scenarios, such as reading to a younger sibling, the whole family, or an individual parent. This instructional activity primarily supports which of the following ESL teaching goals?

(A)   The reading log engenders student ownership of at-home learning

(B)   The reading log allows the teacher to collect quantitative data for the end-of-year subjective report on the students' reading proficiency

(C)   The reading log fulfills state requirements for out-of-school literacy experiences

(D)   The reading log creates collaboration among the teacher, the parents, and the students in promoting students' academic success

The correct response is (**D**). Reading boosts students' language proficiency. This reading-log activity promotes the home environment as an extension of the school learning space and brings parents in as advocates in their children's educational accomplishments. (A) is incorrect because it presents an incomplete explanation of the goal of this activity. (B) and (C) are incorrect because they suggest inaccurately that the reading log is an assessment instrument.

3.   At parent orientation for the school's ESL program, teachers give parents a 3 x 5 card and ask the parents to write *una cartita* (a little letter)—a few lines describing their child, in English or in Spanish. The teachers tell the parents that these notes will be important in helping them get to know their students. The teachers also say that every three weeks, she will send a little letter/*cartita* home with a few sentences about their child's classroom experiences. The little letter will include a blank card so that the parents can write a return note to the teacher. This activity best addresses which of the following essential components of ESL instruction?

(A)   Improving parents' L1 and L2 literacy skills

(B)   Establishing communication and collaboration with parents

(C)   Keeping parents informed about their children's problematic classroom behavior

(D)   Compiling information about students' home life

The correct response is (**B**). The little-letter strategy promotes communication between parents and teachers in an informal, child-centered way. Significantly, the teacher is establishing a two-way route. Ordinarily, letters from school do not require a response, but this activity invites parents to write back. (A) is incorrect because this is not a realistic goal for ESL programs. (C) and (D) are both incorrect responses because they misconstrue the purpose of the little letters/*cartitas*.

PRACTICE TEST 1

TExES English as a Second Language Supplemental (154)

Also available at the REA Study Center (*www.rea.com/studycenter*)

This practice test is also offered online at the REA Study Center. We recommend that you take the online version of the test to simulate test-day conditions and to receive these added benefits:

- **Timed testing conditions**—helps you gauge how much time you can spend on each question

- **Automatic scoring**—find out how you did on the test, instantly

- **On-screen detailed explanations of answers**—gives you the correct answer and explains why the other answer choices are wrong

- **Diagnostic score reports**—pinpoint where you're strongest and where you need to focus your study

PRACTICE TEST 1

TIME: 5 Hours
70 Multiple-choice questions

In this section, you will find examples of test questions similar to those you are likely to encounter on the TExES English as a Second Language Supplemental (154) Exam. Read each question carefully and choose the best answer from the four possible choices. Mark your responses on the answer sheet provided on page 243.

1. Which of the following programs provides federally mandated accountability data on the progress of ELL students in Texas in meeting language proficiency goals?

   (A) The State of Texas Assessments of Academic Readiness (STAAR)
   (B) Texas English Language Proficiency Assessment System (TELPAS)
   (C) Texas Essential Knowledge and Skills (TEKS)
   (D) English Language Proficiency Standards (ELPS)

2. A high school English teacher plans a unit focused on a frequently taught short story from American literature. Because half of his students are intermediate to advanced ESL students, he needs to provide appropriate accommodations to create comprehensible input. Which of the following instructional activities should the teacher select to meet this goal?

   (A) Before starting the unit, the teacher writes 20 vocabulary words on the board and gives students a class period to look them up.
   (B) Students watch a film on the author's novels and stories, focusing on the shared thematic elements.
   (C) The teacher begins the unit with a "book talk" in which he introduces the characters, the initiating event, and touches on the conflict. He then reads a few pivotal passages from the story.
   (D) For homework prior to the first unit day, students are required to read the story and answer a set of questions.

3. A writing teacher has shown intermediate-level ESL students how to brainstorm, how to do webs, and how to pose questions about the topic. An additional strategy that would help students during the planning stage of writing would be to

   (A) create an outline.
   (B) draw a simple illustration.
   (C) write the essay in Spanish and then translate it into English.
   (D) write a thesis statement.

4.   Ms. Contreras is reading a set of student drafts. The following sentence is in Remi's draft: "I knew that if I just had too more minutes, I could of finished." Remi's sentence demonstrates difficulty in

   (A)   using past tense correctly.
   (B)   distinguishing between the oral and written forms of homonyms.
   (C)   using modals correctly.
   (D)   spelling.

5.   Remi's draft ends with this sentence: "You should never feel bad just cuz u didn't finish." Which of the following strategies should Ms. Contreras use to help Remi understand the difference between social and academic registers?

   (A)   She should mark an X through "cuz" and "u" and write "misspelled" in the margin
   (B)   She should use Remi's sentence in the next day's daily oral language exercise and have students try to correct the sentence
   (C)   She should have a minilesson on texting language versus academic language, explaining expectations for each register
   (D)   Since the sentence occurs in a draft, she should expect that Remi will correct the forms during editing and revision

6.   An elementary teacher has a class of beginning ESL students. During oral reading times, the teacher notices that the students are using many L1 phonemes in pronouncing L2 words. The most effective strategy in helping students use their L1 phonological knowledge in producing L2 strings would be for the teacher to

   (A)   correct the students each time they mispronounce a word during oral reading.
   (B)   have students read along silently as she plays an audio recording of a short book they are familiar with. She plays the recording once more, with the students reading along chorally.
   (C)   make a list of all the words the students mispronounced during reading time and give them a spelling test on this list.
   (D)   write simple sentences using words with the L2 phonemes that the students are having trouble with and have the students copy the sentences into their notebooks.

7.   The best rationale for integrating culturally relevant literature into ELL curricula is that

   (A)   students are better able to connect meaningfully with stories and characters that reflect their culture and/or native country environment.
   (B)   books categorized as "multicultural or culturally relevant" literature are easier than canonical literature.
   (C)   culturally relevant literature is written in the students' home language.
   (D)   the only type of literature that ELL students can understand is literature written in language or dialogue that reflects their L1.

8. A third-grade ESL teacher creates a Home Words Homework Page. The teacher tells the students to ask their parents or siblings to help them write down 10 words describing their home or objects in their home. The teacher tells the students to put the words in two columns: one column for the English word and one column for the Spanish translation. This assignment best addresses which of the following ESL instructional strategies?

    (A) The teacher is creating an opportunity for family involvement in the ESL students' education
    (B) By having the students ask for help, the teacher is integrating a homework completion check into the assignment
    (C) The teacher knows that students don't like to do homework, so the assignment is designed to be easy and student-friendly
    (D) By having students write the words in English and in Spanish, the teacher is embedding vocabulary and spelling into this assignment

9. ELL students in a third-grade class are having trouble learning the names of math figures (for example, hexagon, quadrilateral, pentagon, and so on). Which of the following instructional strategies would most effectively promote students' learning in this area of math?

    (A) The teacher devises a quiz in which students have to correctly match the figure to its name. The quiz is administered every day until all the students get 100 percent correct.
    (B) The teacher draws each figure on the board and has students copy the figures into their notebooks. The teacher asks for volunteers to come to the board to label each figure.
    (C) The teacher creates a poster for each figure. In addition to an illustration of the figure, the name is written in large letters, with the root underlined and the corresponding number of sides written in large print on the poster. The poster includes pictures of words with the same root.
    (D) The teacher puts students into groups and assigns a different figure to each group. Their task is to make several models of their figure using a variety of resources such as craft sticks, twigs, pencils, construction paper strips, chenille sticks, and any other materials they can think of.

10. An elementary school teacher has introduced word problems in his ESL class. The teacher knows that word problems pose conceptual difficulties even for native speakers, so he wants to provide appropriate instructional support for his ESL students' understanding of this math concept. Which of the following strategies would best reinforce his ESL students' understanding of math word problems?

    (A) The teacher suggests that students translate the word problems into their L1 before trying to solve them.
    (B) The teacher puts the students in a large circle and has each student read a word problem orally.
    (C) The teacher organizes students into groups and gives each group 12 pencil cap erasers. Each group writes a short word problem focusing on math operations about the erasers.
    (D) The teacher divides the class into two teams. He puts a word problem on the board and gives the teams five minutes to solve the problem. The winning team gets five extra points on their daily math grade.

11. To promote students' understanding of social studies content, a third-grade ESL teacher writes keywords and focal points on the board as he lectures. Which of the following additional strategies would best promote students' understanding of content knowledge during each class lecture?

   (A) The teacher starts each class with a pretest and ends with a quiz on the material covered that day.
   (B) Students read aloud from the textbook, and the teacher corrects any mispronunciations.
   (C) At the end of the class, the teacher asks students to submit questions about anything they didn't understand from the lesson.
   (D) The teacher stops every 10–15 minutes to conduct a "state of the class" session, during which he asks questions about key points and encourages students to explain what they understand and identify what they don't understand.

12. In their August orientation, teachers at a Central Texas school discuss the following statement from the school's Handbook of Daily Operating Procedures: "The teacher creates an environment that values the beliefs, backgrounds, home learning, home language, and sense of belonging to a group that every learner brings to the classroom and fosters a sense of community that brings diverse learners together." In the context of ESL teaching, this statement refers to

   (A) linguistic diversity.
   (B) pedagogical tolerance.
   (C) identity preservation.
   (D) multiculturalism.

13. In a mainstream middle school science class that also includes beginning to intermediate ELL students, which of the following instructional strategies might best promote the teacher's goal to develop the ELL students' academic English proficiency?

   (A) Focusing instruction on the native speakers and having the ELL students participate as best they can
   (B) Assigning supplemental homework to the ELL students to ensure that they catch up with material they did not understand in the day's lesson
   (C) Pairing each ELL student with students of similar language backgrounds so they can help each other understand the science content of each lesson
   (D) Providing a class library of illustrated books at various reading levels to present science concepts at language and cognitive levels accessible to the ELL students

Use the information below to answer questions 14 and 15 that follow.

Ms. Pierce teaches a sheltered class of fifth-grade intermediate ESL students. During their language enrichment period, she hands out the following exercise. Her students are clustered into base groups, but she instructs them to work independently for five minutes and then network with their group members to complete the exercise.

Read the following passage carefully. Fill the blanks with words that make sense in those slots. Remember that to make sense, the words need to fit both in meaning and in grammatical structure.

The playground can _____ kids how to work hard to _____ anything. Whether kids are trying to swing by _____, go down the big slide, or go _____ the monkey bars, they are out there every day working at _____ the task. Once they go down that _____ for the first time, they _____ that when they work at something, they _____ their goal. I still remember the _____ time I was able to swing. _____ I was able to do something on my own!

---

14. What is the label generally given to this type of exercise?

    (A) Cloze exam
    (B) Daily oral language
    (C) Sustained silent reading
    (D) Read-aloud

15. This type of class activity is primarily intended to promote proficiency in

    (A) metacognition.
    (B) syntax and semantics.
    (C) comprehension.
    (D) vocabulary.

16. Ms. Pierce discovers that some of her students are frustrated because they can't figure out the "right answers." Which of the following modifications should she make to support students' efforts to complete this activity effectively?

    (A) She provides a list of possible choices for each blank, including some alternatives that are inappropriate for the context of the blank.
    (B) She asks for volunteers to read the passage aloud in front of the class, saying "blank" every time they come to a blank.
    (C) She tells students who are frustrated to look up words they don't know in the passage.
    (D) She provides picture books and elementary-level storybooks on the general topic of the passage and tells students to read several of these books if they don't understand how to fill in the blanks.

17. Which of the following statements correctly expresses current understandings about ESL students' acquisition of L2 listening and speaking competencies?

    (A) In order to read and write in L2, students must first acquire L2 oral language.
    (B) If they are motivated to learn, ESL students acquire oral language naturally with little or no need for formal instruction. Proficiency in the other language domains follows.
    (C) In learning L2, proficiency in the reading, writing, speaking, and listening domains develops simultaneously rather than sequentially.
    (D) To help students succeed academically, teachers should focus on reading and writing proficiency.

18. A high school with a 75 percent ELL student enrollment has an ESL program in place that meets the following criteria:

    • It promotes language proficiency by addressing the needs learners with a of a diverse range of language competencies.

    • It enhances students' competence in content areas through classroom experiences that reflect the learner's development while fostering readiness for higher levels of learning.

    • It provides instruction through certified ESL instructors who promote learners' L2 competence and uses L2 as a medium for learning in academic subjects.

    Which of the following ESL program models do these criteria describe?

    (A) Content-based program
    (B) Immersion program
    (C) Pull-out program
    (D) Grammar-based ESL and content-area enrichment

19. The Bilingual Education Act, Title VII of the Elementary and Secondary Education Act of 1968, was significant in the history of ESL education in America because it

    (A) implemented federal guidelines for integrating children of undocumented immigrants into American schools.
    (B) established the National Center for Bilingual Education as a resource center for teachers and administrators.
    (C) initiated federal involvement in mandates, funding, rationales, and goals for bilingual/ESL education programs.
    (D) established the "separate but equal" precedent for implementing bilingual education programs in American schools.

20. An elementary school with a large number of students identified as ELL is aiming for 100 percent parental approval for placing students in the district's ESL program. Which of the following strategies would best address the school's goal to facilitate family involvement in ELL students' educational experiences?

    (A) Inviting families to a meeting where several teachers do a class demonstration showing how ESL methods are integrated into daily instruction
    (B) Meeting with each family individually to explain the benefits of ESL education
    (C) Sending a letter to the impacted families explaining the ESL program guidelines stipulated by the Texas Education Code and the No Child Left Behind Act
    (D) Inviting parents to a special parent-teacher organization meeting where a question-and-answer session on ESL is the only item on the agenda

21. A semantic map is considered a good strategy for promoting ESL students' content-area learning because it

    (A) allows students to skim through a new text to identify keywords that will be important in understanding the content.
    (B) provides a graphic structure for anticipating and organizing a core concept and associated subpoints.
    (C) presents all the new vocabulary students will encounter in a content-area lesson.
    (D) provides a graphic organizer for representing text structures.

Use the information below to answer questions 22 and 23.

> Janie is a middle school student whose family recently emigrated from Mexico. On the first day of class, she told her teacher that she had to drop out of school in her native country a year ago. In the interval, she has had no tutoring or formal schooling. She has the following conversation with her English teacher regarding a missed homework assignment.
>
> Janie: Is because I lose…uhmmmm…USB [pronounced "uəsbi"]. Is no finish. Uhmmmmm…the homework.
> Teacher: You were unable to complete your assignment, Janie? [speaking slowly and clearly enunciating]
> Janie: Yes. No do it.
> Teacher: Do you think you could complete your homework during your study period? [speaking slowly and clearly enunciating]
> Janie: Uhmmmmm…Estudy time. Yes. Finish.
> Teacher: That's great, Janie. I hope to get your completed assignment later today.
> Janie: Is good.

22. Based on this brief exchange, which of the following statements offers the best description of Janie's L2 development at this point?

    (A) Janie has virtually no understanding of English grammar.
    (B) Janie's syntactic and phonological output point to interference from Spanish grammatical structures.
    (C) Janie is not capable of completing a logical utterance in English.
    (D) Janie is unable to use her L1 competence as scaffolding for her L2 development.

23. The L2 acquisition strategy that Janie's pronunciation of USB as "uəsbi" is indicative of

(A) transfer.
(B) incorrect translation.
(C) risk-taking.
(D) inactive filter.

24. A high school teacher wants her intermediate and advanced students to write sentences of increasing syntactic complexity. Which of the following instructional strategies would most effectively promote students' ability to construct sentences using subordinate and coordinate clauses in a variety of patterns?

(A) Sentence-combining exercises
(B) Grammar drills in which students correctly identify written compound and compound-complex sentences
(C) Daily oral language sentences that include errors in subordination and coordination
(D) Memorizing lists of subordinate and coordinate conjunctions

25. A high school history teacher wants his ESL class to develop a deeper understand of historical events. He develops the following list of essential questions:

• Who are the pivotal participants?

• How does each participant impact the outcome?

• Why is this event important?

• Could the participants have taken any other course of action?

Following each unit, students discuss the questions in groups and make brief oral reports on their findings. This instructional strategy promotes students' content-area proficiency by

(A) integrating several levels of Bloom's taxonomy.
(B) engaging students in critical thinking through activities that foster communicative competence.
(C) impressing upon students the need to memorize the names of key historical figures.
(D) encouraging students to create a historical timeline that helps them remember when pivotal events happened.

26. A high school teacher works in a newcomer program in her district. She wants to make sure she integrates all of the Texas Administrative Code (TAC) regulations about meeting learners' needs. She knows newcomer ELL students may be shy about asking questions in class, so she puts up a poster showing students raising their hands. The dialogue bubbles show some questions in English and some in Spanish. The teacher in the poster has a smile on her face, and her thought bubble says, "Great questions!" This classroom strategy is designed to address which of the following learner needs?

(A) Conversational
(B) Classroom decorum
(C) Linguistic
(D) Affective

27. According to the Texas Administrative Code (TAC) Chapter 89, the basic requirement for implementing an ESL or bilingual program in a school district is

    (A) a district-wide enrollment of 50 percent or more students whose families are classified as Hispanic, Asian, African American, or other in the U.S. Census Data.
    (B) campus demographics that include 80 percent speakers of languages other than English.
    (C) an enrollment of 20 or more ELL students in any language classification in the same grade level district-wide.
    (D) an audit from the Texas Education Agency that finds disparities in educational approaches used for native and nonnative speakers of English.

28. Ms. Oliver has an elementary class of beginning ESL students. During reading time, she integrates nonfiction picture books that focus on science, history, and social studies topics. She reads a book to her students orally and then rereads it several times. After several rereadings, she stops at key points in the book and asks students to fill in what comes next. Which of the following statements best explains how this teaching strategy reinforces students' content-area learning?

    (A) The repeated readings and student participation reinforces' students familiarity with discipline-specific terms and concepts.
    (B) The oral reading reinforces students' phonological awareness.
    (C) Reading picture books instead of the actual textbooks simplifies the content area material for learners who are not yet ready for challenging content.
    (D) Working with picture books allows students to learn to spell high-frequency words in a meaningful communicative context.

29. A ninth-grade speech communication class is evenly divided among ELL students and native speakers. The teacher has assigned an informal speech. As part of the preparation for this assignment, she shows several movie clips with the sound turned off. The rational that best explains how this activity will promote student achievement in this informal speech assignment is that

    (A) watching film segments with the sound off will provide an opportunity to analyze how nonverbal cues, body language, and gestures contribute to communication.
    (B) watching a film prior to a challenging assignment reduces anxiety and helps students perform at a higher level.
    (C) watching film clips with the sound off and then rewatching with the sound on will enable students to recognize how important good elocution is in being understood by an audience.
    (D) watching film clips will show students how important staging is in delivering a good speech performance

30. A school district in a border area of Texas establishes an ESL program for young students who have recently arrived in the United States and who have limited or no academic background in their native language. The program addresses acculturation, language, affective, and academic aspects of the children's educational experience. The program is a temporary "stop over." The goal is to transition these students into a traditional ESL program. This type of program is typically labeled as a

    (A) transitional ESL program.
    (B) language-intervention program.
    (C) SIFE program (students with interrupted formal education).
    (D) newcomer program.

31. A teacher new to the ESL program in her district wants to learn the state-mandated responsibilities for teachers in required bilingual and ESL programs. Which of the following offers the most thorough resources for ELL teaching in Texas?

    (A) The Language Proficiency Assessment Committee Framework Manual
    (B) The Texas Education Agency's English Language Learner Web Portal
    (C) The Texas Education Code
    (D) The Texas Essential Knowledge and Skills

32. A middle school teacher wants to promote his ESL students' understanding of social studies content-area vocabulary. His students frequently tell him that they think looking up every word they don't know is boring. In order to meet this instructional goal, the teacher

    (A) identifies a focal concept in the next reading assignment and models how to create a semantic map.
    (B) reads part of the next chapter aloud while students read along silently. Every time he comes to a word he thinks that students don't know, he writes it on the board and defines it.
    (C) has a student volunteer read aloud the chapter title and all the subheadings. Then he asks for another volunteer to predict what topics the chapter might cover.
    (D) shows a short video on the key concepts covered in the chapter prior to reading the next chapter.

33. An elementary school teacher with a class of beginning ESL students distributes a card with a consonant blend to each student. The teacher orally reads a list of words. Whenever the teacher reads a word that starts with the consonant blend a student is holding, the student is supposed to hold up the card. This activity promotes language proficiency in

    (A) morphological knowledge.
    (B) vocabulary development.
    (C) phonological knowledge.
    (D) oral language.

34. Which of the following best describes the individual teacher's role in the responsibilities of the LPAC as described in the Texas Education Code and the Texas Administrative Code?

   (A) To inform parents of each students' progress in language acquisition and core course performance at the end of each semester
   (B) To provide a subjective teacher evaluation when the committee considers whether a student is English proficient for exit from the ESL program
   (C) To work closely with the LPAC to determine ELL students placement options at the end of each academic year
   (D) To complete and submit yearly reports on ELL students' academic progress as measured by the TEA Class Performance Matrix

35. According to the *LPAC Framework Manual*, a student is identified as an English Language Learner if he or she

   (A) demonstrates significant deficiencies in writing a short passage in English.
   (B) is unable to respond readily to instructions in English.
   (C) has had no academic experiences in L1.
   (D) is in the process of acquiring English and has a language other than English as a native language.

Use the information below to answer questions 36 and 37.

   A high school teacher presents a unit on the 1960s civil rights movement in a sheltered social studies class. The lesson includes film clips, news stories, magazine pictures published in the 1960s, excerpts from speeches from key civil rights leaders, as well as textbook chapters.

36. Additionally, the teacher creates a Civil Rights Around the World bulletin board and adds a first entry on Nelson Mandela. She tells students that each group needs to contribute a picture and small explanation of civil rights activists from other countries or cultures to add to the bulletin board. She integrates computer-assisted instruction and tells students they may do their computer work in their L1 if they choose. Which of the following explanations best addresses the connection between this instructional strategy and ESL student learning?

   (A) The integration of technology with the option to use Internet resources in their L1 will promote students' content-area knowledge and language acquisition.
   (B) By integrating materials other than the traditional textbook, the teacher demonstrates how history books present limited views of historical events.
   (C) The students will be able to create multimedia products to connect knowledge of this important period in American history to historical events in their home countries.
   (D) By integrating electronic resources, the teacher creates a class environment that reduces the effort that learners need to expend and reduces anxiety over required class work.

37. As a culminating activity, the teacher organizes the class into a large circle for a round-robin discussion. Each student completes the sentence: "I admire _____ (the person the student chose) because _____." Then, the teacher has each student write a letter to the historical figure they mentioned. Which of the following ESL instructional strategies does this activity best reflect?

    (A) The teacher creates an assignment that ESL students can complete effortlessly.
    (B) The teacher creates a learning environment in which students find meaningful connections to content-area knowledge presented in a multicultural setting.
    (C) The teacher creates an assignment that allows for authentic assessment in contrast to the traditional end-of-unit test.
    (D) The teacher makes an assignment that will encourage students to do additional research in order to complete the letter satisfactorily.

38. A middle school teacher shows her ESL class film clips of people from different countries and cultures greeting each other. This instructional strategy primarily focuses on

    (A) showing students that shaking hands is not a universal greeting.
    (B) developing students' awareness of cultural diversity.
    (C) emphasizing the need to watch videos set in other countries.
    (D) reinforcing students' understanding of body language in communicating.

39. To promote her fifth-grade ESL students' academic language proficiency, a science teacher takes her students to the school library once a week and has the students check out books on topics related to the unit they are currently studying. The teacher notices that students talk constantly in the library, showing each other their books, and reading each other's books. She recognizes this as an opportunity to promote her students' communicative language development. Which of the following instructional activities best addresses the teacher's intent?

    (A) Assigning students book reports on the books they pick and posting the reports on the class writing wall
    (B) Having each student do a book talk on his or her book
    (C) Having each student post the title of her or his book on the class notes wall.
    (D) Having a question-and-answer session where the teacher asks each student one question about the book he or she checked out

40. An ELL included the following sentences in her essay: "When one talks about improving the education quality, many ideas such as smaller class sizes, teacher's quality, and lack of resources." "Although increasing funds might be a solution, other ways to improve the educational qualities without more funds." The explanation that the teacher should offer to enable the student writer to understand the L2 problems shown in these sentences is that

    (A) the student is overusing the definite article: "the."
    (B) the student should keep the sentences short so as not to make so many errors in syntax.
    (C) the student needs to proofread the writing more carefully.
    (D) in English, abstract concepts such as education and educational quality generally do not take an article.

Use the information below to answer questions 41 and 42.

A high school English teacher is about to start a unit on Jack London's "To Build a Fire" in her sheltered class.

41. She starts a whole-class discussion by asking: "When the temperature is very high and you feel very hot, what are some things you are supposed to do to stay safe?" She writes their comments on the board and encourages students to follow up on some of the things they say. Then she tells students to work in groups to respond to this question: "When it's very, very cold, what are some things you should do to stay safe?" She gives students five minutes to prepare their group response. How does this oral language activity promote students' communicative language competence?

(A) The teacher activates prior knowledge to help students connect their real-world experiences to the context of the classroom lesson.

(B) Using the students' group responses, the teacher will be able to create a semantic map to introduce the story.

(C) The teacher knows this story will be challenging for ELL students, so she starts with this activity in order to boost their comprehension.

(D) The teacher wants to promote students' active listening skills by making them realize how little they know about extreme cold temperatures.

42. As a follow-up, the teacher takes the class to the school library and assigns the following activity:

• Work with your group members to find three facts about Alaskan geography, topography, and/or temperatures.

• Be ready to do a three-minute summary of your findings tomorrow.

• Your presentation must include at least one photograph. You can show a photograph from a library book, or you and your group members can draw an illustration.

Which of the following descriptions best explains how this activity contributes to students' oral-language proficiency development?

(A) It allows students to connect research-based facts to the events of the story.

(B) It creates opportunities for students to negotiate about which facts are most relevant to the story.

(C) It promotes communicative competence by combining collaboration, research, writing, and oral presentation.

(D) It prepares students to understand the core conflict of the story.

43. Each Monday, a third-grade teacher introduces new content vocabulary to her beginning ESL students. To reinforce their initial understanding of the new words, she posts labeled pictures of the words. She wants to promote their listening and speaking proficiency in the context of content instruction. Which of the following instructional activities most effectively addresses the teacher's goal?

(A) The teacher puts up the lists of new content words, pronounces each one, and then calls on student volunteers to pronounce them, too.

(B) Working in groups, students pick one of the new words to explore by looking in their books, using the dictionary, and using other class resources. Each group does a short presentation to introduce the class to the new word.

(C) The teacher gives students two days to learn the words. They spend a few minutes each day pronouncing the words out loud in unison. On the third day, they have a spelling test on all the new words.

(D) The teacher shows an animated video in which animal characters introduce the new words on the list. After the video, the teacher gives students a short test to determine which words they seemed to understand best.

Use the information below to answer questions 44–46.

Ms. Sahid teaches at a high school that includes *The Great Gatsby* as mandatory reading for all students in eleventh-grade curriculum. Her classes include many intermediate-level ESL students.

44. Which of the following accommodations might best help Ms. Sahid's ESL students understand the novel?

(A) Showing a film version of the novel before reading it

(B) Integrating historical photographs, period music, art, and brief historical overviews to contextualize the themes and events in the novel

(C) Handing out a chapter-by-chapter summary of the novel

(D) Listening to a professional recording of the novel as students follow along in their books

45. To help her students appreciate the literary language in *The Great Gatsby*, Ms. Sahid arranges her class into groups and assigns each group an especially vivid passage from the novel. To promote students' understanding of literary language, she asks each group to dramatize the passage they've been given. The instructional strategy that would be most effective in helping students complete this activity meaningfully and effectively is for the teacher to

(A) model the activity by acting out a passage and explain how her actions, movements, and gestures reflect the language of the text.

(B) ask students to underline and label the literary devices they recognize in their passages.

(C) join each group and ask group members to read the passage aloud and then correct all mispronunciations and incorrect intonations.

(D) ask each group to explain why the passage is important to the reader's understanding of the scene.

46. The accommodations Ms. Sahid makes in teaching *The Great Gatsby* to intermediate ESL students are likely to be most effective if her teaching activities reflect

    (A) sheltered instruction.
    (B) English-language development (ELD).
    (C) specially designed academic instruction in English (SDAIE).
    (D) content-area reading strategies.

47. A high school ESL teacher has students ranging from intermediate to high advanced in his class. He assigns them the following project:

    > Think of your favorite movie in your native language. Create a poster that includes information about the basic plot elements (the characters, the key events, the conflict, and the outcome). Each of you will have five minutes to present your movie poster to the class and explain why this is your favorite film.

    This assignment will take two class periods followed by two presentation periods.

    The teaching goal that this assignment best addresses is to

    (A) create an opportunity for students to practice process writing.
    (B) emphasize the importance of correct pronunciation in a formal speech situation.
    (C) teach students critical viewing skills in the context of international films.
    (D) provide students an opportunity to integrate listening, speaking, and writing skills in an authentic context.

48. ELL students in a middle school English class do quite well on weekly vocabulary tests where they correctly match words and meanings. Which of the following instructional strategies should the teacher use to encourage students to actually use new vocabulary words in oral and written language?

    (A) Students write paragraphs integrating the vocabulary words for that week.
    (B) Working in groups, students pick one word from the week's vocabulary list and create a semantic web poster defining the word in their own words (instead of a dictionary definition) and providing synonyms for their word.
    (C) Working in groups, students pick one word from the week's list and do a scavenger hunt to find examples of the word being used in books and the media.
    (D) Students cut pictures out of magazines and create a collage featuring the meanings of words on the weekly vocabulary list.

49. Which of the following descriptions represents the initial procedure for designating students as Limited English Proficient (LEP) in Texas school districts?

   (A)   The LEP designation is made by individual teachers any time they notice that students demonstrate deficiencies in social and academic language proficiency.
   (B)   When parents request in writing that their child be placed in bilingual or ESL classes, the student is automatically designated LEP.
   (C)   Upon entering a school district, any student whose home language is not exclusively English (as determined by a home language survey) is tested to assess language proficiency. Results are evaluated by the Language Proficiency Assessment Committee (LPAC) to determine LEP or non-LEP status.
   (D)   Initial LEP designations are based on students' performance in the previous academic year. In the case of kindergarten students, the designation is based on teachers' observations of the learner's performance in the first six weeks of school.

50. A third-grade teacher is conducting a phonics lesson in her class of beginning ELL students. She writes the following words on the board, pronouncing each word and having her students respond chorally.

brink	wink
drink	pink
stink	sink
think	link

She has volunteers come to the board to draw a line under the part that is the same in all the words. She asks for other volunteers to draw a vertical line between the underlined part and the beginning sound(s). Which language-learning strategy does this activity reflect?

   (A)   Developing vocabulary
   (B)   Applying morphological knowledge in creating new words
   (C)   Recognizing patterns in language
   (D)   Reinforcing orthographic knowledge

51. Research on ESL instruction shows that use of multiple scaffolds promotes young learners' social adjustment and academic learning. Which of the following descriptions provides the best examples of learning scaffolds?

    (A) The teacher reinforces daily instruction with a quiz at the end of the school day. Students score each other's quizzes and ask questions about the right and wrong responses.
    (B) The teacher uses props and pictures to support new learning in all subjects, makes extensive use of print throughout the room, and structures lessons to integrate cooperative learning.
    (C) The teacher uses short, animated videos to introduce every lesson in content areas and asks students to summarize their understanding of each video.
    (D) The teacher uses instructional materials that offer L1 and L2 versions of every lesson to create a learning environment that addresses the affective needs of all the students.

52. The ESL teachers in a South Texas school district want students and their families to become more familiar with community resources that can promote their students' literacy goals. Which of the following strategies most effectively targets the teachers' goal?

    (A) Teachers send home a flyer from the public library explaining how to apply for a library card. If they get a public library card, students are rewarded with bonus points.
    (B) The teachers set up a book contribution bin in the main school hallway for teachers and staff members to donate books. Teachers display the donated books under a "Free Books" sign during lunch.
    (C) The teachers work with the public library to identify grade-appropriate children's and young adult fiction and nonfiction books. The teachers set up an after-school reading hour for parents and children.
    (D) Teachers create a class-specific supplementary reading program. In order to encourage students to patronize the public library, they select books they want students to read but which aren't available at the school library.

53. The Texas English Language Proficiency Assessment System (TELPAS) is used to provide which of the following types of data about ELL students?

    (A) Information about the effectiveness of classroom ELL instruction in addressing state standards in writing and reading
    (B) Average yearly progress ratings for ELL students as mandated by the Language Proficiency Assessment Committee
    (C) Correlations between state-mandated exam scores and ELL students' end-of-year grades in math, science, social studies, and English
    (D) Individual proficiency level ratings of ELL students (beginning, intermediate, advanced, advanced high) in listening, speaking, writing, and reading

54. Research findings suggest that a key challenge in two-way dual-immersion programs is ensuring that both native speakers and nonnative speakers are receiving comprehensible input during the dual-language lessons. In a two-way dual-immersion setting, the strategy that would best enable a teacher to create comprehensible input for all the learners is

   (A) paraphrasing and repetition to provide redundancy in listening and speaking situations and integrating objects, visuals, dramatizations, and modeling to introduce new concepts.
   (B) setting up class rules that require learners to listen quietly so that they miss no information presented by the teacher.
   (C) providing all instructions and lessons in both L1 and L2.
   (D) separating learners into L1 and L2 groups, providing instruction in the learners' native language, and reconvening to have members of each group share their new knowledge.

55. A middle school teacher is finishing up a unit on a young adult novel in her ELL class. She plans a culminating activity focused on developing oral-language proficiency in the context of discussing the complexities of the novel. Which of the following assignments would best address her goal?

   (A) Working in groups, students create a poster with illustrations of key events in the novel.
   (B) Each student picks his or her favorite passage from the book and reads it aloud, explaining why the passage is important to the story.
   (C) Working in groups, students create and present a five-minute play focusing on key passages from the book, showing how the central conflict develops.
   (D) Working independently, each student writes and then presents a three-minute speech that explains the ending of the novel.

56. Ms. Cisneros, an elementary teacher, has a class of beginning and intermediate ELL students. When she assigns an essay, the students tell her that they don't know how to write an essay. Which of the following strategies would be most effective in developing students' understanding of grade-appropriate writing requirements?

   (A) Using the topic that she has assigned to the students, the teacher models the entire writing process, from prewriting through editing.
   (B) The teacher hands out sample essays and asks for student volunteers to read them aloud.
   (C) The teacher creates new, easier topics and tells students that the essays need to be only one paragraph long.
   (D) The teacher arranges students into groups and assigns a different essay topic to each group. The students in each group collaborate to create a group essay. The groups post their essays and vote on which is the best one.

Use the information below to answer questions 57–59.

> Ms. Newbery is starting a unit on local plants in her middle school science class. Most of the students are beginning and intermediate ELL students. Ms. Newbery wants to make sure the activities in the new unit help students understand science content but also promote their language proficiency

57. The teacher gives each student three resealable zipper storage bags and asks them to collect leaves from three different plants they see each day on the school grounds, in their yards, or in their neighborhoods. This introductory strategy helps to promote students' understanding of the science content in the unit on local plants because

   (A) students can have fun while completing the assignment.
   (B) new content will be reinforced through hands-on activities.
   (C) students will not need to use language strategies in completing this assignment.
   (D) students will demonstrate the extent to which they can follow basic instructions.

58. When they bring in their three leaves, Ms. Newbery gives the students this assignment:

> Each of you is going to present your three leaves and explain where you found them. As you show them to the class, try to identify some of the features that make each leaf distinct from the others or features that the leaves have in common. (Don't say, "They're all green.")

   How does this instructional activity address Ms. Newbery's concerns about her ELL students' content-area learning?

   (A) The oral-language activity forces students to speak in L2 without relying on L1 vocabulary.
   (B) The activity reinforces new science vocabulary for this unit.
   (C) The activity creates a nonacademic environment, which should reduce students' anxieties over participating in class discussions.
   (D) The activity integrates oral language and prior knowledge as a beginning point for new content-area learning.

59. As a culminating activity for this unit, Ms. Newbery asks students to interview one family member about a favorite or special plant. The students are to create a construction-paper poster with a drawing of the plant and a short written account of the interview. Ms. Newbery displays the posters on the wall outside the classroom. How does this instructional activity promote the ELL students' content-area learning?

   (A) Students will use cultural and language background to support new content-area learning.
   (B) Students will integrate new science vocabulary into their written accounts of the interview with a family member.
   (C) Including a drawing of the family member's favorite plant will allow the teacher to test the students' understanding of basic unit information.
   (D) After reading all the interviews, the teacher will be able to determine if reteaching is necessary in this unit.

60. A teacher in a newcomer program has a "Parents Are Stars" segment every Friday. The teacher invites parents to offer demonstrations and instruction in L1 culture-specific topics, which the teacher translates into L2. Which of the following ESL teaching recommendations does this strategy primarily address?

    (A) The teacher is demonstrating that learning takes place at home as well as at school.
    (B) The teacher is providing downtime to keep students from being overwhelmed by the linguistic and academic content of the ESL program.
    (C) The teacher is fostering meaningful parent participation in their children's school activities.
    (D) The teacher is partnering with parents in order to fulfill requirements of the Texas English Language Proficiency Assessment System (TELPAS).

61. A high school advanced ESL student included the following in her essay:

> (1) When one talks about improving the education quality, many ideas such as smaller class sizes, teacher's quality, and lack of resources. (2) One issue that people believe is crucial, the low budget that schools get from the government. (3) Although increasing funds might be a solution, other ways to improve the educational qualities without more funds.

This passage suggests that the student writer has difficulty with

    (A) completing main clause subject-verb combinations in complex sentences.
    (B) using the apostrophe correctly.
    (C) writing effective subordinate clauses.
    (D) maintaining a consistent point of view.

62. A high school teacher is preparing her sheltered class for the mandated state assessment in writing. She displays the following paragraph on the overhead:

> (1) *Dead Poets Society* (Dir. Peter Weir, 1989) illustrates a conflict of father and son. (2) We see this conflict between Neil and his father, it appears every time Neil's father visits him. (3) Neil's father visits Neil when Neil join any extracurricular activities. (4) Like most students at Welton Neil's future is already planned for him by his father.

The teacher tells the students that each sentence has one error in grammar or language use. They have five minutes to find and correct the errors in the sentences. This activity allows the teacher to assess students' proficiency informally in

    (A) editing.
    (B) revision.
    (C) writing on demand.
    (D) comprehension.

63. Homework assignments are sometimes created with the expectation that parents will be able to help students complete the assignment. At a school where the majority of ESL student parents have limited L1 education and no L2 education, which of the following strategies would best promote family involvement in ESL students' homework assignments?

    (A) The teacher sends parents a list of all the homework assignments for the week and asks parents to initial the assignment when the student completes it.

    (B) The teacher sends parents a video explaining how homework reinforces students' progress in content-area classes.

    (C) The teacher sends a package of textbooks to each family so that family members can familiarize themselves with the content-area materials their children are covering in class.

    (D) The teacher invites parents to attend content-area classes and models how they can facilitate their children homework completion even if they don't understand the subject.

64. A middle-school teacher shows her ESL class the "line game" clip from the film *Freedom Writers*. In the film, teacher Erin Gruwell lays down a strip of masking tape on the classroom floor, tells her students (who come from a variety of cultural and ethnic backgrounds) to step up to it, and then asks them a series of questions based on their cultural and family backgrounds. She starts with questions about films they've watched, progressing to questions about friends and family killed through neighborhood violence. They are to step away from the line if they can respond positively to the questions. At the end of the game, only a few students are still standing at the line, and students are looking at each other with apparent new understanding about shared experiences. How does this class activity address the primary components of effective ESL instruction?

    (A) It demonstrates that film offers a highly effective means of presenting meaningful classroom lessons for ESL students.

    (B) It creates a venue for discussion of how sociocultural factors and home environment impact ESL students' classroom experiences.

    (C) It enables the teacher to enrich ESL students' learning experiences by integrating kinesthetic learning into traditional delivery methods.

    (D) It allows ESL students to contrast real-world events with cinematic representations of those events.

65. This sentence below appears in an essay written by a high advanced ELL student in high school: "Some of the valuable lessons that teachers teach us include self-determination, the necessity of education, and the belief that anything is possible if you have the desire to accomplish goals." Which of the following descriptions accurately explains the syntactic structure of this sentence?

    (A) The writer has written a run-on sentence, suggesting a lack of understanding of sentence boundaries.

    (B) The sentence is a compound-complex sentence that includes several embedded clauses and items in a series.

    (C) The sentence demonstrates some redundancy that should have been corrected during revision.

    (D) The sentence includes several subordinate clauses that are incorrectly punctuated.

66. The Texas Administrative Code stipulates that required bilingual and ESL programs in Texas follow one of four program models. Which of the following programs is NOT listed as one of those four models?

    (A) Two-way dual immersion
    (B) One-way dual immersion
    (C) Transitional/bilingual early exit
    (D) Transitional/bilingual stable

Use the information below to answer questions 67 and 68.

Myra is an advanced seventh-grade ESL student. The passage on the next page is an excerpt from an essay she wrote:

> During the week, I would give up my afternoons just to go to band practice. Regardless of me having homework. Our paractice would usually last from six to eight. Except for Wensdays. My weekends were never true because I either had a football game to go too. Sometimes it was because I had to show up for practice the next day. It almost got to the point to where I came close to losing some of my friends. Beeing that I had a busy schedule.

67. Which of the following statements offers the best analysis of the writer's syntactic performance in this excerpt?

    (A) The writer treats subordinate structures as independent elements.
    (B) The writer demonstrates spelling difficulties.
    (C) The writer does not seem to have any strategies for varying sentence structure.
    (D) The writer does not know what constitutes a complete sentence.

68. Which of the following strategies should the teacher use to promote Myra's syntactic performance in writing?

    (A) The teacher should mark all the errors in the passage and have Myra rewrite the passage making all the marked corrections.
    (B) The teacher should give Myra grammar worksheets in identifying complete sentences and fragments.
    (C) The teacher should have Myra read the passage aloud, calling Myra's attention to her intonation and inflection as she reads the sentences.
    (D) The teacher should give Myra a new topic and ask her to write a new draft without making all the errors evident in this passage.

69. A high school biology teacher is starting a unit that addresses state assessment standards on knowledge of interactions among biological systems in plants. Which of the following instructional activities would most effectively promote his ELL students' achievement in this area?

(A) The teacher assigns a group project. Each group identifies a specific plant and uses visuals and props to demonstrate interaction of its biological systems.

(B) The teacher has students fill out a questionnaire about their prior knowledge on plants' biological systems.

(C) The teacher takes his students on a walk around the campus to point out different types of plants growing on the school grounds.

(D) The teacher shows students the state assessment standards in biology and explains the concepts and defines all the content-specific terms in each standard.

70. A fifth-grade teacher wants to promote her intermediate ELL students' understanding of content-area lessons. She has a word wall divided into content areas and each week updates new content vocabulary. She also has content cubicles decorated with posters and realia. Which of the following grouping strategies might further promote her students' content-area learning?

(A) The teacher uses a random grouping approach, creating new groups each Monday morning.

(B) The teacher creates two types of groups: one set includes only ELL students, and the other, only native speakers.

(C) The teacher creates base groups for cooperative learning activities. Each group includes native speakers and ELL students.

(D) The teacher allows students to self-select the groups they want to be in.

PRACTICE TEST 1 ANSWER KEY

1. (B) ✗D
2. (C) ✓A
3. (B) ✗A
4. (B) ✓
5. (C) ✓
6. (B) ✗A
7. (A) ✓
8. (A) ✓
9. (D) ✗C
10. (C) ✗A
11. (D) ✓
12. (D) ✗C
13. (D) ✓
14. (A) ✓
15. (B) ✗A
16. (A) ✓
17. (C) ✗A
18. (A) ✗B

19. (C) ✓
20. (A) ✗D
21. (B) ✓
22. (B) ✓
23. (A) ✓
24. (A) ✗C
25. (B) ✓
26. (D) ✗B
27. (C) ✓
28. (A) ✓
29. (A) ✓
30. (D) ✗A
31. (B) ✓
32. (A) ✓
33. (C) ✓
34. (B) ✗A
35. (D) ✓
36. (A) ✓

37. (B) ✓
38. (B) ✓
39. (B) ✓
40. (D) ✗C
41. (A) ✓
42. (C) ✓
43. (B) ✓
44. (B) ✗C
45. (A) ✗D
46. (C) ✗B
47. (D) ✓
48. (B) ✓
49. (C) ✓
50. (C) ✗B
51. (B) ✓
52. (C) ✗D
53. (D) ✓
54. (A) ✓

55. (C)
56. (A)
57. (B)
58. (D)
59. (A)
60. (C)
C✗61. (A)
D✗62. (A)
63. (D)
64. (B)
65. (B)
C✗66. (D)
67. (A)
68. (C)
69. (A)
70. (C)

48/70

C1   C2   C3   C4   C5   C6   C7   C8   C9
|| ||| ||| || || | | |||| |

C10
||||

PRACTICE TEST 1 ANSWER EXPLANATIONS

1. **(B)** The correct response is (B). TELPAS includes criteria for rating students' yearly language proficiency as beginning, intermediate, advanced, or advanced high. (A) is the state's assessment system for language arts, math, social studies, and science. Accommodations for ESL students are included in STAAR, but it does not target ESL proficiency. Therefore, (A) is an incorrect response. (C) is the state's curriculum for all public schools and therefore not a correct response. (D) is incorrect because it is not an assessment system. ELPS are integrated into TEKS to specify expectations for ESL students' proficiency in reading, writing, listening, speaking, and general academic skills.
   Competency 008

2. **(C)** The correct response is (C). This teacher faces the challenge of ensuring that both his native speakers and the ESL students learn literature content and that the ESL learners have appropriate instructional scaffolding to promote language learning. The book talk would provide scaffolding for all learners, including the native speakers. (A) is incorrect because vocabulary lessons would be more effective integrated into class discussion as the class reads the story rather than prior to reading and prior to establishing a context for the words. (B) is incorrect because the goal is to create a learning environment in which students understand the story. Watching a film of the author's work is a good strategy, but at this point, students need scaffolding to support entry into a literary text such as would be provided by response (A). (D) is incorrect because the pedagogical challenge the teacher faces—making the story comprehensible for his students—would not be addressed by having students read the story independently.
   Competency 002

3. **(B)** The correct response is (B). Illustration is an invention strategy commonly used with very young writers. In suggesting that ELL students draw an illustration as an idea-generation strategy, the teacher would be taking into account the learner's prior literacy experiences. (A) is incorrect because outlining can result in frustration when the writer has not yet generated sufficient content to start an organizational plan. (C) is incorrect because before the writer *writes*, he or she needs to generate ideas. Writing the essay in L1 does not address the original planning problem. (D) is incorrect because a thesis statement cannot be constructed until the writer has generated ideas during planning. This response does not address the writer's problem.
   Competency 005

4. **(B)** The correct response is (B). The student writer confused the forms of two sets of homonyms: to/two/too and have/of. "Could of" is not a verb form error. It indicates interference between oral and written forms. (A) is incorrect because it does not address the language problem: the past tense forms are correct. (C) is incorrect because it suggests that the modal "could" is misused, but it is used correctly. (D) is the wrong answer because all the words in the sentence are spelled correctly. The misused words are not misspelled.
   Competency 001

5. **(C)** The correct response is (C). The student's use of texting forms in academic discourse suggests he sees no distinction between expectations in academic and social registers. Ms. Contreras's explanation should make it clear that correctness is not the issue, but that language choices should reflect the parameters of the discourse environment. (A) reflects an incorrect explanation because understanding register choices is a holistic concern that cannot be addressed through spelling correction. (B) is incorrect because the forms themselves are appropriate in the right discourse environment. (D) is incorrect because there is no guarantee that the writer will self-correct, and even if he does, the core lesson should be not be surface correctness but the understanding of language choices based on registers.
   Competency 001

6. **(B)** The correct response is (B). The teacher needs to promote students' ability to hear the phonemes in L2 contexts. Thus, the audio exercise followed by choral reading of a familiar text would help students boost awareness of target language phonology. (A) is incorrect because, since oral reading is a social activity, correcting students during oral reading would embarrass the speaker and misdirect the intent of the oral-reading activity. (C) is incorrect because it also misconstrues the learning objective. The problem is phonological, not orthographic. (D) is incorrect because writing sentences does not address the phonological problem that the teacher is trying to address.
Competency 003

7. **(A)** The correct response is (A). A foundational argument for the importance of literature in public school curricula is that literature enables us to understand ourselves better. Thus, a core argument for culturally relevant literature is that self-understanding will be facilitated by literature in which students see reflections of themselves. The same argument is used in defending the integration of young adult literature into ELA curriculum. (B) is incorrect because culturally relevant texts present issues and conflicts as complex as those in canonical literature. However, many ELA teachers *do* believe that culturally relevant literature is easier (and therefore inferior) to canonical literature. (C) is true only in some cases. When teachers talk about culturally relevant literature, they are usually referring to stories that reflect the students' culture but which are written in L2. (D) is incorrect because it represents a deficit view of ELL students and misconstrues the value of culturally relevant literature in creating multicultural teaching environment.
Competency 009

8. **(A)** The correct response is (A). The teacher has created an assignment designed to elicit family participation. The targeted students are young and likely to need help completing the assignment. Even if parents cannot help for various reasons, the children could ask an older sibling for help. (B) misinterprets the intent of the assignment as presented by the teacher's instructions. (C) is incorrect because there is no suggestion in the assignment that the assignment is simplified to encourage students to complete it. It is age appropriate rather than simplified to a lower level. (D) is incorrect because creating a vocabulary list is not the primary purpose of the assignment. As a follow-up activity, the teacher could move to a vocabulary activity, but that extension is not reflected in the item stem.
Competency 010

9. **(D)** The correct response is (D). This is the most learner-centered response and most appropriate for the targeted age and ELL level. Working with manipulatives in a math class is considered a learning-inducing strategy: hands-on strategies create engagement and promote understanding. (A) is incorrect because it would force the students to guess rather than to demonstrate competence. The scenario specifies that the students are having trouble learning the names of the figures. A quiz will not promote learning in this scenario. (B) is incorrect because it would be a good way to reinforce students' understanding, but the scenario indicates that the teacher is trying to create understanding. (C) would be more appropriate for students in higher grades and is therefore an incorrect response.
Competency 003

10. **(C)** The correct response is (C). Having students create their own word problems will give them insider knowledge on the structure and rationale of word problems. (A) is incorrect because it will not address the teacher's objective to promote students' understanding of math content. The students are young (elementary level), so the word problems are new knowledge even for students with past schooling in L1. (B) is incorrect because it will not promote understanding of word problems. (D) is incorrect not because it's not a good teaching strategy, but because it doesn't fit the teacher's objective at this point. Later, when students demonstrate comprehensive understanding of word problems, the contest would be a good strategy for reinforcing that math content proficiency.
Competency 006

11. **(D)**   The correct response is (D). By stopping at 10–15-minute intervals and interacting with his students in the manner described in this response, the teacher is developing his learners' metacognitive strategies for monitoring and boosting students' comprehension of content. (A) is incorrect because, while pretesting and posttesting are traditional assessment tools, the teacher is interested in developing knowledge rather than assessment in the scenario described here. (B) is incorrect because simply reading orally from the text (with the teacher interrupting to correct mispronunciations) does not enable learners to glean meaningful content from the lesson. (C) is incorrect because collecting questions at the end of the period provides no opportunity for authentic discussion and clarification of the content covered in the class session.
   Competency 002

12. **(D)**   The correct response is (D). The statement encompasses key aspects of multiculturalism: cultural awareness, respect, and inclusion. (A) presents a limited view of the statement, and so is incorrect. (B) is incorrect because it suggests that teachers need to tolerate aberrations from some hypothetical normalcy. (C) is incorrect because it implies a negative view of the school experience, suggesting that being in school is a threat to one's identity.
   Competency 009

13. **(D)**   The correct response is (D). Because the students in this class are beginning to intermediate level, the teacher needs strategies to make class content comprehensible while also developing the students' language proficiency. Providing the library books in a range of reading levels would give the ELL students a resource to make the course content accessible in language and formats (illustrations and simpler language) appropriate to their current level of L2 proficiency. (A) is incorrect because focusing on the native speakers and ignoring the ELL students would literally create a "sink or swim" approach to ELL content instruction. This approach is counter to federal mandates about providing equitable educational opportunities for ELL students. (B) is incorrect because assigning additional homework on content that is beyond the students' current language and academic proficiency would frustrate the learners, jeopardizing potential development of language proficiency. (C) is incorrect because the ELL learners need strong instructional scaffolding from the teacher. Being paired with students who are themselves trying to improve their language proficiency and understanding of subject matter would also raise frustration levels in the learners.
   Competency 002

14. **(A)**   The correct response is (A). Cloze exams are created from passages in which words are omitted. Usually, the omission formula deletes every fifth or seventh word. However, in this Cloze-type passage, the omitted words have been deliberately picked to make the exercise more accessible to ESL students whose syntactic proficiency in English is still developing. Cloze exams are intended for practice in syntactic and semantic competence. They are not used exclusively in ESL pedagogy, but they adapt very effectively to ESL teaching situations. (B) is incorrect because DOL exercises are typically one or two sentences that students correct. (C) is incorrect because sustained silent reading is a reading activity that allows students to self-select texts for independent reading. (D) is incorrect because the Cloze-exam format generally does not involve oral reading.
   Competency 001

15. **(B)**   The correct response is (B). The blanks in Cloze exams give students an opportunity to determine what word is an appropriate syntactic and semantic fit within the context of the passage. (A) is incorrect because the focus is not the student's thinking about her or his own thinking, but instead recognizing the syntactic and semantic parameters established by the context. (C) is incorrect because Cloze exams do not primarily promote comprehension. Too much information is missing, and the point of the exercise is to attempt to fill in the blanks with appropriate choices. (D) is incorrect because Cloze exams are not focused on knowing meanings but on recognizing what meaning is suggested by the context.
   Competency 001

16.   **(A)**   The correct response is (A). An unfortunate side effect of some Cloze exams is frustration. Providing a list of possibilities for each blank (with appropriate distractors) is a common strategy for making the activity more accessible to students. Having the students choose from the list will make the activity less challenging, but the instructional goal of developing syntactic and semantic proficiency will still be met. (B) is incorrect because a read-aloud should be focused on creating meaning from the text being read. Reading it orally should enhance the students' comprehension. Neither of those objectives applies in reading a Cloze passage orally. (C) is incorrect because telling students to look up other words in the passage will not address the frustration issue. (D) is incorrect because the Cloze activity is not a content-acquisition activity.
    Competency 001

17.   **(C)**   The correct response is (C). ESL theorists and practitioners promote the position that L2 competencies in the speaking, listening, reading, and writing domains develop holistically and simultaneously. Theorists refer to this as the whole-to-part approach which holds that learners construct meaning by processing information contextually. However, this does not mean that learners acquire competency in each area equally. The "opposite" approach—part-to-whole—would have learners acquiring listening skills first, then speaking, then reading, and finally writing. ESL specialists promote learning approaches that focus on the whole communicative context. (A) suggests a sequential, part-to-whole approach to L2 competency with oral language being the foundation of future learning. This belief is no longer supported in ESL literature or practice, so (A) is an incorrect response. (B) is incorrect because it presents a belief not supported by ESL theory or practice. Instruction in oral language is a vital component of acquiring proficiency in L2. (D) suggests that oral language is a peripheral proficiency in L2 acquisition. ESL specialists recognize that listening and speaking proficiencies are vital components of L2 proficiency. Therefore, (D) is an incorrect response.
    Competency 004

18.   **(A)**   The correct response is (A). The program described in the item stem meets the core features of a content-based ESL program as described in the Texas Administrative Code. (B) is incorrect because these are not the features of an immersion program. (C) is incorrect because pull-out programs generally offer supplementary instruction focused on grammar and language use. (D) is incorrect because this term is not used as an ESL program descriptor.
    Competency 008

19.   **(C)**   The correct response is (C). By recognizing the inherent inequity in educational opportunities for language minority students, this act created the foundation for bilingual and ESL programs in schools throughout America. (A) was the result of the Supreme Court case *Plyler v. Doe* in 1982. (B) *does* offer resources for teachers and administrators, but it is a professional organization, not a federally mandated entity. Therefore, (A) is an incorrect response. (D) is incorrect because this term is not used in describing or implementing bilingual programs in the United States. In fact, several court cases have addressed the problems with programs that segregate linguistic majority and linguistic minority students into environments that claim to offer equal education to both sets of students.
    Competency 008

20.   **(A)**   The correct response is (A). If parents are unsure about how ESL instruction will benefit their children, a demonstration should ease their concerns much more effectively than the required consent letter. The Texas Education Agency does not explain why some parents do not provide written approval. This scenario speculates that the reluctance might stem from not knowing how ESL education operates on a day-to-day basis. (B) is unrealistic particularly in schools with a high percentage of ELL students and is therefore incorrect. (C) is incorrect because it extends the letter requirement that is already in place, but information about the ESL mandates is not likely to persuade reluctant parents to provide the written approval. (D) is a good strategy, but the problem with question-and-answer sessions is that if the audience doesn't have sufficient information, they won't be able to ask questions that address their concerns.
    Competency 010

21. **(B)** The correct response is (B). A semantic map is considered a robust strategy for preparing learners for new content. By focusing on a core content term and considering related concepts, learners are primed for processing new knowledge. (A) is incorrect because semantic maps are created prior to reading. (C) is incorrect because, while a semantic map may include new vocabulary, the purpose of the semantic map is to introduce concepts that will show up in new content material. (D) is incorrect because semantic maps are not designed to show text structures.
   Competency 006

22. **(B)** The correct response is (B). Janie's output is comprehensible, but it clearly suggests that she is relying on her L1 grammar to create her L2 output (using "is" without a subject, appending a vowel sound to the initial sibilant in study, and using "no" as a generic negative). (A) and (C) are incorrect because Janie's L2 performance indicates understanding of fundamental English forms even though her output is rudimentary. (D) is incorrect because Janie's L2 output reflects negative transfer of L1 structures.
   Competency 002

23. **(A)** The correct response is (A). Janie's pronunciation of USB demonstrates negative transfer from Spanish phonology. She approximates the initial u sound using her phonological knowledge from L1, pronouncing it /u/ (ŭ), in contrast to the English /ju/ (ū). (B) is incorrect because no translation is involved. (C) is incorrect because risk-taking refers to linguistic choices that indicate the learner is applying new but incompletely acquired knowledge. (D) is incorrect because the transcription of the conversation suggests that Janie's filter is working—the hesitation, the monosyllabic responses—as she tries to construct meaningful responses.
   Competency 002

24. **(A)** The correct response is (A). Sentence-combining exercises are among the best strategies for promoting learners' syntactic maturity. Teachers can create their own sentence-combining exercises tailored to individual learner needs in their classes, or they can use commercially produced exercises from sentence-combining workbooks. (B) is incorrect because research shows that grammar drills do not result in increased syntactic maturity in writing. (C) is incorrect because correcting DOL sentences will not promote students' ability to generate syntactically complex structures. (D) is incorrect because students need to know how to use conjunctions effectively to improve the syntactic complexity of sentences they generate.
   Competency 005

25. **(B)** The correct response is (B). The essential questions and oral presentations promote critical thinking in the context of communicative competence. (A) is incorrect because it describes the activity but doesn't explain which levels of Bloom's taxonomy it addresses. (C) and (D) incorrectly assess the intent of the activity. No memorization or timelines are necessary for completing the assignment.
   Competency 003

26. **(D)** The correct response is (D). The teacher's visuals are focused on easing students' concerns about asking questions, a problem that persists even in mainstream classes made up only of native speakers. The strategy addresses the learner's affective needs by promoting the learners' confidence and self-assurance about asking questions. (A) and (B) are not addressed as learner needs by the TAC and are therefore incorrect. (C) is incorrect because, while the teacher's strategy may promote students' speaking proficiency, that is a side effect of the targeted goal.
   Competency 009

27. **(C)** The correct response is (C). The 20 or more stipulation comes from the Texas Education Code and is reiterated in the *LPAC Framework Manual*. (A), (B), and (D) are incorrect explanations of how bilingual and ESL programs are implemented in Texas.
   Competency 007

28.   **(A)**   The correct response is (A). The teacher is reinforcing content- area knowledge during oral-reading time. Rereading the books familiarizes the young learners with content-area concepts and vocabulary, but it also causes the listeners to "memorize" the text, which is a good language-learning strategy for beginning ESL students. Filling in words and sentences in a familiar text is also an effective language-learning strategy for this ESL level. (B) is incorrect because the teacher's goal is to reinforce content-area knowledge. (C) is incorrect because the teacher is not trying to simplify content, but to reinforce it. (D) is incorrect because the teacher's goal does not target high-frequency words.
   Competency 006

29.   **(A)**   The correct response is (A). This "silent-viewing" activity is a common strategy for helping students understand how nonverbal cues contribute to communication. In an ELL context, this is an excellent strategy for helping students recognize the meaning provided by nonverbals in L2. (B) suggests that this film-viewing activity is unconnected to learning objectives and is therefore incorrect. (C) is incorrect because elocution usually refers to delivery style and is usually taught by studying the style of famous speakers. (D) is incorrect because staging is important in dramatic presentations (like plays) but not a relevant concern in informal class speeches.
   Competency 003

30.   **(D)**   The correct response is (D). The item stem sums up the operational definition of newcomer programs. (A) is incorrect, although many ESL programs, including newcomer programs, are described as "transitional" because the goal is to support students in their L2 literacy and academic development so that they can move to mainstream classes. (B) is not used in describing ESL programs and so is incorrect. (C) is incorrect because, though it is a term that is very likely used to describe the students in newcomer programs, SIFE does not describe the program itself.
   Competency 008

31.   **(B)**   The correct response is (B). TEA's ELL Web portal, accessible through the TEA home page, assembles a wide variety of state documents, professional resources, and teaching materials. (A) is incorrect because this document presents the TEC and TAC mandates for the LPAC responsibilities. However, it does offer a considerable amount of information about the regulations for ESL programs in Texas. (C) is incorrect because the TEC includes official mandates for ESL programs but no resources. (D) is incorrect because TEKS is the state-mandated curriculum for public schools. No ESL resources are included in TEKS, although English Language Proficiency Standards are appended to TEKS.
   Competency 010

32.   **(A)**   The correct response is (A). By modeling how to create a semantic map, the teacher is providing students with an important content-area learning strategy. (B) puts all the responsibility on the teacher. This response teaches learners to rely on the teacher rather than to use strategies that promote independence. Therefore, (B) is an incorrect response. (C) and (D) do not address the content-area vocabulary problem identified in the stem and are therefore incorrect responses.
   Competency 005

33.   **(C)**   The correct response is (C). This is a class of beginning ESL students. The activity reinforces students' ability to hear how distinct phonemes are combined in blends. (A) is incorrect because a consonant blend does not have meaning on its own. Thus students are not demonstrating knowledge of how meaningful word segments are combined (morphology). (B) is incorrect because students are not learning new meanings or new words. Instead, they are demonstrating that they can recognize the consonant blend sounds. (D) is a related side effect of this ac-

tivity. The students would have to listen very attentively, but the focus of the activity is to promote the students' phonological knowledge *through* an oral language activity.

Competency 005

34. **(B)** The correct response is (B). One of the criteria for exiting an ESL program is the teacher's subjective evaluation. (A) is incorrect because informing parents of students' language proficiency progress as determined by the LPAC is not one of the committee's responsibilities. (C) is incorrect because classroom teachers do not work officially with the LPAC except in situations where the student's scores on state-mandated exams and course grades suggest that the student might be English proficient and thus ready to exit the ESL program. (D) is incorrect because there is no such matrix.

Competency 010

35. **(D)** The correct response is (D). The *LPAC Framework Manual* stipulates that the defining characteristic of the ELL student is whether a language other than English is spoken at home either exclusively or in addition to English. (A) and (B) are incorrect responses because they describe levels of achievement that would be manifested in the classroom and that would be addressed through placement in bilingual and ESL classes. (C) is incorrect because it points to the importance of L1 support in acquiring L2 proficiency, but lack of schooling in L1 is not a consideration in the ELL designation as defined by the *LPAC Framework Manual*.

Competency 007

36. **(A)** The correct response is (A). Because this is a sheltered class, the teacher has an opportunity to use L1 scaffolding to promote students' linguistic as well as academic proficiency. (B) and (D) are not correct because they do not reflect the scenario presented in the item stem. (C) is incorrect because the assignment includes no indication that students should choose a historical figure connected to their homelands.

Competency 009

37. **(B)** The correct response is (B). The letter-writing assignment is designed to elicit introspection, analysis, and synthesis, which will enable students to discover meaningful connections to content-area knowledge. The scenario suggests that the teacher wants students to understand the multicultural dimensions of civil rights. (A) is incorrect because it misrepresents the intent of the assignment. The letter-writing activity provides an opportunity for students to think critically about their own ideas about civil rights. (C) is incorrect because the letter-writing assignment is not designed as an assessment instrument. (D) is incorrect because it does not reflect the parameters of the assignment.

Competency 009

38. **(B)** The correct response is (B). Cultural insularity leads students to assume that body language and gestures have universal meaning. This film-viewing activity is designed to extend students' understanding of the importance of nonverbals in conveying meaning in all cultures. (A) is incorrect because it is a related outcome, but not the focus on the activity. (C) is incorrect because it is an oversimplification of the instructional intent of this assignment. (D) is incorrect because it misdirects the goal of the assignment. This could be illustrated by films that reflect a single culture.

Competency 009

39. **(B)** The correct response is (B). Book talks are a recommended strategy for promoting ELL students' oral-language proficiency. This scenario additionally demonstrates the use of a book talk in a content-area lesson. (A) and (C) do not address oral language proficiency and are therefore incorrect. (D) is incorrect because it lacks the complete speaking/listening/content-area connection that the teacher seems to be interested in making.

Competency 004

40.   **(D)**   The correct response is (D). The writer needs help understanding when to use articles with abstract nouns. Providing a grammar-based explanation is a good strategy for helping the learner overcome this common L1 to L2 difficulty. (A) is incorrect because, while it superficially targets the problem, no viable explanation is offered. (B) is incorrect because L2 development should reflect the writer's increasing syntactic maturity. Telling the writer to avoid "long" sentences is antithetical to promoting L2 competence. (C) is incorrect because the writer needs to develop metacognitive understanding of how complex sentences are formed. The fact that all three sentences reflect the same lack of main clause completion suggests the writer would not be able to self-correct during editing.
Competency 002

41.   **(A)**   The correct response is (A). Moving from hot to cold temperature extremes in this prereading activity is an effective approach in this sheltered class. The teacher is providing abundant scaffolding for meaningful discussion and activation of prior knowledge. (B) could be a follow-up activity for the hot-cold extremes discussion, but the activity described in the stem is focused on activating prior knowledge. Therefore, (B) is an incorrect response. (C) is incorrect because this prereading activity does not directly lead to greater comprehension. (D) is incorrect because, while this is an oral-language activity, it is not aimed at exposing students' shortcomings but at helping students collectively compile a "databank" of what they know about temperature extremes.
Competency 004

42.   **(C)**   The correct response is (C). This short research assignment integrates several language domains within the context of content-area knowledge. (A), (B), and (D) are relevant during or after the actual reading of the story. However, the description of the research activity indicates that the teacher is having students do oral language *prereading* activities to enhance the students' prior knowledge in a highly interactive framework. Therefore, (A), (B), and (D) are all incorrect responses.
Competency 004

43.   **(B)**   The correct response is (B). This response shows attention to the teacher's goal to reinforce content-area learning through oral-language proficiency. Working in groups will promote listening and speaking proficiency. The presentations create a learner-centered context for further promoting listening and speaking skills. (A) is incorrect because simply pronouncing the words correctly does not promote content-area learning. (C) is incorrect because it isolates the words from the content-area context by focusing on spelling. (D) does not address the teacher's goal to combine oral-language development with content-area learning.
Competency 004

44.   **(B)**   The correct response is (B). Intermediate ESL students would need extensive instructional scaffolding to read a challenging literary text. Reading a literary text calls for specialized knowledge, so the teacher would have to focus on accommodations designed to develop students' appreciation of literature. The reinforcement provided by art, music, history, and photographs would contextualize the literary text and create an environment for receiving comprehensible input. (A) is incorrect because the teacher's curricular responsibility is to teach the literary text. Showing a film version introduces the additional responsibility of discussing the differences between the two media and analyzing the adaptation. In other words, response (A) deviates from the primary curricular goal. (C) is incorrect because simply knowing the plot does not constitute reading and understanding a literary text. While this strategy might be included in the teacher's strategies for teaching the novel, it does not provide sufficient accommodation to help the ESL student understand the literary aspects of the text. (D) is incorrect because simply listening to a recording will not provide sufficient accommodation to enable students to understand the literary text.
Competency 002

45. (A) The correct response is (A). Even native speakers find making sense of a literary text a challenging academic activity. By focusing on selected passages from the novel, the teacher would create an opportunity for students to explore the nuances of literary language. Modeling the activity would enable the teacher to connect the author's language to reader perception. The teacher would be focusing on metacognitive strategies necessary for reading a literary text. (B) is incorrect because no accommodation is provided in this strategy. Simply labeling a literary device does not promote students' understanding of literary language. (C) is incorrect because simply reading the text aloud does not promote the specialized knowledge necessary in meaningfully reading a literary text. (D) is incorrect because it does not provide accommodation for language learners who need specialized instruction in the way literary language enables readers to construct meaning.

Competency 002

46. (C) The correct response is (C). Reading a literary text calls for specialized instruction that enables students to access and appreciate the text. Accommodations should promote the learners' language development while making the content (in this case, a literary text) meaningful and accessible. The SDAIE approach is best suited for the pedagogical task described in this scenario. (A) is incorrect because sheltered instruction is usually a school-wide initiative rather than a classroom-specific approach. Nonetheless, literature on ESL sometimes refers to certain classroom activities as being sheltered if the activities include substantive support for language development in the context of content acquisition. In this scenario, however, the class includes native speakers and ESL students, so the sheltered approach would not apply. (B) is incorrect because the students described in this scenario are past the ELD level. (D) is incorrect because typical content-area reading strategies are insufficient for the curricular goal that this teacher needs to meet.

Competency 002

47. (D) The correct response is (D). Because this teacher has a wide range of ESL learner levels in his class, he needs an assignment that can be self-adjusted to individual learner levels. This favorite film assignment would create a strong communicative context (authenticity) while providing opportunities for learners to develop writing, reading, speaking, and listening skills. (A) is incorrect because the assignment calls for informal writing that would not require a full-fledged application of writing processes. (B) is incorrect because, while students will be doing a short oral presentation, the highly personal nature of the assignment makes this an informal speech situation in which interest in the speaker's opinions and explanations should outweigh concerns about correctness. (C) is incorrect because this response does not match the parameters of the assignment.

Competency 001

48. (B) The correct response is (B). Before ELL students can make new words part of their lexicon, they need to understand the meaning and appropriate semantic range of the word. (A) is incorrect because, although it is a common classroom vocabulary activity, it does not encourage students to learn the words and use them meaningfully. (C) actually replicates real-world encounters with new words, but simply scavenging in a text for specific words will not promote students' understanding of the meaning. Therefore, (C) is an incorrect response. (D) is incorrect because it would not indicate whether students actually understand the meanings. Additionally, collage-like activities encourage students to settle for impressionistic or inexact connections to the concepts illustrated by the magazine clippings.

Competency 005

49. (C) The correct response is (C). This response correctly summarizes the procedure explained in the *LPAC Framework Manual*. The manual also states that the terms LEP and ELL are used interchangeably in state documents. (A), (B), and (D) incorrectly present the LEP designation process in Texas.

Competency 007

50. **(C)** The correct response is (C). This is a classic onset-rime activity designed to reinforce the learners' recognition of patterns in L2 words (a descriptor in the cross-curricular knowledge English Language Proficiency Standards). Onset-rime reinforces students' phonological as well orthographic knowledge. (A) is incorrect because the activity is not designed for learning new words. The teacher does not define the words. (B) is incorrect because students are not looking at meaning-creating word parts. (D) is incorrect because onset-rime activities are not intended to teach spelling. Orthographic knowledge may be a side effect, but it is not the primary learning goal.
Competency 003

51. **(B)** The correct response is (B). This response offers a concise summary of classroom accommodations designed to promote students' learning in ESL programs. Scaffolding generally refers to instructional activities that offer guidance while learners acquire new knowledge and which are intended to lead the learner toward independence. (A) and (C) are incorrect because they refer to a traditional classroom activities (testing and film-enriched activities), which do not offer the instructional guidance associated with scaffolding in ESL programs. (D) is incorrect because it describes a type of instructional approach that could be used in some ESL programs, but it does not fit the general definition of instructional scaffolding.
Competency 008

52. **(C)** The correct response is (C). Inviting parents to the library with their children is proactive method of encouraging parents to take advantage of community resources for promoting their children's literacy development. (A) lacks the hands-on aspects of (C) and is therefore incorrect. A flyer offers information but does not show parents the actual library experience as response (C) does and is therefore incorrect. (B) is incorrect because it focuses on teacher efforts, not on families making use of community resources. (D) turns the library experience into a class assignment, not a family and community resources opportunity, and so is an incorrect response.
Competency 010

53. **(D)** The correct response is (D). TELPAS includes Proficiency Level Descriptors identifying ELL students according to their current levels of competence and performance in writing, reading, speaking, and listening. The ratings enable teachers to offer differentiated, formative instruction aimed at moving all learners toward the high advanced level. (A) is incorrect because TELPAS targets learner achievement, not instructional methods. (B) is incorrect because TELPAS ratings are not one of the measures stipulated for determining whether students can be declared English proficient and are ready to exit an ELL program. (C) is incorrect because TELPAS does not report correlations between classroom grades and state-mandated exam scores.
Competency 007

54. **(A)** The correct response is (A). Creating comprehensible input is particularly important in two-way dual-immersion programs where two sets of students are learning two different L2's. These strategies are widely suggested as effective means of making sure all learners understand classroom transactions and new content. (B) is incorrect because listening quietly to something that is incomprehensible does not increase comprehension. (C) and (D) are incorrect because they are counter to the theory and practice of two-way dual-language immersion programs.
Competency 008

55. **(C)** The correct response is (C). A five-minute play allows for complex integration of the four language domains within the context of content-area knowledge. Additionally, this collaborative assignment calls for critical thinking skills (analysis and argument). (A) is incorrect because it addresses the teacher's oral-language goal through the collaborative framework, but focuses only on events in the novel, calling for simple narrative retelling. (B) includes oral language, but it calls for a personal response rather than the higher level thinking of the teacher's goal. (B) is therefore an incorrect response. (D) would likely lead to a summary approach because of the "explains" instruction. A summary would not demonstrate students' understanding of the narrative complexities. Additionally,

this approach lacks the collaborative dimension of (C) and is therefore incorrect.
Competency 004

56.   **(A)**   The correct response is (A). Modeling is considered one of the best methods for teaching writing. (B) is incorrect. Looking at mentor texts is also a good writing-instruction strategy, but simply reading mentor texts will not address the problem identified in the stem. (C) and (D) both evade the core problem presented in the stem. The students will still not know how to write an essay, so they are both incorrect responses.
Competency 005

57.   **(B)**   The correct response is (B). The teacher is starting the science unit with a hands-on activity designed to engage the learners right away and to create prior knowledge. (A) is incorrect because it is probably a side effect of the activity but not the main objective in this academic setting. (C) is incorrect because the students will necessarily talk with each other and probably collaborate in collecting their leaves. (D) is incorrect because following directions is not the objective of this assignment.
Competency 006

58.   **(D)**   The correct response is (D). The scenario states that the teacher wants to promote language proficiency in the context of new science content. This activity addresses that goal and encourages learners to rely on what they observe about their leaves (prior knowledge). (A) is incorrect because limiting the students' use of L1 does not figure into the teacher's objective. (B) is incorrect because the new vocabulary has not yet been introduced. The leaf collecting is a preparatory activity. (C) is incorrect because the activity actually extends the academic environment to areas outside the classroom.
Competency 006

59.   **(A)**   The correct response is (A). The interviews and the short oral reports are designed to integrate the students' home life and cultural background into this content area unit. (B) is incorrect because the assignment doesn't specify that new vocabulary needs to be integrated. However, it is likely that students will use their new content vocabulary. (C) and (D) are incorrect because this is not an assessment activity. The teacher seems interested in creating a classroom community and linking home-life experiences to science content.
Competency 006

60.   **(C)**   The correct response is (C). By integrating parents into classroom scenarios, the teacher is facilitating the ESL students' family involvement in their children's education. (A) is incorrect since it misrepresents the intent of the activity because the classroom is the learning site in this teaching scenario even though parents are now in the mix. (B) is incorrect because it suggests parent involvement is an intentional distraction rather than an integral part of the students' learning experiences. (D) is incorrect since it misrepresents TELPAS goals and misconstrues the intent of the activity described in the item stem.
Competency 010

61.   **(A)**   The correct response is (A). None of the sentences has an independent subject-verb clause. (B) is incorrect because, while it could be argued that the phrase "teacher's quality" probably refers to teachers plural, the form shows that the writer knows the function of apostrophes. (C) is incorrect because the writer demonstrates competence in embedding subordinate structures in longer sentence units. (D) is incorrect because the writer maintains a third-person point of view throughout this short passage.
Competency 001

62.   **(A)**   The correct response is (A). The errors in this passage are all surface-level errors that should be identified and corrected during careful editing. They are also obvious enough to allow learners to feel successful about

finding the errors. (B) is incorrect because revision involves holistic concerns such as focus and development, not simple surface-error correction. (C) is incorrect because the students are not actually writing in this activity. (D) is incorrect because the activity is not designed to assess comprehension.

Competency 007

63. **(D)** The correct response is (D). This response involves parents fully in their children's homework responsibilities. With the awareness that the parents do not have the necessary academic or language background to help their children with homework in traditional ways, the modeling would show parents other ways to participate in their children's homework completion. (A) puts the parent in the role of administrator rather than homework coach. (B) does not show parents how to help their children complete homework assignments. (C) does not take into account the parents' limited L2 literacy and academic proficiency described in the item stem. Therefore, (A), (B), and (C) are all incorrect responses.

Competency 010

64. **(B)** The correct response is (B). Showing this film clip offers a platform for discussing the importance of recognizing and respecting sociocultural differences. (A) is incorrect because film-based pedagogy is not a key feature of ESL instruction or the focus of the activity described in the stem. (C) is incorrect because the teacher is not using this film clip as a kinesthetic activity. (D) is incorrect because a limited film clip does not provide sufficient context to examine reality versus cinematic construction of events.

Competency 009

65. **(B)** The correct response is (B). This is an error-free sentence the complexity of which is explained by response (B). (A) is incorrect because the sentence is not a run-on sentence. (C) is incorrect because there is no redundancy and because redundancy is not a syntactic element. (D) is incorrect because the subordinate structures are correctly punctuated.

Competency 005

66. **(D)** The correct response is (D). This term is not used in reference to bilingual and ESL education programs. It implies a permanence that is counter to the intention of bilingual and ESL programs, which strive to promote student language proficiency so that they can exit the program. (A), (B), and (C) are incorrect responses because they are all described in the Texas Education Code and the TAC as the three of the four types of programs that public schools can implement. Transitional/bilingual late exit is the fourth program.

Competency 008

67. **(A)** The correct response is (A). This passage includes eight "sentences," three of which are actually subordinate constructions that are logical continuations of the previous utterance but have been punctuated as complete sentences. (B) is incorrect because the item stem targets syntactic, not orthographic, problems. (C) is incorrect because, even though subordinate clauses are not connected to the corresponding independent clause, the writer demonstrates competence in using a variety of sentence structures. She starts some sentences with adverbial constructions and embeds subordinate clauses in some of the sentences. (D) is incorrect because the writer demonstrates that she is capable of constructing complete sentences. The problem is her recurrent treatment of subordinate constructions as separate structures.

Competency 001

68. **(C)** The correct response is (C). This passage reflects a competence versus performance situation. Clearly, the writer knows how to generate complex structures. However, she is having difficulty demonstrating her knowledge in written language. A typical error-analysis approach is to have writers read their writing orally because they very likely will self-correct through pronunciation, intonation, or inflection. In Myra's case, the teacher can use the

oral reading to reinforce Myra's understanding of dependent and independent clause relationships. (A) is incorrect because marking student errors without explanation does not promote students' understanding of language forms. (B) is incorrect because Myra's writing provides a perfect opportunity for the teacher to teach grammar in the text of the student's own writing. While correctly completing worksheets may imply students' understanding of grammar, research shows that such "understanding" does not transfer to the writing they generate. (D) is incorrect because the problem is not the topic. The teacher needs to address Myra's confusion over written presentation of subordinate structures.

Competency 001

69. **(A)** The correct response is (A). This response calls for a great deal of learner participation in a collaborative project that will take individual interests and abilities into account as well as provide hands-on learning. (B) is incorrect because the questionnaire itself will not promote student learning. (C) is incorrect because identifying the plants does not lead to understanding of how the biological systems work. (D) is a borderline "teaching to the test" activity. Learners do not need to know *about* the standard. They need to understand meaningfully the knowledge measured by the standard.

Competency 007

70. **(C)** The correct response is (C). This scenario focuses on cooperative learning as a boost to ELL student achievement. Integrating native speakers and ELL in base groups (groups that are maintained for a substantive period rather than just for a specific activity) allows students to bond socially. Those social connections, particularly in an ELL setting, promote learning. (A) is incorrect because random grouping initially inhibits the camaraderie that is at the heart of effective cooperative learning. (B) is incorrect since it isolates and marks ELL students as different and possibly deficient. (D) is incorrect as it is discouraged for almost any cooperative learning scenario, the assumption being that students self-select groups of friends. Additionally, self-selected grouping encourages exclusionary practices that teachers should strive to avoid in any teaching situation, but particularly where ELL students are involved.

Competency 003

ANSWERS SORTED BY DOMAIN AND COMPETENCY

Domain	Competency	Question	Answer	Did You Answer Correctly?
I	1	4	B	
I	1	5	C	
I	1	14	A	
I	1	15	B	
I	1	16	A	
I	1	47	D	
I	1	61	A	
I	1	67	A	
I	1	68	C	
I	2	2	C	
I	2	11	D	
I	2	13	D	
I	2	22	B	
I	2	23	A	
I	2	40	D	
I	2	44	B	
I	2	45	A	
I	2	46	C	
II	3	6	B	
II	3	9	D	
II	3	25	B	
II	3	29	A	
II	3	50	C	
II	3	70	C	
II	4	17	C	
II	4	39	B	
II	4	41	A	
II	4	42	C	
II	4	43	B	
II	4	55	C	
II	5	3	B	
II	5	24	A	
II	5	32	A	
II	5	33	C	
II	5	48	B	

Domain	Competency	Question	Answer	Did You Answer Correctly?
II	5	56	A	
II	5	65	B	
II	6	10	C	
II	6	21	B	
II	6	28	A	
II	6	57	B	
II	6	58	D	
II	6	59	A	
II	7	27	C	
II	7	35	D	
II	7	49	C	
II	7	53	D	
II	7	62	A	
II	7	69	A	
III	8	1	B	
III	8	18	A	
III	8	19	C	
III	8	30	D	
III	8	51	B	
III	8	54	A	
III	8	66	D	
III	9	7	A	
III	9	12	D	
III	9	26	D	
III	9	36	A	
III	9	37	B	
III	9	38	B	
III	9	64	B	
III	10	8	A	
III	10	20	A	
III	10	31	B	
III	10	34	B	
III	10	52	C	
III	10	60	C	
III	10	63	D	

PRACTICE TEST 2

TExES English as a Second Language Supplemental (154)

Also available at the REA Study Center (*www.rea.com/studycenter*)

This practice test is also offered online at the REA Study Center. We recommend that you take the online version of the test to simulate test-day conditions and to receive these added benefits:

- **Timed testing conditions**—helps you gauge how much time you can spend on each question

- **Automatic scoring**—find out how you did on the test, instantly

- **On-screen detailed explanations of answers**—gives you the correct answer and explains why the other answer choices are wrong

- **Diagnostic score reports**—pinpoint where you're strongest and where you need to focus your study

TIME: 5 Hours
          70 Multiple-choice questions

> In this section, you will find examples of test questions similar to those you are likely to encounter on the TExES English as a Second Language Supplemental (154) Exam. Read each question carefully and choose the best answer from the four possible choices. Mark your responses on the answer sheet provided on page 244.

1.   Which of the following statements accurately reflects knowledge, research, and practices involving ESL students' acquisition of academic language proficiency in content areas?

   (A)   Acquiring academic language in L2 is a much longer process than acquiring conversational proficiency in L2.
   (B)   Academic language proficiency is significantly promoted when ESL students are taught in an immersion approach.
   (C)   Academic language proficiency proceeds at a faster rate when teaching focuses on distinct L2 skills rather than holistic teaching.
   (D)   Scaffolded ESL instruction provides immediate increases in content-area proficiency but creates dependent learners in the long run.

2.   As part of each experiment, each student has to write a report explaining the results of the experiment. Because Mr. Sauls wants to ensure that his teaching strategies address English Language Proficiency Standards (ELPS) for writing, he invites an English teacher colleague to conduct a writing workshop as the students complete their reports. Which of the following strategies would best enable Mr. Sauls to meet ELPS expectations for writing?

   (A)   During the workshop, the English teacher reviews each report and marks all errors in spelling, punctuation, and word choice. The students then rewrite the reports reflecting the corrections made by the English teacher.
   (B)   As part of the workshop, students exchange reports for peer editing. Mr. Sauls tells students that they need to find at least five errors in each report they read and correct them for their classmates.
   (C)   Because the ESL students probably lack sufficient vocabulary to write their reports correctly, the English teacher encourages them to write their reports in L1 first and then translate their writing into L2.
   (D)   The English teacher and Mr. Sauls conference using directive and nondirective strategies to help the ESL students describe and explain the results of their experiment in well-written sentences using terminology that reflects their understanding of the science content.

3. Idioms pose particular challenges for ESL students because

    (A) idioms frequently are based on sophisticated allusions that ESL students are not likely to recognize.
    (B) the meaning of idioms cannot be derived from the literal meaning of the component words in the expression.
    (C) idiomatic expressions can be understood only if the speaker knows the genesis of the expression.
    (D) idioms usually have ambiguous meanings.

4. A high school chemistry teacher wants his ELL students to pay more attention to the language of the reports they submit after each experiment. His students seem to understand the procedures and outcomes of each experiment, but their grades are low due to problems in language use and mechanics. Which of the following instructional strategies would best promote ELL students' communicative competence in chemistry assignments?

    (A) The teacher starts putting two separate grades on each experiment: a content grade and a grammar grade.
    (B) The teacher distributes a checklist that students must complete before submitting each report. The checklist includes items such as "I looked up words that I might have misspelled," "I used punctuation correctly," and "I spelled all scientific terms correctly."
    (C) The teacher integrates a writing workshop into each experiment unit. Working in small groups, students share their drafts with each other, conference with the teacher, and revise their work in class.
    (D) The teacher stops taking language use, grammatical correctness, and effective expression into account and scores the reports only on chemistry content.

Use the information below to answer questions 5–7.

A middle school social studies teacher has a sheltered class made up of beginning and intermediate ELL students. To introduce a lesson on different terrains in the United States, he shows slides of deserts, woods, lakes, mountain ranges, river valleys, farmland, mountain valleys, and so on in various parts of the United States.

5. As he shows each scene, he asks students to brainstorm about words suggested by each scene (for example, farmland might elicit words such as *rows*, *neat*, *planning*, *harvest*, and so on) and writes the list on the board. Then he asks for student volunteers to describe each scene orally in a few sentences. This activity primarily supports which of the following ELL instructional goals?

    (A) Students practice oral language in a low-stress class activity
    (B) Students gain new knowledge through activities that develop language and content concepts in a meaningful context
    (C) Students learn new vocabulary by connecting images to word lists
    (D) Students demonstrate comprehension of important content-area knowledge.

6. As a follow-up activity, students brings photographs or illustrations of terrains where they have lived or which they have visited. They write short paragraphs describing the area in the photos. Each student is invited to sit in the Author's Chair and briefly talk about his or her picture. This follow-up activity reflects the funds of knowledge approach in which of the following ways?

    (A) Students discover meaningful connections between class activities and their own experiences.
    (B) In listening to each other, students recognize the broad parameters of the topic covered in class.
    (C) In writing paragraphs about their photographs, students are able to use vocabulary they already know instead of struggling with new content-area vocabulary.
    (D) The writing activity prevents learners from relying on L1 words and sentence patterns.

7. Miguel is a student in this social studies class. He brings a photograph of a small wooden house with a mountain looming in the background. When he is writing his paragraph, he raises his hand to ask the teacher for help. He points to his photograph and says, "Uhmmm . . . Very big mountain. Like fall on the house." What language-learning strategy is Miguel demonstrating in this exchange with the teacher?

    (A) Student-initiated question
    (B) Dependence on teacher support
    (C) Resistance to dictionary usage
    (D) Circumlocution

Use the information below to answer questions 8–11.

> Ms. Eams, a high school history teacher, is starting a unit on the Great Depression. The class is mainstream but includes approximately 50 percent intermediate ELL students. She devises several activities designed to prepare students for learning the new concepts in this chapter.

8. On the first day of the unit, the students walk in to discover the class has been transformed: posters of Great Depression scenes are on the walls; old books written in the 1930s are piled on a desk; copies of newspaper articles from the 1930s are tacked on the bulletin board; a small table is covered with an old table cloth; and the table is set with old dishes. By using this instructional strategy to support ESL students' content-area learning, the teacher

    (A) wants students to imagine what it was like to live in the historical period they are about to study.
    (B) wants to demonstrate that learning history is much more than reading a history book.
    (C) is enhancing the contextual support for new history information.
    (D) wants students to connect the new history content to their own backgrounds and experiences.

9. As an introduction to the unit, Ms. Eams shows clips from several movies set in the Great Depression. After she shows all the clips, she has students work in groups to complete this statement: "The Great Depression was a time when…" She tells students to use details from the film clips to support their response. The content-area learning strategy that this activity promotes is that students will

    (A) demonstrate inductive and deductive reasoning.
    (B) activate prior knowledge by comparing what they see in the clips to their experiences.
    (C) demonstrate how carefully they have read the chapter.
    (D) need to rely on strong content-area vocabulary to complete the assignment.

10. Before having students read the chapter, Ms. Eams organizes the class into groups and assigns one of the 1930s articles to each group. She tells the groups that, as they read the articles, they need to come up with at least three questions about the Great Depression. When the groups make their presentations before the whole class, Ms. Eams writes all the questions on a poster board. How will this activity reinforce students' preparation for reading the chapter content?

   (A) The students will have activated some prior knowledge of the historical period they are about to study.
   (B) Students who have difficulties in content-area reading will still know a fair amount about the new history content.
   (C) Students will know the most important points that will be presented in the chapter.
   (D) Students will develop a broad understanding of major issues in the history unit they are about to study.

11. Which of the following metacognitive strategies will promote students' content-area learning as they read the new information in the chapter?

   (A) The teacher reads the entire first section of the chapter aloud before having students read silently.
   (B) The teacher creates questions that students have to answer for homework.
   (C) The students write short summaries of the information in each section of the chapter.
   (D) The teacher asks students to make a list of new words they encounter in the chapter.

12. The entity that is not officially involved in formation of the Language Proficiency Assessment Committee (LPAC) is

   (A) the local school board.
   (B) the school's parent-teacher association.
   (C) the school district.
   (D) The Texas Education Agency.

13. A second-grade ELL teacher asks her students to bring a special object from home (for example, a toy, a photograph, a book, a gift, and so on). On Story Telling Day, each student describes her or his object and tells the story of why it is special to her or him. Which of the following English Language Proficiency Standards expectations for listening and speaking is best addressed by this instructional activity?

   (A) Narrating, describing, and explaining
   (B) Distinguishing sounds and intonations in English
   (C) Integrating new vocabulary into day-to-day language
   (D) Using grade-level content-area vocabulary

14. The document that is not an official, integral component of bilingual and ESL educational policy in Texas public schools is

   (A) the Texas Education Code.
   (B) the No Child Left Behind Act.
   (C) the Texas Administrative Code.
   (D) the National Center for Education Statistics annual Condition of Education Report.

15. In an elementary class of beginning ESL students from various countries and cultures, which of the following strategies would best help students transfer L1 knowledge to L2?

   (A) The teacher posts pictures of events, artifacts, geographical areas, and foods from the students' culture and labels them in L2 terms.
   (B) The teacher insists that students speak only in L2 throughout the day.
   (C) The teacher adds books in the students' L1 to the class library and has students read in their L1.
   (D) After each read-aloud, the teacher asks for a volunteer to translate the story into his or her own L1.

Use the information below to answer questions 16 and 17.

   Ms. Sierra has a class of beginning to intermediate fifth-grade ESL students. She puts the following assignment on the board.

STATE (verb)

Prefixes	Suffixes	New verb forms	New word forms
un-	-s		
re-	-ed		
	-ing		
	-ment		
	-able		

INSTRUCTIONS: With your group, combine the root word *state* with each of the prefixes and suffixes. Write a sentence correctly using each of the words you created. (You may use the dictionary if you need to.) Pick one sentence to add to our Super Sentences Wall.

16. The area of grammar that this activity focuses on is

   (A) syntax.
   (B) semantics.
   (C) morphology.
   (D) phonology.

17. By having each group report the results to the whole class, Ms. Sierra is promoting her ESL students' language proficiency in which of the following ways?

   (A) By using a simple class activity to assess the students' understanding of affixes
   (B) By giving students the opportunity to increase their L2 competence through authentic oral-language classroom experiences
   (C) By shifting responsibility for L2 learning from the teacher to the students through collaborative work
   (D) By using a collaborative approach instead of independent work to keep students from making errors due to limited L2 proficiency

18. A middle school teacher assigns her class of intermediate ELL students an expository essay on the topic "what responsibility means." As a prewriting strategy, she has each student bring a photograph or an illustration that depicts some aspect of responsibility. Students volunteer to be on a panel to discuss the illustrations they brought. Students in the audience ask questions and make comments as the panelists present their illustrations. This teaching strategy prepares students for the writing task in which of the following ways?

    (A) The panel discussion will trigger students' prior knowledge on concepts related to the essay topic.
    (B) The panel discussion will enable the teacher to determine which students are using original ideas when the essays are submitted.
    (C) The discussion will introduce new vocabulary that students should include in their essays.
    (D) The discussion will ensure that all students include correct information in their essays.

19. A high school teacher has his ESL class listen to excerpts from several types of music: a classical piece, a popular rap song, a country-western song, a classic rock song, and a Mexican *corrido*. Each group picks a song and completes the following sentences about the person who might listen to that song:

    My listener's favorite food is _____.

    My listener usually wears _____.

    My listener drives a _____.

    My listener would never, ever _____.

    My listener's hobby is _____.

    This activity is likely to help students understand that cultural bias is connected to

    (A) different preferences.
    (B) closed-mindedness.
    (C) conflicts between old and young persons.
    (D) stereotyping.

20. A high school ELL student routinely says "supposably" instead of "supposedly." This construction indicates that the student

    (A) does not know how to spell "supposedly."
    (B) is approximating the sounds she hears when other speakers utter the word supposedly.
    (C) is not using her monitor in oral-language production.
    (D) has never seen the word "supposedly" in print; if she had, she would not be mispronouncing it.

Use the information below to answer questions 21 and 22.

Mr. Brentwood is collecting data for his yearly classroom assessment of the ELL students in his middle school science class.

21. Mr. Brentwood records the following notes about Rosario, a recent immigrant currently categorized as an intermediate ELL:

- Never asks questions when I introduce a new assignment. Instead, speaking in Spanish, she turns to ask a classmate.

- During informal class activities, she interacts comfortably with classmates but speaks in Spanish.

- When asked a question during class discussions, she responds monosyllabically.

- In group work, she sits quietly, nonparticipatory, but seems to understand what her group members are saying.

- When asked about incomplete homework assignments, she shrugs her shoulders. If I ask for details, she usually says, "Didn't do it."

This teacher's notes will be useful in making an informal assessment about the student's achievement in

(A) academic language proficiency.
(B) listening and speaking
(C) content-area knowledge
(D) general language proficiency

22. Which of the following adjustments should Mr. Brentwood make in his classroom presentations to promote his ELL students' language development?

(A) Whenever he notices students speaking in Spanish, he should interrupt them, tell them they have to speak in English, and have them come to his desk for reteaching.
(B) As he lectures, he should stop occasionally and ask an advanced ELL student to translate the information for classmates who are having trouble understanding the content.
(C) He should model think-alouds that illustrate how to express understanding, confusion, questions, need for more explanation, and other responses to typical class situations.
(D) He should have a question-and-answer session at the end of each lecture, requiring every student in the class to ask one question.

23. A third-grade teacher in a two-way dual-language immersion program is conducting a geography lesson in her class. She has large pictures of geographical sites such as volcanoes, rivers, rain forests, deserts, canyons, and so on. She gives each group a picture and directions for the geography assignment. Which of the following directions for further class activity would best reflect the characteristics of a two-way dual-language immersion program?

   (A) Each group collaborates in writing a paragraph in English describing their picture.
   (B) Each group creates a T-chart showing words that describe the picture with L1 words on one side and L2 on the other.
   (C) The teacher creates a master list of English words that describe geographical sites. Each group selects the words that fit their picture.
   (D) Each group collaborates in writing a paragraph in L1 describing their picture.

24. Which of the following passages shows correct use of a modal?

   (A) He got his first pen when he was eight. He wrote his first story and felt he had grown up. He felt the story or the words he wrote won't be erased.
   (B) He got his first pen when he was eight. He wrote his first story and felt he had grown up. He felt the story or the words he wrote will not be erased.
   (C) He got his first pen when he was eight. He wrote his first story and felt he had grown up He felt the story or the words he wrote would not be erased.
   (D) He got his first pen when he was eight. He wrote his first story and felt he had grown up He would feel the story or the words he wrote won't be erased.

25. A school district on the Texas-Mexico border has implemented a two-way dual-immersion program to meet federal and state mandates for teaching ELL students. Which of the following statements accurately characterizes a key outcome of this district's approach to ESL instruction?

   (A) Native speakers of English will receive 75 percent of their daily instruction in English.
   (B) ELL students will be taught exclusively in Spanish for most of the day but will have to take all tests and complete all homework assignments in English. Additionally, only English will be allowed during class discussions.
   (C) All learners will acquire proficiency (or developing proficiency) in a second language.
   (D) After one year of two-way dual-immersion classes, ELL students will be automatically moved into English-only classrooms.

26. Parental notification that a student has been classified as an ELL and is recommended for placement in the school district's ESL program comes from

   (A) the Language Proficiency Assessment Committee.
   (B) the student's English language arts teacher.
   (C) the school principal.
   (D) the school district's ESL coordinator.

27. An elementary school teacher wants his beginning ESL class to participate meaningfully in an upcoming science unit on insects. A teaching activity that would be an effective introductory strategy for this science unit would be for the teacher to

(A) show a film on common insects and then ask students to talk about which part they liked best.
(B) conduct a short lecture on misconceptions about insects.
(C) put plastic models of insects all around the room and have each student pick an inset and draw it on a 3 x 5 card and on the back write three words that describe the insect.
(D) arrange the students in a circle and have each student complete the following sentence orally: "I think insects are scary because…."

28. The math and science teachers at a South Texas high school tell their principal that they need guidance in assessing their students' oral-language proficiency for spring TELPAS evaluations. Which of the following strategies would best address the math and science teachers' request?

(A) The principal gives the teachers a packet of materials from the Texas Education Agency.
(B) The principal observes each teacher and gives them critiques on how effectively they are integrating oral language into content-area instruction.
(C) The principal gives the teachers a packet of articles on good ESL teaching practices.
(D) The ESL teachers do a demo during the next faculty meeting to illustrate how oral-language assessment can be integrated into daily class instruction.

29. A high school teacher has a class in which almost all the students are intermediate ELL students. Each day, he presents lessons through lectures followed by an end-of-class quiz. The class has a failing quiz average, so the teacher wants to implement an approach that encourages student achievement. An effective, initial change in this teacher's current approach would be for the teacher to

(A) start posting the quiz-grade average each day and to announce that everyone will get a five-point bonus each time the average goes up by five points.
(B) start using a jigsaw approach with each new chapter. Instead of lecturing, he divides the chapter into sections and makes each group responsible for teaching its assigned section to the class.
(C) divide the lecture into mini-lessons of no more than 10 minutes each. At the end of each mini-lesson, the teacher writers the essential points on the board and asks students to write it in their daily notes.
(D) start making audio tapes of each lesson. He has students listen to each lesson as many times as necessary until they pass the quiz for that lesson.

30. The 1974 Supreme Court Case, *Lau v. Nichols*, is important in the history of bilingual and ESL education in America because the court ruled that

(A) bilingual and ESL programs in American schools must be exclusively and entirely funded through federally granted resources.
(B) all students in America are entitled to an education that guarantees fluency both in English and in at least one other language.
(C) establishing separate but equal educational programs for native speakers and nonnative speakers of English adequately safeguards all students' constitutional rights to fair and equal treatment.
(D) without access to education designed to promote proficiency in English, nonnative English-speaking students could not receive equality of treatment in the delivery of education.

Use the information below to answer questions 31 and 32.

Ms. Gorman, a high school English teacher has a ninth-grade class that includes a significant number of ESL students ranging from newcomer to advanced levels. She is introducing a thematic unit on change as the theme, using a frequently taught poem as the anchor text.

31. On the first day of the unit, she writes the word "CHANGE" in big letters on a poster board. She tells students to complete the following sentence: "To me, change means _____. " She marks off a 3-inch x 5-inch box on the poster and models the activity by writing: "To me, change means that something is different." After students complete their sentences, they briefly explain their sentences to the whole class and write them on the poster board. Which of the following statements best explains how this activity promotes English-language proficiency in the context of the teacher's unit?

    (A) This prereading activity promotes oral-language proficiency by allowing students to focus on shared experiences relevant to the unit theme.
    (B) This comprehension activity gives the teacher an opportunity to create a semantic map using some of the concepts suggested by the students' sentences.
    (C) This writing activity allows students to create a short text (the single sentence), which they can expand into a full essay as a culminating unit activity.
    (D) This grammar activity allows the teacher to correct the sentences as the students post them on the poster board.

32. Which of the following teaching activities would enable Ms. Gorman to promote her ESL students' Cognitive Academic Language Proficiency in this poem-based thematic unit?

    (A) The teacher has students visit an Internet site that provides biographical information on the poet. They then submit a short written report on what they learned about the poet.
    (B) The teacher has students memorize the poem, and, for a quiz grade, has them write the poem from memory.
    (C) The teacher reads the poem aloud, and then rereads it, stopping to explain the metaphors and imagery using photographs and other props that reflect the pivotal images in the poem.
    (D) The teacher has students write a response essay explaining what they like or don't like about the poem.

33. A middle school English teacher is having a writing workshop in which students will work on their essay drafts. The class is a mainstream English class evenly divided among native speakers and intermediate and advanced ESL students. On workshop day, the teacher gives each student three colored pencils and gives the class the following directions:

    • Underline the sentence that you are proudest of having written. This may be a sentence that you are proud of because of how you wrote it (the syntactic structure) or because of what it says (the content).

    • With a different color, circle the single word that you are proudest of having included in your essay.

    • With the third color, circle one or more words that you are unsure of (you think perhaps you are misusing them or you're not sure about the meaning or you're not sure if they fit the sentence, and so on).

After the students complete this activity, the teacher has mini-conferences with her students, listening to them as they explain what they underlined and circled in their drafts. This teaching activity reflects the teacher's interest in promoting her ESL students' language proficiency in which of the following ways?

(A) The teacher wants her students to develop independence as writers.
(B) The teacher is providing her students an opportunity to demonstrate metacognitive awareness of their language choices.
(C) The teacher wants to make sure that her students use in-class workshopping to correct their sentences and word choices.
(D) The teacher wants students to understand that every sentence they write must be correctly structured and effectively worded.

34. An elementary school teacher gives her beginning ESL students the following directions:

   • Form your reading circles in your usual areas.

   • Tell your reading circle partners your birth date (month, day, and year).

   • Talk with your reading circle partners to figure out who has the earliest birthday in the year.

   • Whoever has the earliest birthday hands out the reading circle books today.

   The ESL teaching method that this classroom interaction activity reflects is

   (A) total physical response.
   (B) immersion.
   (C) basic interpersonal communicative skills.
   (D) pragmatics.

35. In an elementary class of beginning ELL students, the teacher wants to introduce more writing. However, many of her students live in homes where only L1 is spoken. Consequently, they have not yet developed sufficient L2 vocabulary to write complete sentences. Which of the following strategies would best promote these students' writing development?

   (A) The teacher has each student pick his or her favorite book from the class library. Each student has to copy five sentences from the book into his or her writing notebook.
   (B) The teacher has an Author's Chair day. Each student brings a favorite toy and tells a story about it. After the student tells the story of the favorite toy, the teacher writes a one-sentence summary and has all the students copy it into their writing notebooks.
   (C) The teacher organizes the class into writing circles. Each group picks an object out of the class surprise box. Each writing circle writes a storybook, with illustrations, about the object they picked. Each group presents their story to the whole class.
   (D) The teacher concentrates on reading until students acquire sufficient vocabulary and syntax knowledge to write meaningful sentences.

36. A high school teacher wants his ELL students to understand the importance of using vivid details in writing that describes or explains. Which of the following instructional strategies would best enable students to recognize the power of details in writing?

    (A) The teacher hands out a short passage from a story the class has recently read and asks students to highlight sensory details in green and explanations in yellow.

    (B) During a writing workshop, the teacher puts students in groups of three. The students are to read each other's drafts and underline every detail in the draft. If the peer readers cannot identify any details in their group members' drafts, the writer has to add details.

    (C) Group members collaborate in writing a three-minute description of a chocolate chip cookie. The teacher collects all the descriptions and redistributes them to different groups. Then, he collects all the cookies and arranges them on the front desk. The students try to match the descriptions to the cookies.

    (D) The teacher gives each group of students a simple verb (for example, run, walk, talk, sit, look). Each group is asked to come up with five different synonyms for their assigned verb. Each group picks one of their new words and acts it out for the class.

37. A high school history teacher realizes that his ELL students are having significant difficulties in understanding the content of each new chapter. To introduce the next chapter, he creates an outline of the key points. Prior to starting the chapter, he projects the outline on the overhead and has students copy the outline. Which of the following adjustments should the teacher make to this activity to promote his students' better understanding of history content?

    (A) After they finish copying the outline, the teacher should have several students read the outline orally.

    (B) As a next step, the teacher should model how to create a graphic organizer connecting the key concepts in the outline.

    (C) After the students finish copying the outline, the teacher should check all the outlines to ensure the students copied everything correctly.

    (D) As a next step, the teacher should give students time to work in groups to discuss the outline and then administer a quiz to determine the students' understanding.

38. The following verb forms occur in an essay written by a fifth-grade ESL student:

haded	knowed	ated
thinked	knewed	runned
breaked	broked	had

    These forms indicate that the student

    (A) is overgeneralizing in his use of the past morpheme.

    (B) has limited understanding of verb tense forms in English.

    (C) has not yet internalized rules for irregular verb forms in English.

    (D) lacks phonological understanding to recognize that the -ed suffix sounds "wrong" when attached incorrectly.

39. A teacher is using literature circles in her third-grade ESL class. Which of the following explanations offers the best rationale for promoting literacy through literature circles?

    (A) Because the groups select the text they want to read, the students' interest level in reading is higher.
    (B) Literature circles allow the teacher to integrate more texts into the curriculum.
    (C) Literature circles are based on books that are simple to read, so students have an easier time doing the required work.
    (D) No reading skills are addressed in literature circles, so students enjoy the activity far more than routine reading lessons.

40. Early in the school year, a middle school ESL teacher gives each student a 4 x 6 card and makes the following assignment:

    > On the blank side, please write in large letters a single word that you think describes you perfectly. On the ruled side, write a little story or just a paragraph explaining how and why that word fits you. The word you pick can be either in English or in Spanish.

    After the students complete their cards, the teacher has each student read his or her statement. Then the teacher posts all the cards, word side showing, on the class community board. Which of the following components of creating and maintaining an effective multicultural learning environment does this activity primarily promote?

    (A) By sharing information about themselves, the students will work more effectively in groups.
    (B) By sharing information about themselves, students will develop awareness of and respect for each other's cultural diversity.
    (C) By displaying the cards on the board, the teacher will have readily available examples of L1 and L2 words for grammar and writing lessons.
    (D) By having students read their statements orally, the teacher will establish a baseline for tracking students' speaking skills throughout the year.

Use the information below to answer questions 41 and 42.

A high school teacher is preparing her ELL class for the state-mandated writing exam. She wants to familiarize her students with the format of the writing exam as well as to teach them writing-on-demand strategies.

41. The teacher creates a prompt modeled on the state-mandated writing exam. She leads a discussion on how to break down the topic and do quick planning. To most effectively promote students' understanding of the writing task, the teacher

    (A) does a think-aloud and a demonstration of how she would respond to the prompt, writing her response in front of the class.
    (B) tells students that the exam will require quick writing. She distributes new prompts and gives students 15 minutes to write an essay.
    (C) breaks students into groups and has each group create a collaboratively written essay.
    (D) arranges the class into a large circle. She composes a starting sentence for the essay. In a round-robin approach, each student in the circle contributes a sentence to the developing essay.

42. After the introductory activity, the teacher writes a new prompt on the board. Students are given a class period to respond to the selected prompt. Which of the following would be a good next step in meeting the teacher's goal?

    (A) Students take the drafts home to revise them and submit them the next day for a grade.
    (B) The teacher collects the essays written in class, scores them, and returns them to the students the next day.
    (C) The teacher collects the essays, covers each name with a label, and distributes the essays for students to score using a rubric based on the state-mandated expectations.
    (D) The next day, the teacher has one-to-one conferences with each student to point out the problems in the student's essay.

43. The fundamental purpose of federal and state regulations regarding ESL education is to

    (A) provide equal educational opportunities for all learners.
    (B) develop a citizenry that is fluent in English.
    (C) promote English as the official language of the United States.
    (D) reduce immigrant students' dependence on L1 in everyday social and academic activities.

44. A sixth-grade teacher creates a lesson focused on Sandra Cisneros's story "My Name" and Alice Walker's story "Everyday Use." She introduces the unit with the following book talk:

    These stories present characters who have issues with their names. Esperanza, a Hispanic girl, is named after her grandmother, but she says the syllables in her name feel like they're made of tin and hurt the roof of your mouth. In the end, she says she would like to change her name. In the other story, Dee, a young African American woman, is also named after her grandmother. She changes her name to "Wangero" after she goes to college and studies the civil rights movement.

    After the students read the stories, the teacher leads a class discussion starting with these questions:

    • Why are their names so important to these characters?

    • In what ways are their names more than just names?

    On her lesson plan, the teacher includes an explanation of how this unit addresses important concerns in ESL teaching. The best rationale is that the discussion

    (A) demonstrates the importance of using prior knowledge to launch a literature unit.
    (B) fosters students' respect for cultural and linguistic diversity.
    (C) encourages students to talk about the stories surrounding their own names.
    (D) illustrates the connection between names and individual identity.

45. Which of the following is a cornerstone of dual-language immersion programs?

    (A) All students in the program develop language proficiency in both L1 and L2.
    (B) Paired with one or more L1 students, L2 students serve as literacy coaches for the nonnative speakers.
    (C) The curriculum is modified, allowing teachers to reduce the amount of content-area material that needs to be taught in both languages.
    (D) Dual-immersion programs extend only through the end of elementary grades because the increasing complexity of content is impossible to address in the two-language framework.

46. In an essay, a high school student wrote the following sentence: "I am sitting in class, the geometry teacher up front droning like a cicada on a summer evening." Which of the following terms describes the underlined part of this sentence?

    (A) Absolute
    (B) Subordinate clause
    (C) Participle phrase
    (D) Misplaced modifier

47. A high school ESL teacher is having students take turns reading aloud. Every time someone stumbles or hesitates over a word, the students who know the correct pronunciation laugh at the reader. The teacher continues the read-aloud, but the next time someone laughs at a mispronounced word, she stops and says: "Reading aloud can be scary. You're on the spot. You're sort of performing. Let's listen politely and pay attention to the words we are reading, not to words we're hearing. And if you want to help your classmate, instead of laughing, how about saying the word he or she is trying to pronounce?" The teacher's actions focus on which of the following ESL learner needs?

    (A) By choosing to explain instead of rebuke, the teacher is supporting the students' affective learning domain.
    (B) By continuing the read-aloud, the teacher is demonstrating that linguistic growth occurs by working through a problem independently.
    (C) By choosing not to embarrass the students who are laughing, the teacher is promoting a sense of camaraderie among the students.
    (D) The teacher is supporting the cognitive domain; instead of focusing on the students who are laughing, the teacher keeps the students' concentration on the content.

48. The list that best reflects research- and practice-based instructional practices designed to create educational equity for ESL students is

    (A) grammar drills, frequent testing, and limited L1 support.
    (B) students' prior knowledge, scaffolding, and collaborative work.
    (C) oral-language precedence, simplified curriculum, and targeted teaching to standardized tests.
    (D) parental involvement, curricular accommodations, and L2 immersion.

49. A teacher is using writing circles in her fifth-grade ESL class. She adjusts the typical writing circle framework to have students create stories based on family history and events. She gives the class the following assignment:

> I want each of you to ask a parent or another relative to tell you a story about an important event or person in your family. Make sure you write down some of the details, but you don't have to write down the whole story unless you want to. In class tomorrow, you will work in your literature circles to pick one story to turn into a book that you illustrate and then present to the whole class. Then we will turn our stories into short plays and invite your parents to see your plays.

Which of the following tenets of effective ESL instruction does this class activity primarily address?

(A) The teacher is conveying to students the importance of looking for story material in familiar environments.
(B) The teacher is creating an assignment that integrates reading, writing, speaking, and listening.
(C) The teacher is promoting family involvement in ESL students' education.
(D) The teacher is taking into account the diversity of student abilities; students will be able to collaborate on art, writing, and presentation.

50. A school district has an ESL program in which ELL students are integrated with English speakers for core academic course instruction in L2. The program components include biliteracy, biculturalism, and cross-cultural awareness, but the focus is to provide targeted L2 instruction that promotes academic achievement and L2 proficiency among ELL students. For which ESL education model does this program meet the criteria?

(A) Home-language enrichment
(B) Two-way dual-language immersion
(C) One-way dual-language immersion
(D) Mainstreaming

Use the information below to answer questions 51–53.

Mr. Christopher, a middle school social studies teacher, has a mainstream class that includes a large number of intermediate ESL students. His ESL students are having trouble understanding the basic information in each chapter. Ms. Caranza, a colleague who teaches ESL classes, suggests two things: that he break up his lectures into mini-lessons, and that he create groups that include two or more native speakers in each group and allow students to network with each other after each mini-lesson.

51. The language-learning scaffold that Ms. Caranza's advice to Mr. Christopher reflects is

(A) syllabus-based instruction.
(B) reliance on universal grammar.
(C) the zone of proximal development.
(D) holistic assessment.

52. The value of mini-lessons in helping ESL learners acquire content knowledge is that

   (A) mini-lessons are short in order to keep ESL students from getting bored when they don't understand.
   (B) mini-lessons enable the teacher to divide a lesson into manageable "chunks" of information to help students receive comprehensible input.
   (C) in mini-lessons, difficult concepts are omitted, so even beginning ESL learners are able to understand.
   (D) mini-lessons are delivered very quickly so that the teacher is able to cover a lot more information in a class session.

53. Mr. Christopher plans to use Ms. Caranza's mini-lesson and networking suggestion to promote his ESL students' understanding of social studies content. Which of the following additional classroom activities would help him meet his goal?

   (A) After each networking session, each group offers the following report to the whole class: "We think the most important information in this mini-lesson is _____, but we want more explanation of _____."
   (B) Before each networking session, Mr. Christopher asks each student to write down one word she or he doesn't understand, and he creates a class list of vocabulary words.
   (C) As part of each networking session, students silently reread the section of the chapter just covered in the mini-lesson.
   (D) At the end of each networking session, each student writes a paragraph summarizing the information in the mini-lesson.

54. A teacher is conducting a read-aloud session in a sixth-grade language arts class. George is a newcomer ESL student. When it's his turn to read, the teacher says, "George, how about continuing where Aimee left off?" George says, "No, thank you." George's response can be explained by which of the following language concepts?

   (A) Register
   (B) Semantics
   (C) Monitor hypothesis
   (D) Pragmatics

55. An English teacher reads aloud a chapter from a novel to her middle school ESL students. The chapter is about Rey, a Hispanic boy, who jumps out of a tree to prove to his friends that he's a man. The chapter includes quite a few sentences that show code switching between English and Spanish as the narrator muses about how he has to jump to fulfill cultural expectations. At the end of the read-aloud, the teacher asks, "How many of you have done something similar to what Rey did?" She invites students to share their stories. This teaching activity creates a multicultural learning environment primarily by

   (A) showing students that even a simple childhood event can be turned into a story.
   (B) encouraging ESL students to talk comfortably in a classroom oral-language activity.
   (C) showing students connections between shared common childhood experience and culturally driven behaviors.
   (D) showing students how integrating L1 is essential to presenting an experience in L2 effectively.

Use the information below to answer questions 56 and 57.

Mr. Sauls teaches a high school biology class made up of native speakers and intermediate to advanced ESL students. A good bit of the course work involves conducting experiments in class by following written directions provided by the teacher. Students work collaboratively on each experiment.

56. Mr. Sauls notices that each time a new experiment is assigned, the ESL students turn away from their assigned groups and talk in their native language with the other ESL students. Which of the following strategies would most effectively support the teacher's goal to use collaborative work to promote his ESL students' language competence?

   (A) The teacher tells the ESL students that to learn science content, they must speak in English rather than in their L1.
   (B) The teacher restructures the groups to include two or more ESL students in each group.
   (C) Using an Internet translation tool, the teacher translates the experiments into the students' L1.
   (D) The teacher moves from group to group and reads the instructions orally to each group.

57. Which of the following teaching activities would enable Mr. Sauls to promote his ESL students understanding of science content?

   (A) To help the students understand the scientific concepts addressed by the hands-on experiments, Mr. Sauls has the ESL students read elementary-level books on the relevant science concepts.
   (B) Before the next experiment, Mr. Sauls schedules a computer lab period so that ESL students can search for information on the experiment on websites in their native language.
   (C) Before the next experiment, Mr. Sauls models a similar experiment and posts illustrations throughout the room to reinforce the ESL students' understanding of the procedures.
   (D) Before the next experiment, Mr. Sauls administers a pretest to predict areas in which students may have comprehension problems.

Use the information below to answer questions 58 and 59.

Mr. Reyes teaches fourth grade in a South Texas school district. He wants to create a multicultural and multilingual environment in his math classes. One day, he brings in materials for students to make their own *piñatas*. Mr. Reyes creates a math unit structured around the *piñatas* as manipulatives.

58. In what primary way does the introduction of the *piñatas* contribute to creating a multicultural and multilingual environment?

   (A) The students will be unable to talk about the *piñatas* in English and will have to use Spanish.
   (B) The students will want to talk in Spanish, and this will provide the teacher an opportunity to direct the students into English-only math.
   (C) Because he is using *piñatas* as props, the teacher will have to create the math problems in Spanish.
   (D) The math lessons the teacher creates around the *piñatas* will connect students' funds of knowledge to academic course content.

59. Mr. Reyes writes math problems such as the following on posters and displays them at the front of the classroom. Students work in groups to solve the problems and explain their calculations.

> • Imagine that your *piñata* has to be shipped to Kearney, Nebraska. What size mailing box would have to be used? Report the size in length, height, and width and be ready to explain how you got your answer.
>
> • Assuming that each piece of candy in the *piñata* is about one cubic inch in size, how many candies will it take to fill your *piñata* half full? Three-fourths full? Work with your group members to make sure you can explain to the whole class how you got your answers.

Which of the following explanations best addresses how Mr. Reyes's use of the *piñatas* can facilitate students' cognitive learning and language acquisition in math?

(A) The students will work harder because they will understand what Mr. Reyes is talking about.

(B) Using the *piñatas* as props, the teacher will be able to create simpler math problems than those in the book.

(C) Using a culturally relevant artifact will heighten the students' participation and learning potential in this math lesson.

(D) The students will be able to solve the problems because they will not have to use difficult math formulas. Instead, they can base their answers on past experience.

60. A high school teacher wants to promote his ELL students' vocabulary development but does not want to administer vocabulary tests. To best meet his literacy development goal, the teacher

(A) has students pick vocabulary slips out of a box. Each student creates an illustrated poster to introduce her or his word to the whole class.

(B) makes a list of challenging words from the class texts and has students guess at the meaning of the words.

(C) makes a list of challenging words from the class texts and has students find where the words occur in those texts.

(D) posts a new-word-a-day calendar and has a student volunteer read the word of the day at the beginning of each school day.

61. ESL teachers at a high school with a sheltered instruction program present a workshop on Effective Teaching Strategies for Promoting ESL Student Success in All Content Areas. The workshop is a response to content-area teachers' concerns about not knowing how to adjust their teaching to meet ESL students' needs. Which of the following additional advocacy activities would best enable the ESL teachers to improve their content-area colleagues' instructional effectiveness?

(A) The ESL teachers team teach one or two classes with the content-area teachers to demonstrate how to accommodate instruction and integrate ESL strategies.

(B) The ESL teachers tell the content-area teachers to avoid difficult vocabulary and to repeat everything multiple times because ESL students have trouble hearing things correctly.

(C) The ESL teachers tell the content-area teachers that ESL students often lack parental support in challenging academic areas and explain that this very likely explains students' low achievement in content areas.

(D) The ESL teachers give the content-area teachers several books on teaching ESL.

Use the information below to answer questions 62 and 63.

A high school teacher is having a writing conference with Ana, an advanced ELL student.

62. The teacher asks a question about a sentence in the draft. The student writer responds, "*Pues* I was reading the sample essay. It had a sentence like this one." The student's utterance is an example of

   (A) interference.
   (B) transfer.
   (C) word coinage.
   (D) code-switching.

63. To most likely promote the student's oral-language competence, the teacher

   (A) makes the student repeat the utterance until she uses only L2 language.
   (B) corrects the student orally and has her write down the corrected L2 version.
   (C) doesn't say anything because the insertion of the L1 word does not interfere with the speaker's communicative intent.
   (D) repeats the sentence, correcting the student's L1 usage and tells her never to use L1 words in L2 utterances.

64. In assigning listening and speaking class activities, an ESL teacher needs to take into account individual differences in language and culture because

   (A) in a class with diverse languages and cultures represented, the teacher needs to figure out how to get everyone to understand each other.
   (B) culturally based behavioral and social norms impact oral-language interactions in the class environment.
   (C) most ESL students are very uncomfortable about speaking in public.
   (D) rates of oral-language acquisition vary significantly among individual students.

65. The following sentences are from a high school student's essay about the day he and his classmates made a teacher cry.

> Instead of starting the new lesson like we did every day, she asked us what we thought about her and her teaching. That's when an explosion of comments erupted out of us like lava flowing from a volcano.

Which of the following terms is the best label for the underlined phrase?

(A) Hyperbole
(B) Imagery
(C) Simile
(D) Alliteration

66. Which of the following establishes the federal foundation for ESL programs in Texas schools?

(A) Public Law 107-110 (Elementary and Secondary Education Act)
(B) The U.S. Department of Education
(C) The Texas Education Agency
(D) The Texas English Language Proficiency Assessment System (TELPAS)

67. In an upper elementary class of beginning to intermediate ESL students, the teacher displays the following exercise on the overhead.

> Look at this set of sentences. With your group members, come up with a "rule" that explains a sentence structure that you see repeated in all of the sentences.
>
> • Growing up, I spent a lot of summers with my grandparents in Mexico.
>
> • On my grandparents' ranch, the mesquite trees, dirt piles, and watering holes were my playground.
>
> • Almost every day, I would wake up with the first light, gobble my breakfast, and dash outside.
>
> • At the end of the summer, it was time to return to my home in Texas.

This teaching activity is designed to address which of the following cognitive processes in L2 acquisition?

(A) Syntactic variation
(B) Generalization
(C) Transfer
(D) Error analysis

68. Toward the end of the first grading period of the year, a middle school teacher makes the following assignment in her ESL class:

> I want you to write a short letter to your parents. Write a letter that your parents will understand, so you can write in either English or Spanish or a combination. From your perspective, tell your parents the highlights of this six. Write neatly. Use some details. You might want to add illustrations in the margins. You need to give your letters to your parents. Tomorrow, we will spend some time talking about what your parents said about your letter.

The primary purpose of this assignment is to

(A) provide an authentic writing experience for the students.
(B) create an opportunity for students to self-assess their progress.
(C) communicate with ESL students' parents or guardians regarding school activities.
(D) measure the level of parental interest in ESL student educational activities.

69. Which of the following statements best summarizes the way an ELL teacher can use results of mandated assessment to improve student achievement in the classroom?

(A) Although scores on mandated state exams provide summative assessment data, teachers can use information about performance in discrete areas of the exams to devise formative assessments embedded in day-to-day class activities.
(B) Because mandated state exams create a great deal of anxiety among teachers and students, the teacher should concentrate on improving students' comprehension of academic content instead of integrating state testing requirements.
(C) Because state exams are high stakes for students and teachers, teachers should revise their curriculum to cover only material included on the mandated exams.
(D) Teachers should adapt all course content to reflect the format of state assessments and administer benchmarks every few weeks.

70. An elementary school teacher is planning to introduce a new read-aloud story to a class of beginning and intermediate ELL students. Which of the following prereading strategies would best enable students to understand new vocabulary in the story?

(A) The teacher posts a list of new words and has students look them up prior to the read-aloud.
(B) The teacher posts labeled illustrations of the new words, with each illustration showing the new word in large letters. The teacher explains each new word prior to the read-aloud.
(C) Prior to the read-aloud, the teacher has students skim through the story and write down all the words they don't know.
(D) The teacher gives the students a short summary of the new story prior to the read-aloud and tells the students that once she starts the read-aloud, they should raise their hands each time they hear a word they don't know.

PRACTICE TEST 2 ANSWER KEY

1. (A)	19. (D)	37. (B)	55. (C)
2. (D)	20. (B)	38. (A)	56. (B)
3. (B)	21. (D)	39. (A)	57. (C)
4. (C)	22. (C)	40. (B)	58. (D)
5. (B)	23. (B)	41. (A)	59. (C)
6. (A)	24. (C)	42. (C)	60. (A)
7. (D)	25. (C)	43. (A)	61. (A)
8. (C)	26. (A)	44. (B)	62. (D)
9. (A)	27. (C)	45. (A)	63. (C)
10. (A)	28. (D)	46. (A)	64. (B)
11. (C)	29. (C)	47. (A)	65. (C)
12. (B)	30. (D)	48. (B)	66. (A)
13. (A)	31. (A)	49. (C)	67. (B)
14. (D)	32. (C)	50. (C)	68. (C)
15. (A)	33. (B)	51. (C)	69. (A)
16. (C)	34. (A)	52. (B)	70. (B)
17. (B)	35. (C)	53. (A)	
18. (A)	36. (C)	54. (D)	

PRACTICE TEST 2 ANSWER EXPLANATIONS

1.   **(A)**   The correct response is (A). Practitioners agree that ESL students face an almost daunting task in acquiring general L2 proficiency and content-area knowledge. The task is even more complex for ESL students whose L1 academic background is limited or nonexistent. (B) is incorrect because the immersion approach is generally not considered a learner-centered approach to developing content-area proficiency. (C) is incorrect because ESL experts agree that whole-to-part teaching allows students to develop L2 understanding much more effectively than working "up" through distinct skills. (D) is incorrect because scaffolding is generally considered an excellent means of supporting ongoing learning in ESL.
     Competency 006

2.   **(D)**   The correct response is (D). Conferencing is considered the best method for promoting student competence in writing. As a team, the English teacher and the science teacher could guide the students in using the required written report to reflect their understanding of science content. A good mix of directive conferencing (where the teachers directly explain how to correct errors) and nondirective (where the teachers encourage students to explain their linguistic choices) would help students meet ELPS expectations. (A) is incorrect because marking errors and having students make corrections does not address the level of learner independence suggested in ELPS expectations for writing. (B) is counter to the expectations for a writing workshop environment: peer editing should never be reduced to error hunting. (C) is incorrect because the students in this scenario are at the intermediate and advanced levels, far beyond the proficiency levels where they might have relied on translation from L1 to L2. This approach would be a step back for the learners.
     Competency 001

3.   **(B)**   The correct response is (B). This response accurately explains the root cause of confusion over idioms—expressions that have language-specific meaning, usually figurative, sometimes illogical, that cannot be traced to the semantic and lexical features of the component words (for example, *hit the spot, starting from scratch, can of worms, dog eat dog*, and so on). Typical meaning-constructing strategies, like dictionary definitions, context, and prediction, do not apply with idioms. (A) and (C) are incorrect because, while some idioms can, in fact, be traced to historical or literary origins, knowing the origin is not a necessary part of knowing what the idiom means. (D) is incorrect because, despite the lack of literal meaning in the words themselves, idioms are usually very specific and limited in meaning.
     Competency 002

4.   **(C)**   The correct response is (C). By integrating a writing-improvement strategy, the teacher is creating an environment for improved competence in this content-area class. (A) is incorrect because assigning separate content and writing grades does not address the problem that the teacher has identified. In fact, this strategy ignores the problem. (B) is incorrect because checklists encourage passive attention to the learning task. The problem that the teacher has identified needs to be addressed with interactive, learner-centered tasks. (D) also fails to provide a solution to the students' language-use problems in writing about chemistry. This strategy ignores the problem and so is incorrect.
     Competency 003

5.   **(B)**   The correct response is (B). This item focuses on promoting content-area knowledge in *beginning* and *intermediate* ELL students. The scenario creates a meaningful learning experience for students by integrating listening and speaking proficiencies in the context of prior knowledge. (A) misrepresents the ELL teaching possibilities: oral language should not be "practiced" but should instead be used authentically to promote learning. (C) is incor-

rect because new vocabulary is not the focus of this activity. (D) is incorrect because the activity is not focused on comprehension. It is more of a prereading strategy.

Competency 003

6.   **(A)**   The correct response is (A). The funds-of-knowledge approach values learners' background knowledge and integrates home and other life experiences into classroom environments. (B) suggests that the teacher is using the photograph activity to extend the learners' view of the topic. While comprehensive understanding will likely result, the core intent is to help ELL students connect life experience to class experience. (C) and (D) misrepresent the value of writing as a means of promoting language proficiency in a meaningful context.

Competency 003

7.   **(D)**   The correct response is (D). Circumlocution is a common communication strategy used in L2 acquisition: the learner knows the meaning but hasn't yet acquired the corresponding L2 word. (A) refers to the basic communication strategy that the learner is using, not to a language-learning strategy. (B) misrepresents the learner's strategy. Calling the teacher over suggests the learner sees the teacher as a resource for advancing his L2 understanding, not as a crutch. (C) is incorrect because it would be impossible for the learner to look up a word that is not yet in his lexicon.

Competency 003

8.   **(C)**   The correct response is (C). The transformation of the classroom is the teacher's attempt to expand the context of the content-area material. Instead of just relying on the textbook material, the students will now have realia, visuals, and artifacts to support their new-content learning. (A) is close but not the correct response. The artifacts simply provide context, not a simulation of living in the time period. (B) is a side effect of the teacher's strategy, but it does not reflect the teacher's goal. The transformation of the classroom is not intended to reduce the importance of thorough reading of content-area material. (D) is incorrect because the scenario described here does not take the learners' background into account.

Competency 006

9.   **(A)**   The correct response is (A). Viewing the video clips *before* reading the chapter will allow students to draw inferences and reach conclusions about the period using inductive and deductive reasoning. Giving the students a question to respond to facilitates the integration of higher-order thinking skills called for in this assignment. (B) is incorrect because the students' prior knowledge is very likely limited. In fact, viewing the film clips will create familiarity with the content. (C) is incorrect because this is an introductory strategy, not a postreading assessment. (D) is incorrect because vocabulary development is not the focus of this film-clip-viewing activity.

Competency 006

10.   **(A)**   The correct response is (A). In having students read articles written during the historical period and generate questions, the teacher is helping students develop prior knowledge about the new content material they are about to study. (B) is incorrect because this is not a reading comprehension strategy. (C) and (D) are incorrect because the contemporary newspaper articles are not intended as a preview of chapter content.

Competency 006

11.   **(C)**   The correct response is (C). Writing short summaries of new material presented in chapter sections is considered an important metacognitive strategy for supporting new learning. Metacognition involves knowing how to think about new learning and how to promote retention of new information. (A) and (B) are incorrect because these are teacher-generated activities. Metacognition means that the learner is implementing thinking strategies that promote her or his understanding of the content. (D) is incorrect because simply making a list of new content-area vocabulary is not a metacognitive strategy.

Competency 006

12. **(B)** The correct response is (B). The LPAC is sanctioned by state mandate. The school's parent-teacher association is not officially included in any LPAC-related guidelines. (A), (C), and (D) all play a role in the LPAC as described in the TEC and TAC.

Competency 010

13. **(A)** The correct response is (A). This activity clearly addresses the ELPS that states that ELL students are expected to narrate, describe, and explain with increasing specificity. (B), (C), and (D) target phonology, suprasegmentals, and vocabulary development, but the activity focuses on discourse production.

Competency 004

14. **(D)** The correct response is (D). Bilingual education policies are impacted by federal and state court cases, laws, and codifications. The NCES annual report offers statistics on important aspects of education in American schools, but it is not a policy-setting document. (A), (B), and (C) are all integrally connected to bilingual and ESL policy in Texas public schools.

Competency 008

15. **(A)** The correct response is (A). Seeing images of things they are familiar with and seeing L2 labels will help these young students start transferring their L1 literacy knowledge to new L2 learning. Environmental L2 print, coupled with familiar L1 concepts and scenes, would create a meaningful learning environment for these young learners. (B) is incorrect because it targets the ESL students as delinquents if they slip into L1. (C) keeps students in the comfort and safety of L1. (D) is incorrect because translating an L2 text to L1 does not address the teacher's goal to help students transfer L1 knowledge to create L2 meaning.

Competency 005

16. **(C)** The correct response is (C). The exercise is intended to develop students' practical application of morphological knowledge by giving them an opportunity to combine a root word (state) with inflectional affixes (which change the form of the verb) and with derivation morphemes (which change the part of speech or meaning of the root word). (A) reflects attention to sentence structure. (B) reflects attention to meaning. (D) reflects attention to sounds. Therefore, (A), (B), and (D) are incorrect responses.

Competency 001

17. **(B)** The correct response is (B). By having the students report the results of their collaborative efforts, the teacher is integrating oral-language development into the lesson. To complete the exercise effectively, students would have to consult in their groups, write possible sentences, negotiate about the sentences they construct, and select a group representative to report the results of their effort before the whole class. (A) is incorrect because the exercise is not intended as an assessment instrument. (C) and (D) are incorrect because they inaccurately depict the purpose of collaborative class activities. In a well-constructed collaborative environment, the teacher participates as a coach and resource. Collaboration is intended to increase learner interest in class activities by showing how sharing ideas promotes new learning.

Competency 001

18. **(A)** The correct response is (A). In asking students to bring photographs and talk about them in the panel format, the teacher is facilitating the students' connection to the topic during prewriting. (B) is incorrect because the activity is not an originality check but simply a prior-knowledge-activation activity. (C) is likely to happen as a result of the students' sharing, but it is not the teacher's targeted objective. (D) is incorrect because the panel discussion is intended to generate ideas. Introducing "correctness" implies that some ideas are wrong.

Competency 005

19. **(D)** The correct response is (D). The activity is designed to reveal students' preconceived notions of certain *types* of people, which is the core definition of stereotyping. A lesson on stereotyping will move students toward an awareness of the foundations of cultural bias. (A) oversimplifies the intent of the activity, particularly given the ESL setting, and inappropriately suggests that bias is the result of something as simple as preference. (B) and (C) are incorrect because of the setup of the assignment. The fill-in-the-blank sentences will encourage students to explore preconceptions. A discussion of closed-mindedness or conflict might result, but it is not the primary focus of the assignment.

   Competency 009

20. **(B)** The correct response is (B). This mispronunciation points to the speaker's developing lexical knowledge in L2. The speaker pronounces what he or she *hears* and uses morphological knowledge of derivational morphemes (*-able* + *-ly*) to approximate pronunciation of the L2 word. The result is an "invented" word that is not in the L2 lexicon but that reflects the speakers developing competence. (A) is incorrect because oral production of an invented L2 form does not point to an orthographic problem. (C) is incorrect because the monitor filters incorrect constructions that the speaker *knows* are incorrect. The item stem suggests that the speaker routinely uses this aberrant pronunciation because he or she has not yet learned the correct form. (D) is a possible explanation but not plausible. The construction points to in-progress learning rather than to a careless mispronunciation caused by mismatching print form and spoken output.

   Competency 004

21. **(D)** The correct response is (D). The notes indicate that the learner feels uncomfortable in typical classroom situations, suggesting her basic communication skills in L2 need substantive development. (A) is incorrect because the teacher does not refer to the student's understanding of science-content language. (B) is incorrect because the teacher's notes target attitudinal issues manifested through the student's speaking and listening behaviors. (C) is incorrect because there is no reference to the student's content-area knowledge.

   Competency 007

22. **(C)** The correct response is (C). Think-alouds are considered an excellent means of modeling thinking processes for understanding content-area knowledge. (A) is incorrect because prohibiting students' use of their L1 would single them out in a communicatively nonproductive and personally embarrassing manner. (B) encourages ELL students to become dependent rather than to strive to develop higher levels of L2 proficiency. (D) would possibly lead to recalcitrance in ELL students whose L2 proficiency does not enable them to grasp new content through a traditional lecture.

   Competency 007

23. **(B)** The correct response is (B). This response most effectively addresses the biliteracy goals of two-way dual-language immersion programs, and it is developmentally appropriate for the young learners. (A) focuses on L2 and therefore fails to capture the intent of the dual-immersion model. (C) limits the learners' collaborative efforts and focuses on L2. (D) is incorrect because it focuses on L1. Had the assignment gone further requiring a paragraph written in L2 as well or a translation of the L1 paragraph, this response would be a better fit for the item stem.

   Competency 008

24. **(C)** The correct response is (C). These variations focuses on the logical use of the modal "would." In (C), past tense is used consistently, and "would" reflects a possibility in the future. Choosing "would" is consistent with the past tense in the rest of the passage. (A) and (B) show illogical use of "won't" (a contraction for "will not") and the fully spelled "will not." The past tense in the rest of the passage makes "will" an illogical choice in the sentence because it breaks the consistency of the past tense. (D) is incorrect because "won't" is used in the same manner as in

(B). Additionally, "would" is used illogically to suggest a kind of progressive action not supported by the past tense in the rest of the passage.
Competency 001

25. **(C)** The correct response is (C). In a two-way dual-language immersion program, there are two sets of learners: native speakers and nonnative speakers, both of whom are acquiring a new language. For the native speakers, L1 becomes their L2, while the nonnative speakers retain L1 as their native language but also acquire L2 as a second language. (A) and (B) are incorrect descriptions of approaches used in two-way dual-language immersion programs. (D) is incorrect because exit criteria are linked to official L2 language proficiency ratings and evaluations.
Competency 008

26. **(A)** The correct response is (A). The Texas Education Code places the authority for determining ELL status with the LPAC. (B), (C), and (D) are incorrect because these individuals are not officially involved in students' initial ELL determination.
Competency 010

27. **(C)** The correct response is (C). The teacher's objective is to create a meaningful learning experience in this science unit. Having the learners draw the insect and then describe it in three words creates a connection to content-area material right away. Additionally, this is a hands-on activity. The young students would no doubt handle the plastic models as they draw them. (A) lacks content-specific connection. The students could be responding the way the film presented a certain point, rather than to the science content. (B) is a good strategy for older students. In this scenario, however, the learners are young, so a hands-on introductory is far more appropriate. (D) is a fun activity, but the science teacher is not likely to reinforce the misconception that insects should be feared.
Competency 003

28. **(D)** The correct response is (D). Student advocacy in ESL programs extends to mentoring colleagues as described in this response. When ESL teachers share their knowledge with colleagues, both teachers and students benefit. (A) and (C) are incorrect because these are passive gestures that could be easily ignored. On the other hand, a demonstration such as is suggested by (D) would provide a model that the math and science teachers could emulate. (B) ignores the problem. The math and science teachers' request suggests that they need to learn strategies. A critique would be nonproductive until after the teachers have been given the guidance they requested.
Competency 010

29. **(C)** The correct response is (C). Breaking up the lesson into shorter segments and then reinforcing the information by focusing on key points are strategies likely to help intermediate ELL students master the content. (A) does not take into account strategies for helping students boost the quiz average. (B) overlooks the core problem that students seem to be having difficulty comprehending the information. Asking students to teach each other information that they don't understand will not address the teacher's instructional goal. (D) includes no strategies for promoting the learner's achievement through greater understanding of course content. Audio recordings are considered a good instructional strategy in ELL settings. However, simply listening to incomprehensible input over and over will not make it comprehensible. This response does not address the teacher's goal, and so is incorrect.
Competency 003

30. **(D)** The correct response is (D). This landmark case established the need to address nonnative-speaking students' linguistic needs in addition to academic competencies. (A), (B), and (C) inaccurately summarize the conclusions in *Lau v. Nichols* or any other court case, and therefore, they are all incorrect.
Competency 008

31. **(A)** The correct response is (A). Prereading activities are supposed to help students "enter" a text. In this activity, the sentences about change allow students to discover shared experiences on the topic of the text. By making oral presentation of the sentence a key feature of this activity, the teacher is further promoting the ESL students' oral-language development in a nonthreatening class activity. (B) is incorrect because this is not a comprehension activity. (C) is incorrect because this is a prereading activity, not a prewriting activity. (D) is incorrect because correcting the sentences as they are presented would counter the communicative intention of this oral-language prereading activity.
    Competency 001

32. **(C)** The correct response is (C). Reading a literary text is a specialized academic skill. Even with native speakers, a substantive amount of scaffolding is necessary to help students access literary texts. By reading and rereading the text orally and using visuals to help students understand the figurative language, the teacher is providing needed scaffolding to develop Cognitive Academic Language Proficiency in literature. (A) is incorrect because biographical background will not promote CALP if the teacher's goal is to help students access a literary text. (B) is incorrect because memorizing the poem is pointless if the students do not have the CALP to understand the core meaning of the literary text and how literary language is used. (D) is incorrect because a response paper encourages students to react affectively to a text. To develop CALP, a writing assignment should require cognitive skills. For example, a CALP-centered writing assignment might ask students to explain how the figurative language helps reader visualize the characters.
    Competency 001

33. **(B)** The correct response is (B). Having students explain linguistic and rhetorical choices that they've made in their writing develops their ability to talk about their thinking, and this is the foundation of metacognition. (A) is incorrect because the activity is not about independence but about thinking about linguistic choices. (C) is incorrect because self-correcting during editing is not the goal of this activity. (D) is incorrect because the teacher's instructions do not address syntactic and semantic correctness and furthermore would be counterproductive to the teacher's goal during this drafting activity.
    Competency 002

34. **(A)** The correct response is (A). In this class of young, beginning ESL students, the teacher seems to be focused on developing the students' communicative competence by following simple directions, which is the hallmark of TPR. (B) is incorrect because this isolated activity does not offer sufficient context to classify the approach as immersion (which is characterized by minimal L1–L2 scaffolding). (C) is considered one of the two major "types" of L2 learning: BICS and Cognitive Academic Language Proficiency. The activity is likely to develop BICS, but the stem focuses on a teaching method. (D) is an area of linguistics, not a teaching method, and therefore is an incorrect answer.
    Competency 004

35. **(C)** The correct response is (C). Collaborative writing in a storybook format allows students to "pool" their current writing proficiency and collectively produce a story that they would be unable to do independently. While the teacher can expect invented spellings and typical literacy acquisition strategies in the storybooks, the oral presentations will reinforce the students' ability to produce comprehensible output by creating syntactic structures that are both for the authors and the audience. (A) is incorrect because it does not actively promote students' abilities to generate meaningful writing in L2. (B) focuses on oral-language development rather than writing. (D) is incorrect because it takes the part-to-whole approach, which sees L2 acquisition as segmented and hierarchical.
    Competency 005

36.   **(C)**   The correct response is (C). Describing a chocolate chip cookie and then trying to match different descriptions to different cookies provides a hands-on, learner-centered lesson on how vivid writing creates exactness in writing that is intended to describe and explain. (A) is incorrect. Although this is a common class assignment, it lacks the engagement provided by the hands-on descriptive writing activity. (B) is incorrect because checking for details in a peer's draft does not teach students how to create vivid writing or why vivid writing matters in description and explanation. (D) is incorrect because using vivid verbs is an important strategy in powerful writing. However, as constructed, this response is an exercise in demonstrating nuances in meaning rather than a lesson on the power of details in writing.
  Competency 005

37.   **(B)**   The correct response is (B). The outline will prepare students for the new information they are about to get in the chapter. However, teaching them how to create a graphic organizer from the outline will foster learner independence. They will be able to transfer this knowledge to future new learning. (A) and (C) do not directly support the teacher's objective. Orally reading the outline and checking for correct copying of the outline do not contribute to students' understanding of history content. (D) is incorrect because the outline is supposed to prepare students for new knowledge, so quizzing them on the preparation activity is illogical.
  Competency 006

38.   **(A)**   The correct response is (A). Overgeneralization is common in first-language acquisition and is frequently evident in L2 acquisition as well. Overgeneralization occurs when a learner acquires a language rule but has not yet learned all the parameters for its application and thus "overapplies" it. (B) is incorrect because, despite the errors shown in the list, the learner clearly knows a fair amount about past tense forms. (C) is incorrect because "irregular" verbs cannot be explained through a consistent set of rules (in contrast to regular verbs in which the past tense is formed by affixing the -ed morpheme). (D) is incorrect because phonology is irrelevant in explaining this set of past tense constructions.
  Competency 002

39.   **(A)**   The correct response is (A). One of the keystones of the literature-circle approach to literacy development is the connection between learner choice and engagement. In an ESL classroom, the literature-circle approach allows teachers to take individual differences into account. Additionally, the collaborative environment promotes oral-language proficiency in the context of reading development. (B) may be a side effect of the literature-circle approach, but integrating more texts into the curriculum is not a foundational principle. (C) misconstrues the literature-circle approach. Literature circles can be based on a single curricular text, on texts selected from a list created by the teacher, and sometimes on student-selected texts. (D) is incorrect because the literature-circle approach actually promotes high-level literacy skills: meaning-making, negotiation, conversation, and collaboration.
  Competency 005

40.   **(B)**   The correct response is (B). In writing paragraphs about themselves and sharing them before the whole class, students will learn a fair amount about each other. In this highly personal writing assignment, students will draw on their cultural background. In listening to each other's paragraphs, they will become more aware of the diversity they all bring to the classroom. (A) is a likely consequence of the activity but not the teacher's targeted goal, and is therefore incorrect. (C) and (D) suggest that the activity is intended as a pragmatic, content lesson when, in fact, it is intended to bolster the multicultural learning environment. Therefore, both (C) and (D) are incorrect responses.
  Competency 009

41.   **(A)**   The correct response is (A). Modeling the process of responding to an exam-like prompt would meet the teacher's goals to familiarize students with the exam format as well as to teach how to negotiate the expectations of writing on demand (high-stakes writing done in a limited time frame on an unfamiliar topic). (B) superficially

seems to be a logical choice for preparing students for a state-mandated writing exam. However, without an explanation and targeted instruction on the expectations, this 15-minute writing assignment would lead to a great deal of frustration, anxiety, and possibly resistance in the learners. (C) and (D) fail to meet the teacher's goals. Neither of these options includes actual strategies for managing writing on demand. Instead, these responses present scenarios that might work well in general writing instruction, and are therefore incorrect responses.
Competency 007

42. **(C)** The correct response is (C). Materials for the state-mandated writing exams in Texas encourage teachers to create classroom rubrics to give students feedback on exam-like essays. Having the students use the rubrics to assess their own and their classmates' essays would provide an "insider's view" into the state writing requirements. (A) does not address the writing-on-demand environment. In the test, students will not have time for reflective revision. (B) is not the best strategy for meeting the teacher's goal. Students need "insider information" on what is needed for a satisfactory score. Working with a rubric offers that knowledge. (D) focuses on problems rather than correspondence between the writing task and the student's response and is therefore an incorrect response. If the teacher used the conference to point out how each student's response addresses expectations in the rubric, the strategy would help meet the teacher's goals.
Competency 007

43. **(A)** The correct response is (A). The Elementary and Secondary Education Act (reauthorized in 2001 as the No Child Left Behind Act) broadly established the need to create equitable educational opportunities for language minority and low income students. (B), (C), and (D) offer inaccurate insular and subtractive interpretations of the goals of federally and state-mandated ESL programs, and are therefore incorrect responses.
Competency 008

44. **(B)** The correct response is (B). The conflicts and events in these stories promote students' appreciation of cultural and linguistic diversity. For both characters, their names symbolize cultural issues. (A) is incorrect because the teacher's book talk focuses on a thematic issue in the unit, not on activating students' prior knowledge. (C) is incorrect because the teacher's book talk and postreading questions are not aimed at eliciting class discussion about students' own names (although that is very likely to be a side effect of this discussion). (D) is incorrect because this objective could have been achieved without using culturally based literature and is thus not ESL-specific.
Competency 009

45. **(A)** The correct response is (A). Dual-language immersion programs, both one-way and two-way, strive to develop biliteracy in language-minority and language-majority students. (B) is incorrect as a "cornerstone" of dual-language immersion programs. Research shows that in dual-immersion programs, both L1 and L2 students mentor each other as they each work toward literacy in the other language. (C) is incorrect because dual-language immersion programs do not claim reduced curricular rigor. (D) is incorrect because this response implies that dual-language immersion programs have a reductive effect on content-area learning. Research shows, however, that biliteracy programs have a reinforcing effect on students' conceptual proficiency because of the cross-linguistic environment of the program.
Competency 008

46. **(A)** The correct response is (A). An absolute has no apparent syntactic connection to the independent clause. It modifies neither the subject nor the predicate, but it adds detail to the simple scene presented in the main clause. In other words, it seems to modify the whole sentence. (B) is incorrect because the underlined structure lacks the subject-verb combination necessary for a subordinate clause and because it does not modify the subject or the predicate. (C) is incorrect because, while a participle is included in the absolute ("droning like a cicada"), it modifies only the noun in the absolute, not a noun or verb in the main clause. (D) is incorrect because the underlined structure is

not a traditional adverbial or adjectival modifier. Consequently, it cannot be "misplaced" on the basis of its proximity to the noun or verb that it is supposed to modify.

Competency 001

47. **(A)** The correct response is (A). The teacher supports all learners' affective needs through her response. Significantly, she avoids embarrassing anyone and instead makes comments designed to promote confidence and self-assurance in all learners. (B) ignores the problem and is therefore incorrect. (C) misrepresents the foundations of community that camaraderie is born out of mutual respect and support for group members and is therefore an incorrect response. (D) ignores both the holistic problem (the students' lack of respect for classmates) and the immediate impact (distraction from the content of the lesson) and is therefore an incorrect response.

Competency 009

48. **(B)** The correct response is (B). Prior knowledge, scaffolding, and student collaboration are widely encouraged as practices that promote ESL students' achievement. ESL literature discusses these strategies as means of advocating for students. (A) and (C) are incorrect responses because they list practices that are common in many ESL classrooms but are not defended as effective ESL teaching practices. (D) is not a list of teaching strategies. Parental involvement and curriculum accommodations should be integrated into all ESL programs. L2 immersion varies based on the program model in place. Therefore, (D) is an incorrect response.

Competency 010

49. **(C)** The correct response is (C). In asking students to talk to a family member, the teacher has embedded family involvement into the assignment. The assignment integrates aspects of (A), (B), and (D), but by framing the assignment within a family story, the teacher has created an assignment designed to involve family members in their children's school activities. (A) and (B) are incorrect because the teaching goals presented in these responses do not require family involvement. (D) is incorrect because it is not the primary focus on the assignment as described in the item stem.

Competency 010

50. **(C)** The correct response is (C). This response accurately summarizes the TEC and TAC descriptions of one-way dual-language immersion programs. The core distinction between the one-way and two-way immersion programs is the emphasis on L2 in the one-way program. (A) is not a term used to describe ESL education models. (B) does not match the description in the item stem. (D) is incorrect because mainstreaming places the ESL student in a regular class after the learner meets ESL program exit criteria.

Competency 008

51. **(C)** The correct response is (C). Vygotsky's Zone of Proximal Development theory suggests that learners can be guided toward higher levels of understanding and independent learning through scaffolding offered by teachers and knowledgeable peers. Grouping that ensures the ESL students can network with native speakers will help them negotiate the ZPD. (A) is incorrect because the issue of a syllabus is irrelevant in this scenario. Clearly, the instructor is interested in promoting student learning rather than staying on some sort of schedule. (B) is incorrect because the concept of universal grammar does not figure into this learning transaction. It is a content-based situation. (D) is incorrect because the core issue in this scenario is comprehension, not assessment.

Competency 002

52. **(B)** The correct response is (B). Although the mini-lesson approach is not restricted to ESL teaching, it is particularly suited to language-learning environments because presenting content information in smaller segments (rather than in a single, long lecture or presentation) promotes students' understanding of complex information. Typically, mini-lessons focus on a discrete learning objective and are delivered in 5- to 20-minute segments,

depending on how much discussion and application are necessary. (A) is incorrect, although it could be argued that when students don't understand, they do demonstrate signs of boredom. Averting boredom borne out of a lack of understanding is likely a positive side effect of mini-lessons but not the central rationale for using this approach. (C) is incorrect because the mini-lesson approach does not leave out complexity. Instead, it is designed to make complex concepts accessible. (D) is incorrect because mini-lessons are short but not quickly delivered.

Competency 002

53. **(A)** The correct response is (A). In ending each mini-lesson and networking session with a one-sentence report of each group's understanding, the teacher is promoting English-language proficiency and content knowledge by integrating listening, speaking, reading, and writing skills in a nonthreatening class activity. Furthermore, this feedback while the class is still in session enables the teacher to reinforce learning and to clarify misunderstandings. (B) is incorrect because the teacher has identified comprehension as the issue he is concerned with. A vocabulary exercise would have limited or no impact on the bigger problem. (C) is incorrect because having students independently read something that they already don't understand will not address the teacher's goal to boost comprehension. (D) is incorrect because writing an effective summary requires holistic understanding of the content. Rather than promoting comprehension, writing a summary of content that they don't understand is likely to frustrate the students.

Competency 002

54. **(D)** The correct response is (D). Pragmatics is the area of linguistics that addresses the way we interpret a communicative situation by strongly relying on context. Pragmatics takes into account how we interpret speech acts—language that indirectly expresses the speaker's intention and which a listener is expected to understand on the basis of the context. In the scenario cited in this item, the teacher asks a question but actually intends an imperative meaning: "George, start reading where Aimee left off." George, a newcomer with limited proficiency in L2, interprets the teacher's "question" as a literal question that gives him a choice. (A) is incorrect because George does not misunderstand the register. His polite response indicates that he knows the parameters of this Basic Interpersonal Communicative transaction between teacher and student. Had he responded, "No way, Dude!" that would be construed as a register error. (B) is incorrect because George's response is not due to a semantic issue. (C) is incorrect because, as a newcomer, George's monitor is just developing, so he doesn't have sufficient L2 proficiency at this point to filter incorrect or inappropriate responses.

Competency 001

55. **(C)** The correct response is (C). This activity provides a good opportunity to initiate a discussion on childhood universals and their culturally specific manifestations. (A) and (B) are likely take-aways from this activity, but given the teacher's selection of a culturally relevant story, it is clear that the teacher has much more than story generation or oral language in mind. (D) is an incorrect evaluation of the teacher's instructional goal as presented by the item stem, although students are likely to feel more comfortable about code-switching to create a desired rhetorical or communicative effect.

Competency 009

56. **(B)** The correct response is (B). When ESL students seek each other out during class activities, it is an indication that they need the support provided by fellow L1 speakers. By putting at least two ESL students in each group, the teacher is reducing the anxiety that the students seem to feel. Furthermore, the native speakers can help their ESL classmates negotiate the zone of proximal development. (A) is incorrect because restricting ESL students' use of their L1 is an inappropriate teaching strategy in this particular scenario because the students are likely to feel isolated and excluded. (C) is incorrect because, in providing an L1 translation of the class work, the teacher would not be promoting the students' content-specific language development. (D) is incorrect because reading the instructions orally to each group will not address the underlying problem in this scenario (which is the ESL students' apparent

discomfort over their limited understanding of science content).
Competency 002

57. **(C)** The correct response is (C). Modeling and using visual support will promote this teacher's goal to develop students' Cognitive Academic Language Proficiency in science. (A) is incorrect because the ESL students are at intermediate to advanced levels, indicating that they have substantive proficiency in English, but they need more directive teaching in content. (B) is incorrect because relying on native-language descriptions of the science content will not advance the ESL students' Cognitive Academic Language Proficiency. (D) is incorrect because conducting experiments involves hands-on, active learning rather than paper-and-pencil assessment.
Competency 002

58. **(D)** The correct response is (D). The scenario sets this class in South Texas, an area where the *piñata* and its celebratory associations are well known given the demographics of the area (in South Texas, Hispanics are a demographic majority). Thus, students will be able to draw on their home experiences (funds of knowledge) to complete this academic task. (A) is incorrect because the *piñata* can be described and discussed in any language. (B) is incorrect because it suggests introducing the *piñata* activity is some sort of pedagogical trap to trick ESL students into using Spanish and then reminding them to use English. (C) is incorrect because the *piñatas* are being used as manipulatives, not as language-specific artifacts.
Competency 009

59. **(C)** The correct response is (C). Culturally relevant artifacts help students connect meaningfully with classroom experiences by mirroring their real-world experience, thereby creating an effective multicultural learning environment. (A) presents a deficit view of ESL students by suggesting that unless a cultural connection is made, students will not work hard. (B) and (D) are incorrect because they misrepresent the intent of using the *piñatas* as manipulatives. Manipulatives are intended to provide students hands-on experiences to illuminate content-area concepts, making content knowledge accessible, not easier.
Competency 009

60. **(A)** The correct response is (A). This strategy promotes learner engagement in vocabulary development. The illustrated poster offers a means of reinforcing students' understanding through visual connections with the new word. (B) would be a better strategy if the teacher used a full sentence to encourage students' ability to use context clues. (C) encourages a scavenger-hunt approach, which will not promote the students' understanding of the new words. (D) is incorrect because just reading a new word a day will not promote students' vocabulary development.
Competency 005

61. **(A)** The correct response is (A). Team teaching, even as a mentoring demonstration, is an excellent means of collaborating as advocates for ESL students' success. (B) is a reductive suggestion that does not recognize the importance of content-area terms and that misrepresents repetition as a teaching strategy. (C) is not a teaching strategy. (D) is a passive form of advocacy because there is no guarantee that the content-area teachers will actually read and apply the information.
Competency 010

62. **(D)** The correct response is (D). Code-switching occurs when ESL speakers insert an L1 word or phrase into an L2 string, possibly subconsciously. This speaker appears to be using the L1 word almost in a phatic way. No real meaning is conveyed or lost through the use of this L1 word. (A) is incorrect because the speaker is not borrowing structures from L1 to create an L2 utterance. (B) is incorrect because no transfer is involved here. (C) is incorrect because the speaker did not create a nonexistent L2 word.
Competency 004

63. **(C)** The correct response is (C). The insertion of the L1 word does not interfere with the teacher's comprehension. Calling the speaker's attention to it would be counterproductive since it is likely the speaker does not even realize she inserted an L1 word. (A), (B), and (D) represent error-oriented responses to a meaningful utterance. Code-switching is not an error; it is a communication strategy. Calling unnecessary attention to this structure is likely to embarrass the speaker and possibly set back her progress in oral-language proficiency by causing her to be hypercareful and hesitant in future utterances.

　　　Competency 004

64. **(B)** The correct response is (B). Norms and expectations for oral language differ among cultures, in some cases, significantly. Teachers need to be aware that such variations impact ESL students' attitudes toward oral language in the classroom and significantly affect the way students use oral language in social and academic situations. (A) is incorrect because getting everyone to understand each other on the basis of individual L1 is not a viable communicative competence goal in ESL classrooms. (C) expresses a myth about ESL students. It is much more likely that any observed discomfort is due to lack of familiarity with L2 oral-language behaviors and classroom expectations. (D) is a correct statement about ESL students' individual rates of acquisition of oral language, but it does not address differences in language and culture and is therefore an incorrect response.

　　　Competency 004

65. **(C)** The correct response is (C). The phrase is a classic example of a simile—a comparison using *like* or *as*—with the writer comparing the power of the students' response to the power of a volcanic eruption. (A) is incorrect because the writer is exaggerating, but the exaggeration occurs because of the comparison created by the simile. (B) is incorrect because imagery is supposed to allow the reader to visualize a scene. There is no actual volcano in the scene. (D) is incorrect because it is a rhetorical feature created by repeating initial sounds in a string of words. That does not occur in this structure.

　　　Competency 001

66. **(A)** The correct response is (A). The 1965 Elementary and Secondary Education Act (reauthorized by Congress in 2001 as the No Child Left Behind Act) includes provisions for ensuring that ESL students receive necessary educational support. (B) is incorrect because ESL programs do not originate in the U.S. Department of Education. (C) and (D) are not federal agencies and are therefore incorrect responses.

　　　Competency 007

67. **(B)** The correct response is (B). The sentences all include an introductory element with a comma separating it from the main clause. The objective in this activity is to encourage students to generalize about the structure and appropriate punctuation. The teacher wants students to recognize that English marks introductory phrases with a comma. (A) is incorrect because the sentences are basically identical in core structure—an introductory phrase followed by the independent clause. (C) is incorrect because punctuation systems are usually language dependent, and transfer from L1 to L2 is not a viable strategy for understanding punctuation expectations. (D) is incorrect because the activity is not aimed at getting students to explain the likely cause of errors. Furthermore, there are no errors in the four sentences.

　　　Competency 002

68. **(C)** The correct response is (C). This letter-writing activity is intended to involve students in informing their parents about their school experiences. It promotes family involvement and communication with parents about school activities. (A) is incorrect in the framework of the item stem. The assignment is not constructed primarily to provide an authentic writing experience, although it clearly *does* involve the student writers in a realistic, meaningful writing task. (B) is incorrect because this activity is not intended as an assessment instrument. (D) is incorrect because it does not reflect the parameters of the item stem. Although the students are supposed to discuss their

parents' responses to the letters, the assignment does not integrate mechanisms for measuring the parents' interest level.

Competency 010

69.   **(A)**   The correct response is (A). Because state exam score reports include holistic as well as discrete information, teachers can create class activities that help learners develop greater understanding in areas that the scores suggest are challenging or problematic. Formative assessment does not mean more testing. It means that the teacher is adjusting lessons and activities to integrate ongoing, authentic assessment to promote student learning. (B) and (C) are incorrect because this attitude suggests there is a mismatch between what is being taught in the classroom and what state exams assess. (D) reflects a complete "teaching-to-the-test" approach. Research and anecdotal evidence from students point to the academic limitations of tailoring course content to reflect the testing approach and format.

Competency 007

70.   **(B)**   The correct response is (B). This response targets the instructional goal and the ELL level. The visual support and the reinforcement of the spelling of the new words is a good prereading strategy for young ELL students. (A) lacks the multiple types of reinforcement offered by (B). This response isolates the learners and turns vocabulary into a rote activity. (C) is incorrect because beginning and intermediate ELL learners at the elementary level would not yet have learned skimming skills. (D) is incorrect because it interferes with the continuity of the read-aloud. Read-alouds are social reading times rather than direct instruction time.

Competency 005

ANSWERS SORTED BY DOMAIN AND COMPETENCY

Domain	Competency	Question	Answer	Did You Answer Correctly?
I	1	2	D	
I	1	16	C	
I	1	17	B	
I	1	24	C	
I	1	31	A	
I	1	32	C	
I	1	46	A	
I	1	54	D	
I	1	65	C	
I	2	3	B	
I	2	33	B	
I	2	38	A	
I	2	51	C	
I	2	52	B	
I	2	53	A	
I	2	56	B	
I	2	57	C	
I	2	67	B	
II	3	4	C	
II	3	5	B	
II	3	6	A	
II	3	7	D	
II	3	27	C	
II	3	29	C	
II	4	13	A	
II	4	20	B	
II	4	34	A	
II	4	62	D	
II	4	63	C	
II	4	64	B	
II	5	15	A	
II	5	18	A	
II	5	35	C	
II	5	36	C	
II	5	39	A	

Domain	Competency	Question	Answer	Did You Answer Correctly?
II	5	60	A	
II	5	70	B	
II	6	1	A	
II	6	8	C	
II	6	9	A	
II	6	10	A	
II	6	11	C	
II	6	37	B	
II	7	21	D	
II	7	22	C	
II	7	41	A	
II	7	42	C	
II	7	66	A	
II	7	69	A	
III	8	14	D	
III	8	23	B	
III	8	25	C	
III	8	30	D	
III	8	43	A	
III	8	45	A	
III	8	50	C	
III	9	19	D	
III	9	40	B	
III	9	44	B	
III	9	47	A	
III	9	55	C	
III	9	58	D	
III	9	59	C	
III	10	12	B	
III	10	26	A	
III	10	28	D	
III	10	48	B	
III	10	49	C	
III	10	61	A	
III	10	68	C	

ANSWER SHEET FOR PRACTICE TEST 1

1. Ⓐ Ⓑ Ⓒ Ⓓ
2. Ⓐ Ⓑ Ⓒ Ⓓ
3. Ⓐ Ⓑ Ⓒ Ⓓ
4. Ⓐ Ⓑ Ⓒ Ⓓ
5. Ⓐ Ⓑ Ⓒ Ⓓ
6. Ⓐ Ⓑ Ⓒ Ⓓ
7. Ⓐ Ⓑ Ⓒ Ⓓ
8. Ⓐ Ⓑ Ⓒ Ⓓ
9. Ⓐ Ⓑ Ⓒ Ⓓ
10. Ⓐ Ⓑ Ⓒ Ⓓ
11. Ⓐ Ⓑ Ⓒ Ⓓ
12. Ⓐ Ⓑ Ⓒ Ⓓ
13. Ⓐ Ⓑ Ⓒ Ⓓ
14. Ⓐ Ⓑ Ⓒ Ⓓ
15. Ⓐ Ⓑ Ⓒ Ⓓ
16. Ⓐ Ⓑ Ⓒ Ⓓ
17. Ⓐ Ⓑ Ⓒ Ⓓ
18. Ⓐ Ⓑ Ⓒ Ⓓ
19. Ⓐ Ⓑ Ⓒ Ⓓ
20. Ⓐ Ⓑ Ⓒ Ⓓ
21. Ⓐ Ⓑ Ⓒ Ⓓ
22. Ⓐ Ⓑ Ⓒ Ⓓ
23. Ⓐ Ⓑ Ⓒ Ⓓ
24. Ⓐ Ⓑ Ⓒ Ⓓ
25. Ⓐ Ⓑ Ⓒ Ⓓ
26. Ⓐ Ⓑ Ⓒ Ⓓ
27. Ⓐ Ⓑ Ⓒ Ⓓ
28. Ⓐ Ⓑ Ⓒ Ⓓ
29. Ⓐ Ⓑ Ⓒ Ⓓ
30. Ⓐ Ⓑ Ⓒ Ⓓ
31. Ⓐ Ⓑ Ⓒ Ⓓ
32. Ⓐ Ⓑ Ⓒ Ⓓ
33. Ⓐ Ⓑ Ⓒ Ⓓ
34. Ⓐ Ⓑ Ⓒ Ⓓ
35. Ⓐ Ⓑ Ⓒ Ⓓ

36. Ⓐ Ⓑ Ⓒ Ⓓ
37. Ⓐ Ⓑ Ⓒ Ⓓ
38. Ⓐ Ⓑ Ⓒ Ⓓ
39. Ⓐ Ⓑ Ⓒ Ⓓ
40. Ⓐ Ⓑ Ⓒ Ⓓ
41. Ⓐ Ⓑ Ⓒ Ⓓ
42. Ⓐ Ⓑ Ⓒ Ⓓ
43. Ⓐ Ⓑ Ⓒ Ⓓ
44. Ⓐ Ⓑ Ⓒ Ⓓ
45. Ⓐ Ⓑ Ⓒ Ⓓ
46. Ⓐ Ⓑ Ⓒ Ⓓ
47. Ⓐ Ⓑ Ⓒ Ⓓ
48. Ⓐ Ⓑ Ⓒ Ⓓ
49. Ⓐ Ⓑ Ⓒ Ⓓ
50. Ⓐ Ⓑ Ⓒ Ⓓ
51. Ⓐ Ⓑ Ⓒ Ⓓ
52. Ⓐ Ⓑ Ⓒ Ⓓ
53. Ⓐ Ⓑ Ⓒ Ⓓ
54. Ⓐ Ⓑ Ⓒ Ⓓ
55. Ⓐ Ⓑ Ⓒ Ⓓ
56. Ⓐ Ⓑ Ⓒ Ⓓ
57. Ⓐ Ⓑ Ⓒ Ⓓ
58. Ⓐ Ⓑ Ⓒ Ⓓ
59. Ⓐ Ⓑ Ⓒ Ⓓ
60. Ⓐ Ⓑ Ⓒ Ⓓ
61. Ⓐ Ⓑ Ⓒ Ⓓ
62. Ⓐ Ⓑ Ⓒ Ⓓ
63. Ⓐ Ⓑ Ⓒ Ⓓ
64. Ⓐ Ⓑ Ⓒ Ⓓ
65. Ⓐ Ⓑ Ⓒ Ⓓ
66. Ⓐ Ⓑ Ⓒ Ⓓ
67. Ⓐ Ⓑ Ⓒ Ⓓ
68. Ⓐ Ⓑ Ⓒ Ⓓ
69. Ⓐ Ⓑ Ⓒ Ⓓ
70. Ⓐ Ⓑ Ⓒ Ⓓ

1. Ⓐ Ⓑ Ⓒ Ⓓ
2. Ⓐ Ⓑ Ⓒ Ⓓ
3. Ⓐ Ⓑ Ⓒ Ⓓ
4. Ⓐ Ⓑ Ⓒ Ⓓ
5. Ⓐ Ⓑ Ⓒ Ⓓ
6. Ⓐ Ⓑ Ⓒ Ⓓ
7. Ⓐ Ⓑ Ⓒ Ⓓ
8. Ⓐ Ⓑ Ⓒ Ⓓ
9. Ⓐ Ⓑ Ⓒ Ⓓ
10. Ⓐ Ⓑ Ⓒ Ⓓ
11. Ⓐ Ⓑ Ⓒ Ⓓ
12. Ⓐ Ⓑ Ⓒ Ⓓ
13. Ⓐ Ⓑ Ⓒ Ⓓ
14. Ⓐ Ⓑ Ⓒ Ⓓ
15. Ⓐ Ⓑ Ⓒ Ⓓ
16. Ⓐ Ⓑ Ⓒ Ⓓ
17. Ⓐ Ⓑ Ⓒ Ⓓ
18. Ⓐ Ⓑ Ⓒ Ⓓ
19. Ⓐ Ⓑ Ⓒ Ⓓ
20. Ⓐ Ⓑ Ⓒ Ⓓ
21. Ⓐ Ⓑ Ⓒ Ⓓ
22. Ⓐ Ⓑ Ⓒ Ⓓ
23. Ⓐ Ⓑ Ⓒ Ⓓ
24. Ⓐ Ⓑ Ⓒ Ⓓ
25. Ⓐ Ⓑ Ⓒ Ⓓ
26. Ⓐ Ⓑ Ⓒ Ⓓ
27. Ⓐ Ⓑ Ⓒ Ⓓ
28. Ⓐ Ⓑ Ⓒ Ⓓ
29. Ⓐ Ⓑ Ⓒ Ⓓ
30. Ⓐ Ⓑ Ⓒ Ⓓ
31. Ⓐ Ⓑ Ⓒ Ⓓ
32. Ⓐ Ⓑ Ⓒ Ⓓ
33. Ⓐ Ⓑ Ⓒ Ⓓ
34. Ⓐ Ⓑ Ⓒ Ⓓ
35. Ⓐ Ⓑ Ⓒ Ⓓ

36. Ⓐ Ⓑ Ⓒ Ⓓ
37. Ⓐ Ⓑ Ⓒ Ⓓ
38. Ⓐ Ⓑ Ⓒ Ⓓ
39. Ⓐ Ⓑ Ⓒ Ⓓ
40. Ⓐ Ⓑ Ⓒ Ⓓ
41. Ⓐ Ⓑ Ⓒ Ⓓ
42. Ⓐ Ⓑ Ⓒ Ⓓ
43. Ⓐ Ⓑ Ⓒ Ⓓ
44. Ⓐ Ⓑ Ⓒ Ⓓ
45. Ⓐ Ⓑ Ⓒ Ⓓ
46. Ⓐ Ⓑ Ⓒ Ⓓ
47. Ⓐ Ⓑ Ⓒ Ⓓ
48. Ⓐ Ⓑ Ⓒ Ⓓ
49. Ⓐ Ⓑ Ⓒ Ⓓ
50. Ⓐ Ⓑ Ⓒ Ⓓ
51. Ⓐ Ⓑ Ⓒ Ⓓ
52. Ⓐ Ⓑ Ⓒ Ⓓ
53. Ⓐ Ⓑ Ⓒ Ⓓ
54. Ⓐ Ⓑ Ⓒ Ⓓ
55. Ⓐ Ⓑ Ⓒ Ⓓ
56. Ⓐ Ⓑ Ⓒ Ⓓ
57. Ⓐ Ⓑ Ⓒ Ⓓ
58. Ⓐ Ⓑ Ⓒ Ⓓ
59. Ⓐ Ⓑ Ⓒ Ⓓ
60. Ⓐ Ⓑ Ⓒ Ⓓ
61. Ⓐ Ⓑ Ⓒ Ⓓ
62. Ⓐ Ⓑ Ⓒ Ⓓ
63. Ⓐ Ⓑ Ⓒ Ⓓ
64. Ⓐ Ⓑ Ⓒ Ⓓ
65. Ⓐ Ⓑ Ⓒ Ⓓ
66. Ⓐ Ⓑ Ⓒ Ⓓ
67. Ⓐ Ⓑ Ⓒ Ⓓ
68. Ⓐ Ⓑ Ⓒ Ⓓ
69. Ⓐ Ⓑ Ⓒ Ⓓ
70. Ⓐ Ⓑ Ⓒ Ⓓ

References

"A Brief History of ESL and Bilingual Education." *teachingasleadership.org/.../HistoryofESLandBilingualEducation.doc*

Anderson, L. W. and D. R. Krathwohl. *A Taxonomy for Learning, Teaching and Assessing: A Revision of Bloom's Taxonomy.* New York: Longman Publishing, 2001.

Anstrom, K. et al. *A Review of the Literature on Academic English: Implications for K–12 English Language Learners.* Arlington, VA: The George Washington University Center for Equity and Excellence in Education, 2010.

Asher, James J. *Learning Another Language Through Actions.* Los Gatos, CA: Sky Oaks Productions, 1982.

Associations for Supervision and Curriculum Development *www.ascd.org/research-a-topic/english-language-learners-resources.aspx#twitter*

August, D. M. et al. "The Critical Role of Vocabulary Development for English Language Learners." In *Learning Disabilities: Research and Practice.* 20 (1), 2005.

August, D. and T. Shanahan (Eds.) *Developing Literacy in Second-Language Learners: Report of the National Literacy Panel on Language-Minority Children and Youth.* Mahwah, NJ: Lawrence Erlbaum, 2006.

Beck, I., M. G. McKeown, and L. Kucan. *Bringing Words to Life: Robust Vocabulary Instruction.* New York: Guilford 2002.

Bialystok, E. *Bilingualism in Development: Language, Literacy, and Cognition.* Cambridge, UK: Cambridge University Press, 2001.

Bransford, J. et al. *How People Learn: Brain, Mind, Experience, and School.* National Research Council, 2000.

Bravo, M. A., E. H. Hiebert, and P. D. Pearson. *Tapping the Linguistic Resources of Spanish/English Bilinguals: The Role of Cognates in Science.* Berkeley CA: Lawrence Hall of Science, University of California, 1995.

Calderón, M. et al. "Bring Words to Life in Classrooms with English-Language Learners." In *Teaching and Learning Vocabulary: Bringing Research to Practice.* E. H. Hiebert and M. L. Kamil (Eds.). Mahwah, NJ: Erlbaum, 2005.

Canale, M. "From Communicative Competence to Communicative Language Pedagogy." In *Language and Communication.* J. C. Richards and R. W. Schmidt (Eds.). 2–27. London: Longman, 1983.

Canale, M. and M. Swain. "Theoretical Bases of Communicative Approaches to Second Language Teaching and Testing." *Applied Linguistics,* 1 (1980): 1–47.

Carlo, M. S. et al. "Closing the Gap: Addressing the Vocabulary Needs of English Language Learners in Bilingual and Mainstream Classrooms." *Reading Research Quarterly* 39 (2) (2004):188–215.

Carnine, D. W. et al. *Teaching Struggling and At-Risk Readers*. Upper Saddle River, NJ: Pearson, 2006.

Castro, D. C., B. Ayankoya, and C. Kasprzak. *The New Voices/Nuevas Voces: Guide to Cultural and Linguistic Diversity in Early Childhood*. Baltimore, MD: Paul H. Brookes, 2010.

Center for Applied Linguistics
www.cal.org/resources/

Center for Research on Education, Diversity, and Excellence
manoa.hawaii.edu/coe/crede/?page_id=35

Chamot, A. and J. O'Malley. *The CALLA Handbook*. Reading, MA: Addison-Wesley, 1994.

Chomsky, C. *The Acquisition of Syntax in Children From 5 to 10*. Cambridge, MA: MIT Press, 1969.

Cloud, N. "Special Education Needs of Second Language Students." In *Educating Second Language Children: The Whole Child, the Whole Curriculum, the Whole Community*. F. Genesee (Ed.). Cambridge, UK: Cambridge University Press, 1994.

Coelho, E. "Social Integration of Immigrant and Refugee Children." In *Educating Second Language Children: The Whole Child, the Whole Curriculum, the Whole Community*. F. Genesee (Ed.). Cambridge, UK: Cambridge University Press, 1994.

Colorín Colorado
www.colorincolorado.org/educators/

Colorín Colorado (Resources for Texas Teachers)
www.colorincolorado.org/web_resources/by_state/texas/

Cummins, J. "Interdependence of First- and Second-Language Proficiency in Bilingual Children." In *Language Processing in Bilingual Children*. E. Bialystok (Ed.). Cambridge, UK: Cambridge University Press, 1991.

Cummins, J. *Bilingualism and Minority Language Children*. Toronto, Ontario; Ontario Institute for Studies in Education, 1981.

de Jong, E. *Toward a Monolingual USA? The Modern English-Only Movement*, 2011.
www.colorincolorado.org/article/49656/

Díaz-Rico, L.T. and K. Z. Weed. *The Cross-Cultural, Language, and Academic Development Handbook, Fourth Edition*. Boston, MA: Allyn & Bacon, 2010.

Durgunoglu, A. Y., W. E. Nagy, and B. J. Hancin-Bhatt. "Cross-Language Transfer of Phonological Awareness." In *Journal of Educational Psychology* 85 (3), 1993.

Echevarria, J., M. A Vogt, and D. J. Short. *Making Content Comprehensible for English Learners: The SIOP Model, Second Edition*. Boston, MA: Allyn & Bacon, 2004.

Ellis, R. *Second Language Acquisition*, Oxford, UK: Oxford University Press, 1997.

English Language Proficiency Standards (ELPS)
ritter.tea.state.tx.us/rules/tac/chapter074/ch074a.html#74.4

Equity and Excellence in Education
www.ceee.gwu.edu

Escamilla, K. "Developing Literacy in Second Language Learners: The National Panel on Language-Minority Children and Youth: Book Review." The *Journal of Literacy Research*, Vol. 41(4): 2009.
jlr.sagepub.com/content/41/4/432.refs.html

Francis, D. J. et al. Practical Guidelines for the Education of English Language Learners: Research-Based Recommendations for instruction and Academic Interventions. Portsmouth, NH: RMC Research Corporation, Center on Instruction, 2006.

Gay, G. *Culturally Responsive Teaching: Theory, Research, and Practice.* New York: Columbia University, Teacher's College Press, 2010.

Genesee, F. et al. *Educating English Language Learners: A Synthesis of Research Evidence.* NY: Cambridge University Press, 2006.

Gersten, R. et al. *Effective Literacy and English Language Instruction for English Learners in the Elementary Grades: A Practice Guide* (NCEE 2007–4011). Washington, DC: National Center for Education Evaluation and Regional Assistance, Institute of Education Sciences, U.S. Department of Education, 2007.
ies.ed.gov/ncee/wwc/pdf/practiceguides/20074011.pdf

Gibbons, P. *Scaffolding Language, Scaffolding Learning: Teaching Second Language Learners in the Mainstream Classroom.* Portsmouth, NH: Heinemann, 2002.

Gillon, G. T. *Phonological Awareness: From Research to Practice.* NY: Guilford Press, 2004.

Goldenberg, C. "Teaching English Language Learners: What the Research Does—and Does Not—Say." In *American Educator*. Summer 2008.

Graves, M. and J. Fitzgerald. (2003). "Scaffolding Reading Experiences for Multilingual Classrooms." *English Learners: Reaching the Highest Level*

English Literacy (2003): 96–124. Newark, NJ: International Reading Association.

Greene, J. "A Meta-Analysis of the Russell and Baker Review of Bilingual Education Research." *Bilingual Education Journal*, 21(2) (1997): 103–122.

Halliday, M. A. K. *Introduction to Functional Grammar, Second Edition.* London: Arnold, 1994.

Harris, T. L. and R. E. Hodges. *The Literacy Dictionary.* Newark, DE: International Reading Association, 1995.

Hart, B. and T. R, Risely. *Meaningful Differences in the Everyday Experience of Young American Children.* Baltimore, MD: Paul H. Brookes, 1995.

Heath, S. B. *Ways with Words*. Cambridge, UK: Cambridge University Press, 1983.

Henry, M. K. *Unlocking Literacy: Effective Decoding and Spelling Instruction*. Baltimore, MD: Paul H. Brookes, 2003.

Honig, B., L. Diamond, and L. Gutlohn. *Teaching Reading Sourcebook*. Novato, CA: Arena Press, 2008.

Howard, E. R. et al. *Guiding Principles for Dual Language Education, Second Edition*. Washington, DC: Center for Applied Linguistics, 2007.

Hymes, D. "Competence and Performance in Linguistic Theory." In *Language Acquisition: Models and Methods.* R. Huxley and E. Ingram (Eds.). London: Academic Press, 1971.

Jenks, J. W. and W. J. Lauck. *The Immigration Problem: A Study of American Immigration Conditions and Needs.* New York: Funk & Wagnalls, 1926.

Jiménez, R. "The Strategic Reading Abilities and Potential of Five Low-Literacy

Latina/o Readers in Middle School." In *Reading Research Quarterly*, 32 (1997): 224–243.

Jiménez, R. T. "Understanding and Promoting the Reading Comprehension of Bilingual Students." In *Bilingual Research Journal*, 18 (1 & 2), 1994.

Johnson, D. "Grouping Strategies for Second Language Learners." In *Educating Second Language Children: The Whole Child, the Whole Curriculum, the Whole Community.* F. Genesee (Ed.). Cambridge, UK: Cambridge University Press, 1994.

Krashen, S. D. and T. D. Terrell*The Natural Approach: Language Acquisition in the Classroom.* San Francisco, CA: The Alemany Press, 1983.

Krashen, Stephen D. *Principles and Practice in Second Language Acquisition. English Language Teaching Series*. London: Prentice-Hall International (UK) Ltd., 1981.

Lee, O. and M. A. Avalos. "Promoting Science Instruction and Assessment for English Language Learners." *Electronic Journal of Science Education*, Vol. 7, No. 2 (December 2002). *wolfweb.unr.edu/homepage/crowther/ejse/lee.pdf*

LeLoup, J. W. and R. Ponterio. "Language Acquisition and Technology: A Review of the Research." *CAL Digest*. Washington, DC: Center for Applied Linguistics. December 2003.

Levine, D. U., and L.W. Lezotte. Effective Schools Research. In *Handbook of Research on Multicultural Education.* J.A. Banks and C.A.M. Banks (Eds.) 525–547. New York: Macmillan, 1995.

Liu, M. et al. "A Look at the Research on Computer-Based Technology Use in Second Language Learning: A Review of the Literature from 1990–2000." *Journal of Research on Technology in Education, 34*(3) (2002): 250–273.

Long, M. H. *Problems in SLA*. Mahwah, NJ: Erlbaum, 2007.

Lyster, R. *Learning and Teaching Languages Through Content: A Counterbalanced Approach.* Philadelphia, PA: John Benjamins, 2007.

Marzano, R. and J. Marzano. "The Key to Classroom Management." *Educational Leadership*, 61 (1) (2003): 6–13.

Marzano, R. J. *What Works in Schools: Translating Research into Action*. Association for Supervision and Curriculum Development. 2003.

May, S. "Bilingual/Immersion Education: What the Research Tells Us." In *Encyclopedia of Language and Education, Second Edition*. J. Cummins and N.H. Hornberger (Eds.). Vol. 5: Bilingual Education (2008): 19–34: Springer Science+Business Media LLC.

McCrum, R., W. Cran, and R. MacNeil. *The Story of English*. New York: Viking Penguin, 1986.

McKeon, D. "Language, Culture, and Schooling," In *Educating Second Language Children: The Whole Child, the Whole Curriculum, the Whole Community*. F. Genesee (Ed.). Cambridge, UK: Cambridge University Press, 1994.

Met, M. "Teaching Content Through a Second Language." In *Educating Second Language Children: The Whole Child, the Whole Curriculum, the Whole Community*. F. Genesee (Ed.). Cambridge, UK: Cambridge University Press, 1994.

Moats, L. C. *Language Essentials for Teachers of Reading and Spelling (LETRS). Module 10, Reading Big Words: Syllabication and Advanced Decoding*. Longmont, CO: Sopris West, 2005.

Moats, L. C. *Speech to Print: Language Essentials for Teachers*. Baltimore, MD: Paul H. Brookes, 2000.

Moll, L., C. Amanti, C., D. Neff, and N. Gonzalez, N. "Funds of Knowledge for Teaching: Using a Qualitative Approach to Connect Homes and Classrooms." In *Theory Into Practice,* 31(2), 1992.

Mora, J. K. *Identifying Fallacious Arguments in the Bilingual Education Debate.moramodules. com/Prop227/BERoadmap.htm*

Mora, J. K. *Legal History of Bilingual Education moramodules.com/pages/historyBE.htm*

Nash, R. *Dictionary of Spanish Cognates Thematically Organized*. Sylmar, CA: National Textbook Company, 1999.

National Clearinghouse for English Language Acquisition *www.ncela.gwu.edu*

National Institute of Child Health and Human Development (NICHD). Report of the National Reading Panel. *Teaching Children to Read: An Evidence-Based Assessment of the Scientific Literature on Reading and Its Implications for Reading Instruction*. (NIH Publication No. 00–4769). Washington, DC: U.S. Department of Health and Human Services, 2000.

Norris, J. and L. Ortega (Eds.). *Synthesizing Research on Language Learning and Teaching*. Philadelphia, PA: John Benjamins, 2006.

Pacific Policy Research Center. *Successful Bilingual and Immersion Education Models/Programs*. Honolulu: Kamehameha Schools, Research & Evaluation Division, 2010.

Piaget, J. *Origins of Intelligence in the Child.* London: Routledge & Kegan Paul, 1936.

Quinn, H. and O. Lee. *A Framework for K–12 Science Education: Practices, Crosscutting Concepts and Core Ideas Implications for English Language Learners (ELLs).* Webinar Presentation, September 19, 2012.
ell.stanford.edu/publication/language-demands-and-opportunities-relation-next-generation-science-standards-ells

Robinson, P. and N. C. Ellis (Eds.). *Handbook of Cognitive Linguistics and Second Language Acquisition.* New York: Routledge, 2008.

Rolstad, K., K. Mahoney, and G. Glass. "The Big Picture: A Meta-Analysis of Program Effectiveness Research on English Language Learners." *Educational Policy*, 19 (2005): 572–594.

Scarcella, R. *Academic English: A Conceptual Framework (Technical Report No. 2003–1: No. 1).* Irvine, CA: The University of California Linguistic Minority Research Institute, 2003.

Scarcella, R. "Academic Language: Clarifying Terms." *AccELLerate! the Quarterly Newsletter of the National Clearinghouse for English Language Acquisition (NCELA),* 1(1) (2008): 5–6.

Scarcella, R. "Some Key Factors Affecting English Learners' Development of Advanced Literacy." In *Developing Advanced Literacy in First and Second Languages: Meaning with Power.* M. J. Schleppegrell and M. C. Colombi (Eds.). Mahwah, NJ: Lawrence Erlbaum Associates, 2002.

Scarcella, R. "Defining Academic English." NCELA Web Conference. August 21, 2008.

Shaywitz, B. A., et. al. "Development of Left Occipitotemporal Systems for Skilled Reading in Children after a Phonologically-Based Intervention." *Biological Psychiatry* 55 (9) (2004): 926–933.

Sherris, A. "Integrated Content and Language Instruction." In *CAL Digest.* Washington, DC: Center for Applied Linguistics. Summer 2008.
www.cal.org/resources/digest/integratedcontent.html

Slavin, R. and A. Cheung. "A Synthesis of Research on Language of Reading Instruction for English Language Learners." *Review of Educational Research,* 75 (2005): 247–281.

Snow, C. E., S. M. Burns, and P. Griffin. *Preventing Reading Difficulties in Young Children.* Washington, DC: National Academies Press, 1998.

TELPAS Assessment
www.tea.state.tx.us/student.assessment/ell/telpas/

Texas Education Agency. *A Chronology of Federal Law and Policy Impacting Language Minority Students. 2011.*
www.colorincolorado.org/article/50856/

TEA Web Pages

Chapter 89. Adaptations for Special Populations, Subchapter BB. Commissioner's Rules Concerning State Plan for Educating English Language Learners.
ritter.tea.state

Limited English Proficiency Initiatives
www.tea.state.tx.us/index4.aspx?id=5081&menu_id=814

Texas English Language Learners Portal
elltx.org

Tong, F. et al. "Accelerating Early Academic Oral English Development in Transitional Bilingual and Structured English Immersion Programs." *American Educational Research Journal 45*(4) (2008): 1011–1044.

Torgesen, J. K. and R. F. Hudson. "Reading Fluency: Critical Issues for Struggling Readers." In *What Research has to Say about Fluency Instruction*. S. J. Samuels and A. E. Farstrup (Eds.). Newark, DE: International Reading Association, 2006.

Trieman, R. and B. Kessler. "The Role of Letter Names in the Acquisition of Literacy." In *Advances in Child Development and Behavior*. R. Kail (Ed.). 31 (2003): 105–135.

Turkan, S., J. Bicknell, and A. Croft. *Effective Practices for Developing Literacy Skills of English Language Learners in the English Language Arts Classroom*. Princeton, NJ: Educational Testing Services, 2012.
www.ets.org/research/contract.html

Vygotsky, L. S. *Mind in Society: The Development of Higher Psychological Processes*. Cambridge, MA: Harvard University Press, 1978.

Wenglinsky, H. *How Teaching Matters: Bringing the Classroom Back into Discussions of Teacher Quality*. Princeton, NJ: Educational Testing Service, 2000.

What Works Clearinghouse
ies.ed.gov/ncee/wwc/topic.aspx?sid=6

Wolk, S. "Hearts and Minds: Classroom Relationships and Learning Interact." *Educational Leadership* 61(1) (2003): 14–18.

Young, S. *A Brief History of Adult ESL Instruction*. 2008.
www.cal.org/caela/esl_resources/eslhistory.ppt

Index

NOTES

NOTES

NOTES

NOTES